# FROM
# GIBBON
## TO
# AUDEN

# FROM
# GIBBON
## TO
# AUDEN

### ESSAYS ON THE
### CLASSICAL TRADITION

## G. W. BOWERSOCK

OXFORD
UNIVERSITY PRESS
2009

# OXFORD
UNIVERSITY PRESS

Oxford University Press, Inc., publishes works that further
Oxford University's objective of excellence
in research, scholarship, and education.

Oxford  New York
Auckland  Cape Town  Dar es Salaam  Hong Kong  Karachi
Kuala Lumpur  Madrid  Melbourne  Mexico City  Nairobi
New Delhi  Shanghai  Taipei  Toronto

With offices in
Argentina  Austria  Brazil  Chile  Czech Republic  France  Greece
Guatemala  Hungary  Italy  Japan  Poland  Portugal  Singapore
South Korea  Switzerland  Thailand  Turkey  Ukraine  Vietnam

Copyright © 2009 by Oxford University Press, Inc.

Published by Oxford University Press, Inc.
198 Madison Avenue, New York, New York 10016

www.oup.com

Oxford is a registered trademark of Oxford University Press

Library of Congress Cataloging-in-Publication Data
Bowersock, G. W. (Glen Warren), 1936–
From Gibbon to Auden : essays on the classical tradition / Glen W. Bowersock.
p. cm.
ISBN 978-0-19-537667-8
1. Europe—Civilization—Classical influences.  2. Europe—Civilization—18th century.
3. Europe—Civilization—19th century.  4. Europe—Civilization—20th century.  I. Title.
CB203.B677 2009
940.2—dc22     2008026676

9 8 7 6 5 4 3 2 1
Printed in the United States of America
on acid-free paper

# PREFACE

THE SEVENTEEN ESSAYS THAT COMPRISE THIS VOLUME
have their roots in more specialized studies on the ancient world and
its history. They not only reflect my own personal interests and areas
of competence but exemplify a firm belief that classical antiquity has
been consistently important in modern thought and literature, and
that it continues to be important today. The essays collected here range
across three centuries, the eighteenth to the twentieth, and are divided
chronologically. But they have an internal coherence that arises from the
research that engendered them.

It would hardly be surprising for a historian of the Roman Empire
to turn to Gibbon. From my earliest work, on the Augustan empire, the
*Decline and Fall* has provided a standard of historical interpretation and
exposition that remains as extraordinary today as it was when it was written. The papers I have devoted to Gibbon span three decades, and two
other eighteenth-century pieces, included here, are closely connected
with them—one on Suetonius and Samuel Johnson, and the other on
the discoveries at Herculaneum and Pompeii. Samuel Johnson showed
little interest in Gibbon, and Gibbon showed little interest in Campanian
archaeology. Yet Johnson set a new standard for biography in European literature, and he did so under the influence of a master classical biographer,
who was a contemporary of Plutarch. And the discoveries in the vicinity of
Naples had an enormous impact on eighteenth-century art and thought,
particularly through the British Dilettanti. Biography and archaeology
have much occupied me in the past, and that is how I came to these topics. I dare to hope that the papers on Suetonius and Pompeii will deepen
the presentation of the eighteenth-century's interest in the Roman world.

Gibbon stands no less behind the essays on the modern Greek poet Cavafy, whose annotations on Gibbon have now been brilliantly published by my friend Diana Haas (*Folia Neohellenica* 4 [1982]: 25–96). Cavafy was not only a poet of the erotic, for which he is perhaps most notorious, but also of the complex Greek world of the Roman and Byzantine empires. My own studies on late antiquity have brought me into contact with Cavafy's interpretations over and over again. For Cavafy Gibbon, together with the Greek historian Constantine Paparrigopoulos, was a fundamental modern historian of the late antique and Byzantine worlds. Naturally this meticulous and imaginative poet did not rest content with secondary sources. He insisted on going back to the ancient texts. But Gibbon often guided him. Auden's suppressed paper on the fall of Rome, which I had the honor of publishing for the first time, is, in its quirky way, another tribute to the problem of decline that Gibbon had posed, and as a poet himself he views it explicitly through the lens of Cavafy's verse.

If Gibbon provides the skeleton for this corpus, the flesh is embellished with exotic adornments that derive from years of research on eastern Mediterranean society, especially among the Arabs. This is what lies behind the discussion of Mediterranean gestures at Naples in a review of a famous old book by Andrea de Jorio. This research also led me to Edward Lear, who visited the eastern Mediterranean and did many precious drawings that include invaluable testimony for the rose-red city of Petra in the nineteenth century.

The contemporaneity of my work on pre-Islamic Arabia, not only in libraries but also in the region, sharpened my sense of the impact of the modern world upon the changing interpretations of antiquity, and hence the relevance of ancient history to the present day is another strand that binds this book together. My friendship with Arnaldo Momigliano led to many fruitful discussions about trends in classical scholarship over the centuries, and here again Gibbon played an important role. I have reflected often on the shifting popularity of the Greeks and the Romans in modern European and North American history. That is why Berlioz's espousal of Virgil, the Germans' worship of the Greeks (until Hitler, who admired the Romans), and the Americans' move from the Jeffersonian model of the Roman republic to the democracy of Athens all assume a place in this volume. This is also why the infatuation of a contemporary Polish journalist with Herodotus appears in these pages. Inevitably an investigation into the wide-ranging thought of Momigliano in his later years has found a place here.

These essays have appeared in many places, in journals and books, and they all evoke inspiring colleagues and friends. Several come from *The New Republic*, whose editor, Leon Wieseltier, has not only shown an uncanny instinct for what would interest me but an exceptional tolerance in letting me say what I wanted at whatever length I chose. My longtime friend Bernard Knox sent the suppressed Auden piece in my direction. Joseph Epstein commissioned several articles for *The American Scholar*, when he was its luminous editor for a long and distinguished term during which Momigliano and I had the privilege of serving together on its editorial board. The work on Cavafy reflects my friendship with the late George Savidis, who was my colleague at Harvard as well as the owner of the surviving Cavafy archive and the distinguished editor of its many treasures. Savidis generously turned over the hitherto unknown poems on Julian for my analysis just as Renata Lavagnini in Palermo was preparing the texts of those poems. My association with her in this project was a memorable experience, and she has continued to benefit all serious readers of Cavafy with her magnificent edition of the unfinished poems, published at Ikaros in Athens in 1994. Despite many versions of the "canon," these astonishing poems are still not available in any translation. Lavagnini's edition was the template for my paper on the "new Cavafy," and it provided the texts for my own provisional renderings of excerpts from a few of the pieces. Fortunately, Daniel Mendelsohn has now translated all of them into English and will publish them with Knopf in 2009 as a supplementary volume to his translations of the canonical poems.

In this book translations from French, German, Latin, and Greek that are not explicitly ascribed to a translator are mine. There is nothing here that I did not discuss in advance with Christopher Jones, George Martin Lane Professor of Classics and History at Harvard University. His judgment, learning, and imagination have enriched me for almost fifty years. And now, early in the new millennium, I have to thank Aldo Schiavone and Stefan Vranka for their encouragement to bring together these miscellaneous essays in a single volume. Some of them appeared in Italian under the title *Saggi sulla tradizione classica dal Settecento al Novecento* in 2007 (Einaudi). The chapters that follow mirror not only my own intellectual tastes and scholarly research but those of a whole circle of friends without whom my life and work would have been infinitely poorer.

Bibliographical details for each of the chapters are as follows. References have been updated, texts have been revised to take account of more recent publications, and quotations in foreign languages have been translated.

1. "Gibbon's Historical Imagination," *The American Scholar* 57 (Winter 1988): 33–47.

2. "Gibbon on Civil War and Rebellion in the Decline of the Roman Empire," *Daedalus* (Summer, 1976): 63–71, reprinted in *Edward Gibbon and the Decline and Fall of the Roman Empire*, ed. G. W. Bowersock, J. Clive, and S. R. Graubard, 27–35 (Cambridge, Mass.: Harvard University Press, 1977).

3. "Some Reflections on Gibbon's Library," *Gazette of the Grolier Club* 52 (2001): 49–59.

4. "Watchmen," Essay on D. Womersley, *Gibbon and the Watchmen of the Holy City, Essays in Criticism* 53 (2003): 82–91.

5. "Suetonius in the Eighteenth Century," *Biography in the Eighteenth Century*, ed. J. D. Browning, 28–42 (New York: Garland, 1980).

6. "The Rediscovery of Herculaneum and Pompeii," *The American Scholar* (Autumn 1978): 461–70.

7. "Sign Language: A. de Jorio, Gesture in Naples and Gesture in Classical Antiquity," *The New Republic*, April 9 and 16, 2001, pp. 57–61.

8. "Berlioz, Virgil, and Rome," original English text, not previously published. Italian translation in *Saggi sulla tradizione classica* (Turin, Italy: Einaudi, 2007), 91–99.

9. "Edward Lear in Petra," *Proceedings of the American Philosophical Society* 34 (1990), 309–20.

10. "Burckhardt on Late Antiquity from the *Constantin* to the *Griechische Kulturgeschichte*," in *Begegnungen mit Jakob Burckhardt* (Beiträge zu Jakob Burckhardt, Bd. 4), ed. A. Cesana and L. Gossman, 215–28 (Basel/Munich: Schwabe/Beck, 2004).

11. "The New Old World: C. Winterer, The Culture of Classicism," *The New Republic*, Nov. 4, 2002, pp. 27–31.

12. "The Julian Poems of C. P. Cavafy," *Byzantine and Modern Greek Studies* 7 (1981): 89–104.

13. "Cavafy and Apollonios," *Grand Street* (Spring 1983): 180–89.

14. "The New Cavafy," *The American Scholar* 65 (1996): 243–57.

15. "The Later Momigliano," *Grand Street* (Autumn 1989): 197–209.

16. "A Modern Aesop," *The New Republic*, Sept. 24, 2007, pp. 53–55.

17. "'The Fall of Rome' by W. H. Auden," *Auden Studies* 3 (Oxford: Oxford University Press, 1995), 111–19.

# CONTENTS

PART I

# THE EIGHTEENTH CENTURY

# CHAPTER ONE

# GIBBON'S HISTORICAL IMAGINATION

THE REPUTATION OF EDWARD GIBBON IS EVEN MORE secure now than when he died. In posterity as in life, the historian of the Roman Empire was the antithesis of Dr. Johnson. He had no Boswell but hardly needed one because he left behind a supremely great masterpiece. Without his biographer, Dr. Johnson would probably be remembered most of all for his dictionary. Important as it is, that is certainly not a work frequently read today. But the *History of the Decline and Fall of the Roman Empire* continues to be reprinted, read, and admired throughout the Western world. It is Gibbon's one great triumph, the cause of his fame and at times notoriety.

The *Decline and Fall* is indisputably a work of history, but just as indisputably it is not what is known today as a scholarly resource. Its information is not always exact, nor was it when it appeared. Its author had read widely in the original sources but contributed nothing in the way of scholarly analysis beyond what he found in the studies of scholars. For the facts and problems, a serious reader intent upon research would have to turn elsewhere—in the eighteenth century to the very sources that Gibbon himself used (Tillemont, the Abbé de la Bléterie, Muratori, Pocock, and many more) and in modern times to Mommsen, Syme, the *Prosopographia Imperii Romani*, and the like. The *Decline and Fall* is generally reliable, but that is certainly not why it is read.

Nor again is the vast panorama of history, so often admired and so very rare in historiography, the reason why Gibbon continues to be read.

His boldness in composing an account of more than a thousand years of history made him a pioneer in the comparative treatment of Rome, Byzantium, the early Church, and Islam. So comprehensive a vision is as uncommon now as it was in the eighteenth century, and yet few read Gibbon from beginning to end at one time and experience at firsthand his magnificent juxtapositions of culture. Moreover, those who do read the work through discover a far greater optimism as it draws to a close than they had been led to expect from the first part of a work titled *Decline and Fall.* Gibbon's perspective and even his interpretations changed as he moved along during the fifteen years or so of composition. His positive estimate of Western civilization in his own day was bound to cast some sunlight on the fallen monuments of ancient Rome, and the genuine alarm and pessimism that arose from his observation of the French Revolution came too late to be reflected in the *Decline and Fall.*

Gibbon's readers do not therefore consult his work in search of references to the facts of ancient history, nor do many of them read it through from beginning to end as they would a novel, a biography, or even a shorter work of history. The *Decline and Fall* is compelling at virtually any point in its long course. It can be read with pleasure; but equally, because it has no complex and interwoven plot, it can be put down at any moment without a feeling of incompleteness. It is always inescapably there, and it is probably fair to say that reading Gibbon is addictive. The more one does it, the more one wants to do it; and the supply gives the impression of being inexhaustible, even though it is not.

It is no secret that Gibbon's magnificent language has long beguiled his readers, but there is far more to Gibbon than a rhetorician. The extraordinary influence of the *Decline and Fall* over some two centuries on creative artists and scholars alike—for many of whom English was not a native language—must obviously be due to something more than felicity of language. Nor, as we have seen, can it be due to a repertoire of facts that could be more easily and accurately found elsewhere. Theodor Mommsen, the greatest historian of ancient Rome in modern times, said to his students in the nineteenth century, as we have recently learned from the sensational discovery of detailed lecture notes, that Edward Gibbon's history was "the most important work that had ever been written on Roman history." These newly discovered lecture notes, prepared by a highly intelligent adult student of Mommsen, reveal that the interpretation of Roman imperial history that he presented showed striking parallels with the interpretation in Gibbon, particularly the comparison of Constantine with Augustus. It is clear that Mommsen's assessment had nothing to do with Gibbon's language or with his facts but with his overall view of imperial history, or what I should prefer to call his historical imagination. When Mommsen won the Nobel Prize for literature in 1902, just a few months before his death, the *Roman History* for which the prize was awarded had been in existence for some fifty years. It was a work begun by the young Mommsen but actually never completed. The fourth volume was to have contained his narrative of the Roman Empire, and it has always been a mystery why he was never able to write it, even though he regularly lectured on the Roman Empire. The answer seems to be that he not only stood in awe of his great English predecessor but was afraid of competing with him. Mommsen must have known that he was a better scholar than Gibbon but feared that Gibbon was the better historian.

Elsewhere in nineteenth-century Germany, two other highly cultivated but otherwise very different people were reading Gibbon with equal appreciation. The diaries of Richard Wagner's wife Cosima show that the two of them read Gibbon to one another off and on in the evenings from 1869 to 1876. They always read Gibbon with pleasure, according to Cosima's notes, and marveled several times at the dramatic power of Gibbon's exposition. In 1871 they contemplate a Gibbonian tragedy on Julian the Apostate, and in the next year they admire the conflict of power and character represented by the confrontation of Ambrose and Theodosius. Although the Wagners had a lively appreciation of Gibbon's English style because they read his work in the original and contrasted it favorably to Carlyle's, what impressed them above all was Gibbon's insight into the character of historical figures and his dramatic presentation of their struggles. Once more it is Gibbon's historical imagination that comes to the fore.

In the twentieth century, another reader for whom English was not a native language read Gibbon with close attention. This was the Alexandrian Greek poet Cavafy, whose detailed marginal notes in his copy of the *Decline and Fall* were published a few decades ago.[1] Cavafy reads Gibbon with a critical eye, corrects his facts, finds fault at times with his methods, but overall admires the historical vision. As the Wagners find drama in Gibbon, Cavafy finds poetry. Of a scene in chapter 31 in which

---

1. For details see chapter 12 in this volume.

a defeated emperor plays the flute in the midst of a crowd of Gothic conquerors, Cavafy wrote in the margin, "The subject for a beautiful sonnet, a sonnet full of sadness such as Verlaine would write, *je suis l'empire à la fin de la décadence* [I am the empire at the end of its decline]." Or again, when he reached chapter 57, Cavafy wrote beside the account of Mahmud the Gaznevide, "still venerable in the East" according to Gibbon, that this tale is the subject of a beautiful poem by Leigh Hunt, and Cavafy explicitly remarks, "The poet acknowledges his indebtedness to Gibbon," as was indeed the case. Cavafy's marginalia in the *Decline and Fall* constitute his own extensive acknowledgment; and several of his poems, notably those on Julian the Apostate, are proof of what he owed to Gibbon's narrative.

If we look at the greatest historian of Rome in the twentieth century, Sir Ronald Syme, we see that Gibbon made as profound an impression upon him as upon Mommsen in the previous century. And, it should be noted, the influence is not stylistic, for of course Syme's unusual style is an English reworking of the inconcinnity of Tacitus. But Syme's perspective—his historical outlook, his historical imagination—is thoroughly Gibbonian. The portrait of Augustus in *The Roman Revolution* owes something to Tacitus and Asinius Pollio but far more to Gibbon in the third chapter of the *Decline and Fall*. The ancient writers had provided hints of a hostile portrait of the first Roman emperor, but it was Gibbon who created that portrait. Syme's indebtedness to his eighteenth-century predecessor even extends beyond the *Decline and Fall*. Taking Gibbon's long and eloquent reply to a serious critic of his two chapters on early Christianity (the so-called *Vindication*) as his model, Syme replied to an equally serious critic at comparable length with similar irony and memorable phrasing. Syme's pamphlet, entitled *The Historia Augusta: A Call for Clarity*, is a Gibbonian vindication from our own time.

Finally, before we try to look at the fundamental components of Gibbon's historical imagination, another twentieth-century writer, very different from Syme and Cavafy, has a small claim on our attention for what is perhaps the most trenchant and brief critical observation on Gibbon to have been made in a long time. John Lahr in his biography of the brilliant comic dramatist Joe Orton reports that one of Orton's literary agents observed that Orton had once produced "a very funny and penetrating piece of literary criticism." This man had asked Orton whether he and his friend Halliwell had read Gibbon, and the reply came back, "What an old queen she is! Send up, send up, send up the whole time."

This is obviously not simply a reference to Gibbon's style or to his irony: it is far more than that. It touches upon Gibbon's whole technique of presenting historical personalities and events. That a comic dramatist, in the English tradition of Sheridan and Wilde, should have perceived this quality in Gibbon is as impressive in its way as the comments of Richard Wagner on the dramatic characteristics of the *Decline and Fall*.

Let us, then, try to work out what is so special about Gibbon's historical imagination in the *Decline and Fall*, what makes his work so much more than an aggregate of facts or a treasure of well-turned and quotable sentences. Fortunately for us, Gibbon wrote when he was twenty-five a remarkable assessment of his own character. After acknowledging that his fundamental virtue and generosity were corrupted to some extent by pride, he notes, "Wit I have none. My imagination is rather strong than pleasing, my memory both capacious and retentive. The shining qualities of my understanding are extensiveness and penetration; but I want both quickness and exactness." In her biography of the young Edward Gibbon, Patricia Craddock rightly explains the strictures against wit as no more than Gibbon's failure to aspire to what Samuel Johnson called "good things" in conversation. No one, least of all Gibbon himself, could have doubted his sense of humor and his powerful irony, but equally it is true that no Boswell would have been able to compile a volume of aphorisms emitted by Gibbon in social settings. Gibbon talked at length and mellifluously, but he was not a man to reply pungently to someone else's talk. This may have been one of the many reasons that he and Johnson disliked each other.

Gibbon's introspective candor about what he calls wit encourages one to believe that he was equally perceptive in describing his imagination as strong rather than pleasing. Gibbon's writings throughout his career leave a powerful impression, but his early work, such as the aborted history of the Swiss Republics, certainly does not afford such pleasure as the *Decline and Fall* does. No one could question Gibbon's belief that his memory was capacious and retentive: his entire oeuvre proves the point. When he says that the shining qualities of his understanding are extensiveness and penetration, this seems a quite astonishing anticipation of the writer who could encompass more than a thousand years of history with a rich supply of new observations. And when the twenty-five-year-old Gibbon says at the same time that he lacks both quickness and exactness, no working scholar who has studied the *Decline and Fall* could disagree. Gibbon was not a compiler; he was not an industrious researcher. He was, in short, no Le Nain de Tillemont, and that is undoubtedly why he needed to rely upon such a scholar.

Gibbon's self-conscious lack of precision is clearly part of his alignment with the *philosophes* against the *érudits* in the debates of eighteenth-century Europe. As a bilingual Englishman whose education and life in a French-speaking environment gives a curious foreignness to much of his work, Gibbon believed that mere erudition and antiquarian learning were not what really mattered in his time. The philosophic historian should speak to the needs of his age in a form that was as agreeable as it was instructive. In other words, Gibbon warmly espoused the Horatian precept of commingling the *dulce* (or sweet) with the *utile* (or useful). As early as 1758, when the young Gibbon was still living in Lausanne and known to have been studying the date of Horace's *Art of Poetry*, he took time to study the Abbé de la Bléterie's account of the succession of the Roman emperors. In Gibbon's observations, which look forward to views later expressed in his Francophone essay on literature, the young Gibbon, writing in French and already allying himself with the *philosophes*, said of La Bléterie's work, "To bring a spirit of clarity into the shadows of antiquity suffices for the man of letters who wishes to instruct himself; to scatter flowers on the thorns of knowledge is the plan of the wit who seeks only to amuse himself. To unite the useful and the agreeable is all the most demanding reader can ask: let him ask it of M. de la Bléterie without fear."

This view of history, which is the engine that set his strong imagination in motion, remained with Gibbon throughout his life. In the introductory remarks to the first of the final two volumes of the *Decline and Fall* (in other words, at the beginning of chapter 48), Gibbon observed that, after he had narrated the history of five centuries of the decline and fall of the Empire, a period of more than eight hundred years still awaited his attention. "Should I persevere in the same course," he wrote, "should I observe the same measure, a prolix and slender thread would be spun through many a volume, nor would the patient reader find an adequate reward of instruction or amusement." Accordingly, since the history to follow was less suited to these twin objectives, Gibbon would compose the narrative in less detail in order to avoid tedium. Annalistic writing as such was utterly contrary to his historical aims. For that final period of his work he justified a summary treatment by observing, "These annals must continue to repeat a tedious and uniform tale of weakness and misery; the natural connection of causes and events would be broken by frequent and hasty transitions, and a minute accumulation of circumstances must destroy the light and effect of those general pictures which compose the use and ornament of a remote history." The observation is exceptionally helpful. We should note the emphasis that Gibbon gives to "light and effect" in "those general pictures which compose the use and ornament of a remote history." Use and ornament remind us once again of *dulce* and *utile*.

In writing, similarly in French, in the *Mémoires Littéraires de la Grande Bretagne*, which Gibbon published for a few years at the end of the 1760s with his friend Deyverdun, Gibbon remarked, with a recognizably continental perspective (and undoubtedly an eye on Montesquieu), "The other nations of Europe had outstripped the English in the progress of history. England possessed poets and philosophers, but she was reproached with having only cold annalists and impassioned declaimers." But Gibbon then goes on to mention two exceptions, and these are the two exceptions that continued to provide contemporary models for his own work as he began the project of the *Decline and Fall*. They were Robertson and Hume. And we should attend carefully to the way in which he chooses to praise these two writers in this early passage in the *Mémoires Littéraires*. "Two great men have silenced this reproach. A Robertson has adorned the annals of his homeland with all the graces of the most vigorous eloquence. A Hume, born to instruct and judge mankind, has carried into history the light of a profound and elegant philosophy." So to annalistic history Robertson brought grace and Hume instruction. It is well known that when the first volume of the *Decline and Fall* appeared it was warmly praised by Hume himself, not long before his death. As for Robertson, Gibbon paid him the ultimate tribute—paraphrasing Robertson's own words in what has become probably the most famous passage in the whole of Gibbon's work. In chapter 3 of the *Decline and Fall*, we read, "If a man were called to fix the period in the history of the world during which the condition of the human race was most happy and prosperous he would, without hesitation, name that which elapsed from the death of Domitian to the accession of Commodus." Only eighteenth-century specialists today will know that in Robertson's history of the emperor Charles V, published seven years before the first volume of the *Decline and Fall*, he had written, "If a man were called to fix upon the period in the history of the world during which the condition of the human race was most calamitous and afflicted, he would without hesitation name that which elapsed from the death of Theodosius the Great to the establishment of the Lombards in Italy." For Gibbon this resemblance is not plagiarism but homage. He was concerned to explain as forcefully as possible his beginning with the Antonines, and he was following a system of thought, identifying the age of happiest felicity in comparison with the age of greatest misery, that constituted a mechanism for providing both the instruction and the elegance that he sought in his historical writing.

What we might consider plagiarism was of no great concern to Gibbon. He assembled his facts where he could find them, and he tried without undue strain to identify the most reliable purveyors of them. He was well acquainted with many of the great works of classical and late antiquity, and he was prepared within limits to check out sources to which he was referred by his modern authorities. But he had no desire to waste his time in protracted antiquarian research. As he readily acknowledged at the beginning of the chapter in which he proposed to expound theological debates on the incarnation, it was simply just too much trouble to document all that he was about to lay before the general public. He did not hesitate to put his problem directly before his readers: "By what means shall I authenticate this previous enquiry which I have studied to circumscribe and compress?" In other words, he is going to provide a synthesis of what he has read. He then declares:

> If I persist in supporting each fact or reflection by its proper and special evidence, every line would demand a string of testimonies, and every note would swell to a critical dissertation. But the numberless passages of antiquity which I have seen with my own eyes are compiled, digested, and illustrated by Petavius and Leclercq, by Beausobre and Mosheim. I shall be content to fortify my narrative by the names and characters of these respectable guides.

Nowhere does Gibbon make quite so plain his lack of interest in the minutiae of traditional scholarship.

Attentive readers of the *Decline and Fall* will find many a passage in which Gibbon's paraphrase of ancient authors comes through the text of a modern writer he had consulted rather than from the ancient author directly. In the case of Julian the Apostate, I have been able to prove that some of Gibbon's quotations from Ammianus Marcellinus and from Julian himself were in fact directly translated from the French paraphrase of the Abbé de la Bléterie and not from the originals.[2] In the outcry over

2. See chapter 4 in this volume.

the notorious fifteenth and sixteenth chapters on the origins of Christianity, one critic, the unfortunate Henry Edwards Davis, B.A., of Balliol College, Oxford, was able to set up in parallel columns a huge series of direct borrowings by Gibbon. And Mr. Davis, of course, categorized these as plagiarisms.

Now Mr. Davis is best known as the helpless target of Gibbon's powerful reply to his critique. The famous *Vindication of Some Passages in the Fifteenth and Sixteenth Chapters* is, from start to finish, a vigorous rebuttal of the charges made by Mr. Davis in his very detailed book. We all know the ironic beginning of the *Vindication* in which Gibbon observes in apparent bewilderment that Mr. Davis "styles himself a Bachelor of Arts, and a member of Balliol College in the University of Oxford," and we all know that Gibbon in the same work declared, "I cannot profess myself very desirous of Mr. Davis's acquaintance; but if he will take the trouble of calling at my house any afternoon when I am *not* at home, my servant shall show him my library, which he will find tolerably well furnished with the useful authors, ancient as well as modern, ecclesiastical as well as profane, who have *directly* supplied me with the materials of my history."

But these palpable hits should not make us forget that Gibbon felt called upon to write the *Vindication* in the first place. Davis's attack was a genuine threat to the integrity of Gibbon's work. The section on plagiarisms, which runs to dozens of pages, is the most damaging, and yet it is that section to which Gibbon devotes the least space in his reply. Under the rubric of plagiarisms Gibbon simply tells his readers that he should be congratulated for choosing to rely upon the most reputable scholars and in any event can scarcely be expected to waste a great deal of time in looking up material that others have looked up before him. "It would surely be unreasonable," protested Gibbon, "to expect that the historian should peruse enormous volumes, with the uncertain hope of extracting a few interesting lines, or that he should sacrifice whole days to the momentary amusement of his reader. Fortunately for us both, the diligence of ecclesiastical critics has facilitated our enquiries." In other words, there was substance to the charges brought by Davis; and Gibbon knew that, if they went unanswered, they could detract substantially from the readership of his work. His *Vindication* is not so much a reply to Davis's charges as a powerful affirmation that these charges simply do not matter. The rhetorical fireworks with which Gibbon destroyed Henry Edwards Davis for all time have tended to make readers forget that he was one of many who attacked Gibbon's fifteenth and sixteenth chapters.

Yet it was only this attack that provoked Gibbon to issue a detailed reply, although, to be sure, he took the opportunity in doing so to comment on some other critics as well.

If Gibbon's insouciance about correct scholarly method must be judged blameworthy to some extent, it nonetheless allowed him to exercise his talents as a *philosophe* without exposing the inadequacies he undoubtedly felt as an *érudit*. In his *Vindication*, when he addresses the plagiarisms alleged by Davis, Gibbon says with an almost disarming candor that if the public should think his two chapters on early Christianity contained materials that are of interest and value, "it is of little moment to whom they properly belong." He then goes on to say, "If my readers are satisfied with the form, the colours, the new arrangement which I have given to the labours of my predecessors, they may perhaps consider me not as a contemptible Thief, but as an honest and industrious Manufacturer, who has fairly procured the raw materials, and worked them up with a laudable degree of skill and success." This is an astonishingly open and unblushing description of Gibbon's perception of himself as a historian for the *grand public*. Scholars provide the raw materials, but he works them up with due attention to form, colors, and arrangement. It is necessarily in the elaboration of the raw materials that Gibbon's historical imagination can assert itself. I have dilated upon Gibbon's rather dismissive view of scholarship because it is evidently the very strength of his imagination that has moved him to prefer form, colors, and arrangement to scholarly precision. The author of the *Vindication* appears, therefore, as very much the same writer as the young man of twenty-five years of age who admitted that he lacked exactness but judged the shining qualities of his understanding to be "extensiveness and penetration."

Gibbon thus treated the raw materials of ancient and medieval history much as a novelist treated the plot line. Many will recall his famous tribute to Fielding in the *Memoirs*, when he declared that "the romance of Tom Jones, that exquisite picture of human manners, will outlive the palace of the Escorial and the imperial eagle of the House of Austria." But Gibbon never dreamt of writing fiction himself. In a famous footnote in the *Decline and Fall* he observed, "The *Cyropaedia* [of Xenophon] is vague and languid: the *Anabasis* is circumstantial and animated. Such is the eternal difference between fiction and truth." Yet Gibbon shaped his truth as if it were fiction, preserving thereby the animation of human history and the art of the novelist. In this sense Gibbon could describe himself in the *Vindication* as a Manufacturer.

For Gibbon, the manufacturing process not only included discarding boring material, such as much of the history of the last eight hundred years with which he had to deal. It also required him to flesh out those important episodes on which the ancient tradition was, for his purposes, regrettably inadequate or even altogether silent. Gibbon was, as always, candid about his procedures, and at the beginning of chapter 10 of the *Decline and Fall* when he approaches the exceptionally ill-documented time of the mid-third century A.D., he declares, "The confusion of the times, and the scarcity of authentic memorials, oppose equal difficulties to this historian, who attempts to preserve a clear and unbroken thread of narration." Yet the period is a pivotal one in the transition from Roman Empire to the early Byzantine age, and Gibbon's problem has been acutely felt by all historians who have followed him, The first edition of the *Cambridge Ancient History*, for example, turned over the whole period to numismatists because there were more interesting coins from this period than there were texts. Yet Gibbon's solution to the problem of insufficient evidence was simply free invention. Here is the way he describes that solution: "Surrounded with imperfect fragments, always concise, often obscure, and sometimes contradictory, he [the historian] is reduced to collect, to compare, and to conjecture: and though he ought never to place his conjectures in the rank of facts, yet the knowledge of human nature, and of the sure operation of its fierce and unrestrained passions, might, on some occasions, supply the want of historical materials."

And with this justification Gibbon drew from his knowledge of human nature some of the most unforgettable portraits of fierce and unrestrained passion in Western literature. His famous description of Augustus, constructed upon a few intimations in Tacitus and so fundamental to Syme's vision of the Roman revolution, is almost entirely invented on the basis of inference. No ancient texts tell us what Gibbon tells us about the character of Augustus:

> The tender respect of Augustus for a free constitution, which he had destroyed, can only be explained by an attentive consideration of the character of that subtle tyrant. A cool head, an unfeeling heart, and a cowardly disposition, prompted him, at the age of nineteen, to assume the mask of hypocrisy, which he never afterwards laid aside. With the same hand, and probably with the same temper, he signed the proscription of Cicero, and the pardon of

Cinna. His virtues, and even his vices, were artificial; and according
to the various dictates of his interest he was at first the enemy, and
at last the father, of the Roman world.

This masterly and compelling portrait—whether true or false, we shall
probably never know—not only supplied, in Gibbon's words, "the want
of historical materials," it also gave the historian an organizing principle
for his entire work. As the great narrative moves on across the centuries, Gibbon returns at crucial moments to make a comparison with the
founder of the Roman Empire, and he never loses sight of the characterization he provided in the third chapter. We have already observed
that Mommsen was profoundly impressed by the parallel that Gibbon
drew between Augustus and Constantine, a parallel in which the founder
of the Byzantine Empire was represented (as no ancient source ever
represented him) as a master of artifice and the author of the second
Roman revolution. But Gibbon enhances the dramatic contrast between
Augustus and Constantine by emphasizing the rise of the first emperor
from tyranny to the fatherhood of humankind and the descent of the
founder of Constantinople from heroism to cruelty and dissolution. It
obviously served Gibbon's view of the influence and effects of Christianity to observe dissolution after conversion.

Again, many chapters and many hundreds of years later, Augustus is
once more brought back to make a comparison with the pathetic Charles
IV in the fourteenth century: "If we annihilate the interval of time and
space between Augustus and Charles, strong and striking will be the contrast between the two Caesars: the Bohemian who concealed his weakness
under the mask of ostentation, and the Roman who disguised his strength
under the semblance of modesty." Richard Wagner said to Cosima one
evening in July of 1872 that Gibbon had created powerfully dramatic
characters in his work. "All the figures are there" for a great drama, but
"only the dramatists are missing." What Wagner seems to mean is that the
memorable characters are presented in splendid tableaux without much
interacting with one another, as would be required in an integrated piece
for the theater. Just as scholars provided raw material for Gibbon, Gibbon
in Wagner's view provided raw material for dramatists.

In addition to creating historical characters out of the wealth of his
understanding of human passion, Gibbon was able to develop his narrative still further through the deliberate and sometimes downright startling transposition of materials from one historical period to another.

He was more interested in the usefulness of an ancient source for his purpose than he was in historical accuracy. This characteristic of Gibbon's method has been noticed more than once, but it needs to take its place here as another means by which his imagination was given free play. In describing the Persian nobility in chapter 8 of the *Decline and Fall*, Gibbon pieced together a memorable account from a variety of ancient and modern texts, and his justification for doing so was simply that human nature tended to remain the same and that what was true of the Persians in the fifth century B.C. was likely to be true of the Persians in the third century A.D. In the final footnote to that chapter he says, without embarrassment, "From Herodotus, Xenophon, Herodian, Ammianus, Chardin, etc., I have extracted such *probable* accounts of the Persian nobility, as seem either common to every age, or particular to that of the Sassanids." In other words, sources that mention the Sassanids were included in his account of that Persian dynasty, and sources that did not were included because of characteristics common to every age. In a particularly notorious instance that was vigorously censured by Cavafy in his marginalia to Gibbon, a direct quotation from Xenophon's *Anabasis* is included in Gibbon's account of the victory of Galerius over the Persians in the late third century A.D. Again, in Gibbon's description of the Battle of the Golden Horn in 1453, he does not hesitate to avail himself of the testimony of Thucydides, who wrote in the late fifth century B.C. In a footnote to a vivid description of Muhammed II sitting on horseback on the beach, Gibbon calmly acknowledges, "I must confess that I have before my eyes the living picture which Thucydides has drawn of the passions and gestures of the Athenians in the naval engagement in the great harbour of Syracuse." Thus was Gibbon's imagination nourished by the ancient sources but wholly unconfined by them.

Yet, despite the great descriptive passages that reflect Gibbon's reading of books and of men, his reconstructions are essentially dramatic or theatrical rather than purely visual. There is very little in the *Decline and Fall* to suggest that Gibbon's aesthetic appreciation contributed much to his visual imagination. His rare allusions to art and architecture are undistinguished. Monuments interest him principally for their symbolism and historical significance, so that when he comes to such discoveries of the eighteenth century as the remains at Palmyra or the palace of Diocletian at Split, he is uncharacteristically speechless. For Palmyra he can only make an admiring but banal reference to the work of Dawkins and Wood, and for the palace at Split he feels obliged to quote directly from Adam's account of the palace. There is no hint of the archaeological discoveries at Pompeii and Herculaneum that were of such concern to eighteenth-century artists and connoisseurs. But this should perhaps come as no surprise in an author who visited the Naples area when he was on the Grand Tour in 1764—the very tour on which he believed that he was inspired to write the *Decline and Fall*—and never took the trouble to visit Pompeii. It is clear from Gibbon's journals of that year that he tried valiantly to study and observe the artistic masterpieces in the museums of Italy. But most of the observations ring hollow, and his failure to make contact at Rome with Winckelmann and his circle of artists and dealers (whom Boswell met), to say nothing of his disinterest in the archaeology of the age, are incontrovertible evidence that he had no serious interest in art for its own sake.

But, despite this lack of visual imagination in relation to art or objects, Gibbon was nonetheless as excited by topography as he was by the spectacle of human passion. His description of Constantinople is still one of the best ever written, even though he had never been there. His ability to imagine the layout of the great city on the Bosporus where much of his history took place is staggering, but it was the city as a scene for events that fired his imagination. His description of Poggio sitting on the Capitol amid the ruins of the Temple of Jupiter at the beginning of the final chapter of the *Decline and Fall* is artfully paired with Gibbon's description of himself sitting amid the ruins of the Capitol at the fateful moment in which he is supposed to have conceived the idea of writing the history. In fact, in the description of that memorable moment in the various drafts of his *Memoirs* Gibbon was misled by Poggio's dream of the past into believing that he, like Poggio, was seated by the remains of the Temple of Jupiter, even though he was not. His error was undoubtedly due more to a desire for an artful parallel with which to conclude his work than to a recollection of an error in Nardini, whom he had read many years before. Poggio's reverie did indeed take place on the remains of the Temple of Jupiter; but, when Gibbon went to Rome, the Palazzo Caffarelli had already been built over the remains, and Gibbon was obliged to sit musing by the site of the Temple of Juno (not of Jupiter) where the barefooted friars were singing vespers. But despite inaccuracies, the description of the Capitol stands like the description of Constantinople as a brilliant testimony to Gibbon's use of topography for setting a scene.

His interest in such descriptions was not at all aesthetic. He lavished so much of his talent upon them to provide a suitable stage for great events. Wagner was right in detecting the dramatic quality of Gibbon's historiography. But it was not only the characters who were dramatic: the descriptions were dramatic too. Topography was a kind of a mise-en-scène, a stage set for the momentous events that were to be presented. In modern times it was the distinguished German historian and thinker Friedrich Meinecke, who in a brief essay on Gibbon accurately defined the theatrical character of Gibbon's historical writing. "Again and again," wrote Meinecke, "one is reminded in his historical work of the theatrical scenes of a classical drama." Meinecke goes on to suggest, probably correctly, that, although the rhetorical brilliance of Gibbon's diction can sometimes become a little tiresome, the theatrical power of his narrative moves the reader forward. We see once again that the greatness of Gibbon's work was apparent to non-Anglophone readers not so much for the brilliant style as for the presentation of the material. And we may recall that this is what Gibbon himself believed to be his greatest achievement in the writing of history. Let us remember, too, that from his youthful reading in Lausanne onward Gibbon was steeped in the classic historical theater of Racine and Corneille. *J'aime le théâtre*, wrote Gibbon in 1764, *mais j'ai peu de goût pour la farce* [I like the theater, but I have little taste for farce].

Theodor Mommsen, indisputably the most knowledgeable of German readers of Gibbon, acknowledged, as we saw, the enduring value of the *Decline and Fall* and seems to have felt, even at a distance of a hundred years, a certain competition from its author. Mommsen was far too intelligent not to have recognized that the imagination Gibbon brought to his narrative presupposed a certain arbitrary and superficial handling of the original sources. The young Mommsen, in his Nobel Prize–winning *Roman History*, had proved himself a master of historical narrative, but the older Mommsen must have realized increasingly the tension, verging on incompatibility, that arose from giving free rein to historical imagination while attempting to maintain scholarship at the highest level. When Mommsen visited England, his praise of Gibbon was as lavish as it evidently was in the lectures to his students in Berlin, so that it was not unnatural for the Camden Professor of Ancient History at Oxford, Henry Pelham, to invite Mommsen to the celebrations of the hundredth anniversary of Gibbon's death held in London in 1894 or, if he could not attend, to send an appropriate statement. Mommsen sent a letter that was read out by Professor Pelham at the time and widely reported as one of many tributes to the author of the *Decline and Fall*.

Dr. Brian Croke of Australia has tracked down the publication of the brief missive that Mommsen sent to Pelham. It is at once a surprising and perceptive document, for it turns out that Mommsen refused to supply a public tribute. In his own excellent English Mommsen wrote as follows:

> I feel immensely honoured by the request you have made to me in the name of the Gibbon committee; but you must excuse me if I cannot accept. I have been obliged to undertake new and very serious tasks for my inscriptions, and it is absolutely impossible for me to leave Berlin this winter. If it were not, I might try to overcome the horror I have always felt for congress-going, and in this instance it would have been compensated by the pleasure of revisiting England and seeing once more my English friends.
>
> As for the paper you want me to write, it is not easy for me to say No; but after long, and too long, consideration, I cannot say Yes. Acknowledging in the highest degree the mastery of an unequalled historian, speaking publicly of him, I should be obliged to limit in a certain way my admiration of his work. He has taught us to combine oriental with occidental lore; and he has infused in history the essence of large doctrine and theology; his "solemn sneer" has put its stamp upon those centuries of civilization rotting and of humanity decaying into civil and ecclesiastical despotism. But his researches are not equal to his great views: he has read up more than a historian should. A first-rate writer, he is not a plodder. This must be said, and will be said; but you understand that such saying would not become this festival, and would come with a bad grace from me.

So here we have a definitive statement from Mommsen about the unequaled historian. The scholar in Mommsen fueled the rival, and he had at last to fault Gibbon where he could easily be faulted—for scholarly inadequacies. Mommsen is right when he says that Gibbon's researches were not equal to his great views. He is right when he says that Gibbon read up—or, as we might say nowadays, mugged up—more than a historian should. Gibbon did not regularly work at firsthand and with a critical eye. But Mommsen must have known perfectly well that if Gibbon had done the kind of research expected of a thoroughgoing scholar, the great views would in all probability never have taken shape or found expression. This, I suspect, is a paradox that confronted and troubled Mommsen in his old age.

If Gibbon had been the kind of scholarly historian that Mommsen wanted, he would not, indeed he could not, have been the historian that we admire today. He might have been another Tillemont, or even another Hume or Robertson. By recognizing the weaknesses of Gibbon we can see why he was great. Those very weaknesses allowed that strong imagination to run its course, to create the matchless characterizations, the high drama, and the vivid scenes that constitute the *Decline and Fall.* These are all manifestations of a historical imagination that overrides Gibbon's industry and eloquence and makes his work far more than an anthology of memorable quotations. Mommsen's opinion of Gibbon was essentially right; but if he had rephrased it a little differently, it would by no means have been graceless of him to pronounce it publicly. But had he done this, he would have had to admit that Gibbon's work was not scholarship but something that surpassed scholarship: literature of genius. Without the research of his predecessors, Gibbon could certainly not have undertaken the manufacture of which he spoke in his *Vindication,* but he had neither the desire nor the capacity to do the same kind of research himself. What he did was something much more remarkable. If Mommsen was not prepared to face up to this, it was probably for the same reason that he was never prepared to write the missing volume in his *Roman History.* Although the greatest Roman historian of modern times, Theodor Mommsen could have had no hope of matching Edward Gibbon on the history of the Roman Empire.

# CHAPTER TWO

# GIBBON ON CIVIL WAR AND REBELLION IN THE DECLINE OF THE ROMAN EMPIRE

NEAR THE BEGINNING OF THE TWENTY-SIXTH CHAPTER of the *Decline and Fall*, Gibbon alludes to "the disastrous period of the fall of the Roman empire, which may justly be dated from the reign of Valens." Although he thereby inaugurates the fall some four centuries after the time of Caesar Augustus, his own narration of the decline opens, as everyone knows, with the dissolution of the supposed Antonine peace. In the winter of 1790–91, Gibbon realized that he had made a terrible mistake: he had misapprehended the causes of decline and in so doing had started his great work at the wrong point. But it was too late. Gibbon's papers for a seventh volume, which was to contain revisions of the *Decline and Fall*, preserve the following eloquent words: "Should I not have deduced the decline of the Empire from the Civil Wars, that ensued after the fall of Nero or even from the tyranny which succeeded the reign of Augustus? Alas! I should: but of what avail is this tardy knowledge? Where error is irretrievable, repentance is

*Note*: References to the *Decline and Fall* (*DF*) are given by chapter number and page in the three-volume Penguin edition of David Womersley (London: Penguin, 1994).

useless."[1] It is a strange irony that Gibbon's admired Roman predecessor, Tacitus, "the first of historians who applied the science of philosophy to the study of facts,"[2] had similarly recognized, though not when it was too late, that his initial work on imperial Rome had to be supplemented by another on the preceding reigns. By late 1790, Gibbon had seen two major uprisings, one in America and one in France, and we may imagine that he was moved enough to attach more importance than before to civil war and social tumult. The readjustment was difficult for Gibbon, who by 1793 had abandoned all hope for the French rebels, now become in his judgment "the new barbarians."[3] But they rose from within and did not invade from without.

If one reads Gibbon's chapters on the decline of Rome with an eye to his observations on civil war and uprisings, it becomes easy to see why this great and scrupulous historian came to castigate his own work so unambiguously. Gibbon's vast reading and philosophic reflection had served only to persuade him that disturbances in society were but an ugly disfigurement—a stain on the social fabric or a wound in the body politic. They were essentially external; they were disagreeable but susceptible of cleansing or healing. It is not impossible that Gibbon's sharp mind had been dulled by the potency of his own metaphors.

The stain and the wound occur with almost equal frequency and in contexts that rarely represent the historian's most profound thought. For example, in chapter 3 we find one of Gibbon's most breathtaking inaccuracies (to which we shall return): "Excepting only this short, though violent eruption of military licence [A.D. 69], the two centuries from Augustus to Commodus passed away unstained with civil blood, and undisturbed by revolutions."[4] In chapter 4 we are told that because of the love of power "almost every page of history has been stained with civil blood."[5] The old Gordian in chapter 7 begs his supporters to let him

---

1. *The English Essays of Edward Gibbon*, ed. P. B. Craddock (Oxford: Oxford University Press, 1972), p. 338. On the date of these notes, see Craddock, p. 211.

2. *DF*, chap. 9, p. 230.

3. *The Letters of Edward Gibbon*, ed. J. E. Norton (London: Cassell, 1956), III, p. 321. This extreme judgment comes at the end of the crescendo of despair that follows Gibbon's initially sympathetic reaction to the revolutionaries. Already in December 1789, he wrote, "How many years must elapse before France can recover any vigour, or recover her station among the powers of Europe?" (*Letters*, III, p. 184).

4. *DF*, chap. 3, p. 98.

5. *DF*, chap. 4, p. 110.

die "without staining his feeble age with civil blood."[6] And in chapter 26 Gibbon declares that the cause of a successful aspirant to power "is frequently stained by the guilt of conspiracy or civil war."[7]

For Gibbon, the Roman Empire was "that great body,"[8] like the *immensum imperii corpus* of Galba's speech in Tacitus's *Histories*.[9] It could be wounded, but the wounds could be healed. Augustus "hoped that the wounds of civil discord would be completely healed."[10] The emperor Tacitus in the third century "studied to heal the wounds which imperial pride, civil discord, and military violence had inflicted on the constitution."[11] In the last years of Constantius, barbarians moved into Gaul "before the wounds of civil discord could be healed."[12] In one important passage, concerning the establishment of Septimius Severus as emperor, Gibbon acknowledged that appearances could be deceptive: "Although the wounds of civil war appeared completely healed,"[13] they were not. A "mortal poison" was left in the vitals of the constitution,"[14] and with this remark the "slow and secret poison," which had been introduced "into the vitals of the empire" well before Severus, received a booster shot.[15] It may be that Gibbon himself was not altogether free from the fault he discovered in Ammianus: "It is not easy to distinguish his facts from his metaphors."[16]

Disruptive, disfiguring, even poisonous on occasion, civil strife and social upheaval in the period of Rome's decline rarely seemed to Gibbon much more than a superficial occurrence due to a widespread love of power. A consideration of the relevant occurrences, as they are chronicled by Gibbon, makes his attitude embarrassingly clear. To take a particularly striking example, from A.D. 132 to 135 the Jews, under the leadership of Bar Kochba, rose in a mighty rebellion against Roman authority.

6. *DF*, chap. 7, p. 194.
7. *DF*, chap. 26, p. 1073.
8. *DF*, chap. 15, p. 446.
9. Tacitus, *Hist.* 1.16. Neither Gibbon in modern times nor Tacitus in ancient was alone in preferring this imagery for the state. See my remark in note 43 below.
10. *DF*, chap. 3, p. 87.
11. *DF*, chap. 12, p. 331.
12. *DF*, chap. 19, p. 694.
13. *DF*, chap. 5, p. 145.
14. *DF*, chap. 5, p. 145.
15. *DF*, chap. 2, p. 83.
16. *DF*, chap. 26, p. 1023 n. 1.

The uprising was fierce and protracted, ultimately requiring the presence of the Emperor Hadrian himself. By its end, Jerusalem was transformed into the Roman colony of Aelia Capitolina. No historian would deny the significance of these events not only in the annals of Rome but also of European civilization down to the present. In the opening pages of his *Decline and Fall*, Gibbon appears to have forgotten completely about this four-year war: "If we except a few slight hostilities that served to exercise the legions of the frontier, the reigns of Hadrian and Antoninus Pius offer the fair prospect of universal peace."[17] But Judaea was not on the frontier, nor were the hostilities slight. Gibbon certainly knew about the rebellion of Bar Kochba, and when in the course of his work his subject drifted close to the history of the Jews he was able to write in chapter 15: "But at length, under the reign of Hadrian, the desperate fanaticism of the Jews filled up the measure of their calamities."[18] By chapter 16, Gibbon refers to "that furious war which was terminated only by the ruin of Jerusalem," and he labels it "that memorable rebellion."[19] Yet he himself had not remembered it when he was writing the text of chapter 1.

Gibbon was perfectly capable of distinguishing popular uprisings and revolts from "those civil wars which are artificially supported for the benefit of a few factious and designing leaders."[20] On the whole, he neither liked nor trusted the people. He attributed the peace and prosperity of Europe in 1776 to a general recognition of "the superior prerogative of birth," which he declared to be "the plainest and least invidious of all distinctions among mankind."[21] He had no patience with the tensions and disturbances of the highly complex society of ancient Alexandria: "The most trifling occasion, a transient scarcity of flesh or lentils, the neglect of an accustomed salutation, a mistake of precedency in the public baths, or even a religious dispute, were at any time sufficient to kindle a sedition among that vast multitude, whose resentments were furious and implacable."[22] Gibbon's outlook coalesced easily and naturally with

17. *DF*, chap. 1, p. 38. In the footnote he wrote for this text Gibbon somewhat lamely reminded himself and his reader of the omission of Bar Kochba's revolt.

18. *DF*, chap. 15, p. 454.

19. *DF*, chap. 16, p. 526.

20. *DF*, chap. 7, p. 198.

21. *DF*, chap. 7, p. 198.

22. *DF*, chap. 10, p. 293.

that of his model and predecessor, Tacitus, who scorned the *plebs sordida* that was accustomed to spectacles and theatrical entertainments.[23] For Tacitus, the mob abused the body of Vitellius with the same perversity (*pravitas*) with which they had fawned upon him as emperor;[24] the enthusiasms of the Roman people were short-lived and ill-omened (*breves et infaustos populi Romani amores*).[25] Compare Gibbon: "The resolutions of the multitude generally depend upon a moment; and the caprice of passion might equally determine the seditious legion to lay down their arms at the emperor's feet, or to plunge them into his breast."[26]

Gibbon's opinion of the movements of multitudes caused him to dismiss one of the more significant events in the social history of the later Roman Empire. The peasant revolt of the so-called Bagaudae in Gaul began under the Tetrarchy and had long-lasting influence. Gibbon introduces the subject by making a facile and false comparison of the Bagaudae insurrection with "those which in the fourteenth century successively afflicted both France and England";[27] he then observes drily: "They asserted the natural rights of men, but they asserted those rights with the most savage cruelty."[28] When they yielded to the armies of Rome, "the strength of union and discipline obtained an easy victory over a licentious and divided multitude."[29] It is impossible to tell from reading Gibbon that in the peasant revolt under the Tetrarchy lay the origins of an independent Brittany ruled by the Bagaudae in the fifth century. When Gibbon himself finally reaches, at the end of chapter 35,[30] the fortunes of Brittany, or Armorica as it was called, he shows no sign of recalling that "the confederations of the Bagaudae" who created the "disorderly independence" in the fifth century were the descendants of the licentious multitude he has already written about. It is simply not true to say of the revolt of Armorica, "the Imperial ministers pursued with proscriptive laws, and ineffectual arms, the rebels whom they had made." It was the revolt of America, not Armorica, that Gibbon had in

23. Tacitus, *Hist.* 1.4.
24. Tacitus, *Hist.* 3.85.
25. Tacitus, *Ann.* 2.41.
26. *DF*, chap. 6, p. 177.
27. *DF*, chap. 13, p. 363.
28. *DF*, chap. 13, p. 364.
29. *DF*, chap. 13, p. 364
30. *DF*, chap. 35, p. 356.

mind as he concluded chapter 35. As we know, for example, from his celebrated "General Observations on the Fall of the Roman Empire in the West," Gibbon relished making parallels and predictions; but, owing to some fundamental attitudes, he was not always at his most perceptive in doing so. Although contemporary affairs interested and moved him, he responded to them as the man of letters he was, insulated by his library. Gibbon's seat in Parliament exposed him directly to the excitement of current history and yet never altered his bookish temperament.

If Gibbon was contemptuous of popular rebellions and upheavals, he viewed with equal contempt the efforts of Roman factional leaders to raise the standard of revolt and to curry favor with the people or with the legions. It is astonishing that he could describe the two centuries from Augustus to Commodus as "unstained with civil blood, and undisturbed by revolutions"—with the sole exception of the "military licence" of A.D. 69.[31] Gibbon goes on to admit that he is aware of "three inconsiderable rebellions," which he enumerates in a footnote. Yet the rebellion of Camillus Scribonianus was a sinister adumbration of the coming proclamations of claimants to the throne as they served at the head of legions in the provinces. The rebellion of Antonius Saturninus under Domitian signaled the alliance of Roman usurpers with primitive tribes on the frontiers. And the rebellion of Avidius Cassius in Syria in A.D. 175 marked the first attempt of a provincial Roman to exploit the allegiance of his home territory in making a desperate claim to the purple. How could Gibbon miss all this? For him the uprisings are inconsiderable for one reason only: they failed. They "were all suppressed in a few months, and without even the hazard of a battle."

The view of almost uninterrupted peace from Augustus to Commodus depends not only on the depreciation of disturbances Gibbon mentions but on the omission of others. We have already noted the absence of the Jewish revolt in Gibbon's account of Hadrian; he likewise omits, in his survey of the first century A.D., the Jewish revolt that broke out in A.D. 66 and ended with the Fall of Masada. We hear nothing of the revolt of Tacfarinas in Africa under Tiberius, nothing of the great popular support for the pretenders who claimed to be Nero after Nero was dead, nothing of the uprising of the Jewish diaspora at the end of Trajan's reign (now better documented through archaeology but amply attested in sources

---

31. *DF*, chap. 3, p. 98.

that Gibbon knew). Gibbon's deep persuasion that the early centuries of the Roman Empire were a time of relatively unviolated peace can perhaps best be traced to the author he revered, Tacitus. Gibbon's language is like his—*immota quippe aut modice lacessita pax* [an undisturbed or modestly disrupted peace].[32] In composing the *Annals*, covering A.D. 14–68, Tacitus could say this with a certain aptness, especially as a reinforcement of his view that the price of peace was monarchy: Augustus gave *iura quis pace et principe uteremur; acriora ex eo vincla*: the laws by which we enjoy both peace and monarchy—the result was a more acute bondage.[33] Although valuing monarchy more highly, Gibbon fully imbibed this lesson and these words. Yet not even Tacitus himself would have described the years from 68 to 96 as *modice lacessita pax*, as the opening chapters of his *Histories* make very plain.

Gibbon took Tacitus as the model of a philosophic historian, blending *érudit* and *philosophe* before the opposition had ever been thought of. We are in no doubt as to what a philosophic historian should, in Gibbon's view, be able to accomplish, namely, to discover secret causes and connections. When the soldiery submitted to Severus Alexander, Gibbon was moved to remark, "Perhaps, if the singular transaction had been investigated by the penetration of a philosopher, we should discover the secret causes which on that occasion authorized the boldness of the prince and commanded the obedience of the troops."[34] Later, in reviewing ancient assessments of the character of Theodosius, Gibbon wrote, "There are few observers who possess a clear and comprehensive view of the revolutions of society; and who are capable of discovering the nice and secret springs of action which impel, in the same uniform direction, the blind and capricious passions of a multitude of individuals."[35] This conception of the philosophic role of a historian was firmly rooted in Gibbon and appears clearly articulated in his early *Essai sur l'étude de la littérature*, published in 1761 but written in 1758–59. There the young Gibbon dilates upon *l'esprit philosophique* and designates Tacitus as its embodiment: "To my knowledge only Tacitus fulfils my idea of the philosophic historian."[36] Only the philosopher can perceive amid

32. Tacitus, *Ann.* 4.32.
33. Tacitus, *Ann.* 3.28.
34. *DF*, chap. 6, p. 177.
35. *DF*, chap. 27, p. 69.
36. *Essai*, chap. 52.

the chaotic mass of historical facts "those that prevail overall by virtue of intimate connections and the generation of activity."[37] Montesquieu is singled out, not surprisingly, for particular praise. Gibbon's conviction that there were always secret springs of action in human history naturally inclined him to consider events so public and obvious as civil war or rebellion to be purely external, superficial, and ultimately insignificant. These were to be numbered among the innumerable facts "qui ne prouvent rien au-delà de leur propre existence."[38] In alluding to Constantius's struggle with Magnentius, Gibbon opens a sentence, "As long as the civil war suspended the fate of the Roman world...."[39] The war merely interrupted the fulfillment of a fate set in motion by hidden causes; it is presented as external to them.

In writing the *Decline and Fall*, Gibbon's search for the hidden springs of action not only diverted his attention from tumultuous events but also led him to postulate a secret cause for the whole decline of Rome. Gibbon, as often, turned to metaphor: "This long peace, and the uniform government of the Romans, introduced a slow and secret poison into the vitals of the empire."[40] Although the visible decline did not begin before Commodus, Gibbon is obliged to explain what happened then in terms of the poison of peace. By the end of the fourth century a kindred poison is transfused from one organism to another: "The effeminate luxury which infected the manners of courts and cities had instilled a secret and destructive poison into the camps of the legions."[41] And we can recall that, between the long peace and the effeminacy of the Theodosian court, Septimius Severus had added a "mortal poison" from the civil wars of 193—not, however, a secret poison. It is remarkable enough that Gibbon should have considered the disturbances of 193 poisonous at all in view of his dismissive attitude toward the comparable vexations of 69. But Gibbon was by no means consistent in his vast work, and he had a special reason to give more weight to 193. With the death of Commodus at the end of the preceding year and the eventual emergence of Severus at the end of the civil strife of 193, the visible decline of Rome, in Gibbonian terms, was launched. The era of public felicity was over, and Gibbon saw

37. *Essai*, chap. 49.
38. *Essai*, chap. 49.
39. *DF*, chap. 19, p. 688.
40. *DF*, chap. 2, p. 83.
41. *DF*, chap. 27, p. 70.

in Severus "the principal author of the decline of the Roman empire."[42] Gibbon had forced himself into this remarkable opinion.

By the time of the "General Observations" in chapter 38, Gibbon's notions of Roman decline had changed noticeably in favor of an interpretation redolent of Montesquieu: "The decline of Rome was the natural and inevitable effect of immoderate greatness." There is no word of the secret poisons of peace and effeminacy, no harking back to the impact of Septimius Severus. Barbarians and Christianity had come to engage Gibbon's attention. The secret cause he had tried to find eluded him. His problem consisted in the continuing search for a single secret cause. Had he looked only for various secret springs of action, his interpretations might have cohered better. It is unclear why Gibbon's concept of the philosophic spirit kept driving him to find a secret poison, a single hidden cause to explain the whole story of Rome's decline. But one can hazard a guess. It may once again have been Gibbon's great evil genius, Tacitus.

In chapter 4 of the first book of his *Histories*, Tacitus declared that at the death of Nero the secret of empire was revealed (*evulgato imperii arcano*): an emperor could be made in another place than Rome. Gibbon, misjudging the influence of the legionary troops that made it possible for emperors to be raised up in the provinces, tried to go beyond Tacitus's identification of the *arcanum imperii*; but, just as with the *modice lacessita pax*, Tacitus's formulation seemed to have been embedded in his thought. There had to be, for the historian of Rome's decline, an *arcanum imperii*. Refusing to see in civil war and revolt anything secret, Gibbon had to look elsewhere. As he did so and as his reflections naturally found expression in metaphor, the *arcanum imperii* of Tacitus became transformed into a poison that infected the immense *corpus* of the empire.[43]

Naturally it would not have been necessary for Gibbon to look to Tacitus for the concept of a secret cause. The thought of the eighteenth century was full of it, as is evident not least in Gibbon's early *Essai sur l'étude de la littérature*, where he discusses the importance—which he later

---

42. *DF*, chap. 5, p. 148.
43. Cf., for the phraseology *venenum adfusum* (in a different context), Tacitus, *Ann.* 1.10. I am not, of course, suggesting that Gibbon owed the idea to Tacitus, but rather that a writer imbued with Tacitean language would choose this terminology from the diction of decline.

forgot—of searching for many hidden causes rather than one.[44] Although Tacitus himself had a powerful influence in shaping post-Renaissance theories of causation, it is more significant that Gibbon worked closely from the original ancient sources.[45] His renewed study of Tacitus for the *Decline and Fall* was more than sufficient to put him in search of a secret cause for Rome's decline. Gibbon's intellectual heritage was imperceptibly metamorphosed into the attitude of his classical master.

It may be, too, that somewhere in Gibbon's extraordinary mind there echoed the *tam grande secretum* proclaimed by the eloquent fourth-century pagan Symmachus. But Gibbon's treatment of Symmachus's pleading discourages such a notion: "Even scepticism is made to supply an apology for superstition. The great and incomprehensible *secret* of the universe eludes the enquiry of man."[46] That was obviously not the kind of secret a philosophic historian labored to discover. The secret of empire was.

It has sometimes been said that between the discussion of *l'esprit philosophique* in the *Essai* and the *Decline and Fall* Gibbon passed through a phase, connected with his Italian journey, of almost pure antiquarianism. Yet the journal does not bear this out. It reveals a voracious scholar, reading and digesting every learned treatise he could lay his hands on, but doing so with an admirable sense of the ultimate objectives of research. Writing in French, he observed, "It is a dry and ungrateful work, but when one builds an edifice it is necessary to dig the foundations. One is obliged to play the role of mason as well as architect."[47] Of the epigraphical collections of Muratori, Reinesius, and Gruter, Gibbon wrote, "Above all they will amply supply me with material for customs, practices, curious anecdotes, and all that interesting history that is hidden in ordinary history."[48] These reflections, written in Florence in the summer of 1764, display an arresting, even startling, sense of the historian's task. The concept of hidden history (*qui est cachée*) betrays the philosophic writer

44. *Essai*, chap. 49, "ce n'est qu'en rassemblant qu'on peut juger."

45. I have returned to this subject, with reference to Julian, in *Gibbon et Rome à la lumière de l'historiographie moderne.* Publications de la Faculté des Lettres de l'Université de Lausanne 22 (Geneva: Droz, 1977), 210–212.

46. *DF*, chap. 28, p. 75.

47. *Gibbon's Journey from Geneva to Rome: His Journal from 20 April to 2 October 1764*, ed. Georges A. Bonnard (London: Nelson, 1961), p. 129.

48. *Gibbon's Journey*, p. 221.

still mindful of his duty, but the attention to social behavior and customs illustrates a maturity absent from the *Essai*. At the same time Gibbon was busy with work on the geography and economy of Roman Italy as the direct result of an intensive study of Muratori's dissertation on an inscription, recently uncovered at Veleia, which provided precious details about the alimentation system of Trajan. Gibbon even fancied that he could improve on Muratori, whom he much admired. The inscription provides "the most useful illumination on the history, geography, and economy of that age."[49]

It is evident that the philosophic historian was at work on Roman history before he even reached Rome in the year 1764. His plan had been to compose *Recueils géographiques sur l'Italie*, but that original plan was gradually altered during the summer of 1764 as Gibbon was studying his inscriptions and observing the art of Italy. On the thirtieth of August he wrote in his journal about texts that would be useful "pour mes Desseins sur la géographie de l'Italie qui subsistent toujours quoique le plan en soit un peu changé."[50] It was on the same day that he penned his lines on the revelations of society concealed *dans l'histoire ordinaire*. By the time Gibbon reached Rome, the thought of a larger history of Rome and its empire may well have been in his head. If we must reject as romantic fiction Gibbon's later account of what started to his mind amid the ruins of the Capitol on October 15, 1764, it is nevertheless by no means impossible that the *Decline and Fall* had its origins in Gibbon's labors and ruminations on the Italian journey.

Gibbon's approach to the subject at that time was, as we can readily judge from the diary, substantially different from what was to appear in 1776. One finds, to be sure, the same scrupulous attention to ancient sources, the same taste for geography, the same alert wit, the authentic Gibbonian tone. But the deep interest in society and economic life is unparalleled in the *Decline and Fall*. Gibbon's painstaking work on the

---

49. *Gibbon's Journey*, p. 122. The Veleia inscription is no. 6675 in H. Dessau's *Inscriptiones Latinae Selectae*.

50. *Gibbon's Journey*, p. 221. It has sometimes been wrongly assumed that Gibbon's description of Italy was completed before he visited the country, because the work was started as a preparation for the visit. But it is clear from the passage in the *Journal* as well as from a letter written in Florence on June 20, 1764 (*Letters* [see note 3 above], p. 181), that he continued to work on the project, begun in Lausanne, during his Italian tour.

inscription of Veleia finds no resonance in his later masterpiece, where there is not even a passing allusion to Trajan's alimentation scheme. In the *Decline and Fall*, there is little sign of the sifting of *histoire ordinaire* to recover the secret history of society. The gulf between the would-be historian of 1764 and the author of the *Decline and Fall* is nowhere as apparent as in the following lines written at Turin on May 3, 1764: "A court for me is simultaneously an object of curiosity and of disgust. The servility of courtiers revolts me, and I see with horror the magnificence of palaces that have been cemented with the blood of peoples."[51] These remarks may be compared to Gibbon's reaction to a bust of Nero at Florence: "Ought I to say it, and say it here? Nero has never revolted me so much as Tiberius, Caligula, or Domitian. He had many vices, but he was not without virtues."[52] Gibbon had studied too much ancient history not to have known the high esteem in which people and soldiers held the emperor Nero. In 1764, Gibbon would not have ignored completely the three pretenders to Nero's name and their supporters. In 1764, Gibbon's attitude to an imperial court, to the first-century Roman emperors, to social history in general was manifestly not that of 1776. The Bagaudae might have held more interest for a historian who viewed with horror the magnificence of palaces "cemented with the blood of peoples."

What caused the change? Gibbon's personal circumstances may properly be invoked, particularly his social position in London and his seat in Parliament. But again there is Tacitus. To write his *Decline and Fall*, Gibbon steeped himself in the works of a writer with whom he must have felt increasingly sympathetic and whom he had judged since the days of the *Essai* to be the very model of a philosophic historian: "The revolution of ages may bring round the same calamities; but ages may revolve without producing a Tacitus to describe them."[53] Under the spell of the old Roman, Gibbon moved away from the sympathies and interests of the Italian journey. The Roman court and its vivid personalities, on which Tacitus laid such brilliant emphasis, enliven many of the most polished pages of Gibbon. His scorn of the multitude resembles that of Tacitus and underlies his refusal, which is not Tacitean, to allow any special importance to the upheavals of society. Revolts and civil wars play an often colorful but essentially superficial role. When they occur

51. *Gibbon's Journey*, p. 18.
52. *Gibbon's Journey*, p. 168.
53. *DF*, chap. 36, p. 399 n. 110.

in Gibbon's narrative, fate is suspended, history stained, the body politic wounded; but for him they have almost nothing to do with the explanation of decline.

Yet, sometime after the outbreak of the French Revolution—and conceivably under its influence—Gibbon was moved to write that he had been wrong to trace the decline of Rome from the collapse of the Antonines. He had attempted to write the history of the Roman Empire from the end of that era of felicity at which Tacitus had left off.[54] But instead, by his own admission, he should have "deduced the decline of the Empire" either from the civil wars of A.D. 69 or perhaps even from "the tyranny which succeeded the reign of Augustus" in A.D. 14. This constitutes an entirely new assessment of the first century A.D. and attaches a significance to the civil wars and "inconsiderable" rebellions altogether alien to Gibbon's earlier outlook. Yet the confession of irretrievable error has a curious and chilling aspect. It is not the bold declaration of rethinking that it seems at first to be. In minimizing the civil war after Nero's death, Gibbon had parted company with his Roman mentor in search of a more profound *arcanum*. When, in the winter of 1790–91, he acknowledged that he ought to have begun at one of those two first-century dates, he did no less than make the ultimate submission to Tacitus; for Tacitus had actually begun one major work, the *Histories*, with the civil wars of 69, and the other, the *Annals*, with "the tyranny which succeeded the reign of Augustus." In the shadow of the American and French revolutions, the old Roman claimed his disciple.

54. Observe Tacitus on his own time at *Agricola* 3 (*felicitatem temporum*) and *Hist.* 1.1 (*rara temporum felicitate*). The wording of Gibbon's celebrated judgment of the Antonine age is remarkably parallel to Robertson's reference to the century and a half after Theodosius: "If a man were called to fix upon the period in the history of the world during which the condition of the human race was most calamitous and afflicted, he would without hesitation name that which elapsed from the death of Theodosius the Great to the establishment of the Lombards in Italy" (*History of the Emperor Charles V* [1769], I, p. 10). I am inclined to think this parallel more significant for style than substance. Cf. D. Jordan, *Gibbon and His Roman Empire* (Urbana: University of Illinois Press, 1971), p. 216 n. 8.

# CHAPTER THREE

# REFLECTIONS ON GIBBON'S LIBRARY

IN 1773 EDWARD GIBBON SETTLED INTO HIS NEWLY renovated house at 7 Bentinck Street in London, where he could savor the independence and comfort that provided the luxuries he deemed indispensable for the creation of his *History of the Decline and Fall of the Roman Empire.* By taking refuge in his library, furnished with painted white bookcases and blue wallpaper with gold trim, Gibbon found, as he wrote in his *Memoirs,* that he could "divide the day between Study and Society." When he needed more books for his researches, he had not far to go to find them. "To a lover of books," he wrote, "the shops and sales in London present irresistible temptations; and the manufacture of my history required a various and growing stock of materials." He depicted his collection as a working library, and his books were themselves a vindication of his integrity as a historian. When Gibbon undertook to refute the allegations of the hapless Henry Davis, of Balliol College, who had attempted to discredit the fifteenth and sixteenth chapters of the *Decline and Fall,* their author declared, in a passage that every bibliophile will know and cherish, "I cannot profess myself very desirous of Mr. Davis's acquaintance; but if he will take the trouble of calling at my house any afternoon when I am *not* at home, my servant shall shew him my library,

*Note*: This lecture was delivered on the occasion of the Grolier Club's journey to the Gibbon exhibition at the Chapin Library in Williamstown, Massachusetts, November 11, 2000.

which he will find tolerably well furnished with the useful authors, ancient as well as modern, ecclesiastical as well as profane, who have *directly* supplied me with the material of my History."

Artfully deploying the backs of playing cards, Gibbon and others employed by him constructed a catalogue of this great library, which numbered some six thousand or more volumes by 1783. In that year Gibbon moved to Switzerland to join his dear friend and intellectual comrade, Georges Deyverdun, in Lausanne. In a letter to Deyverdun he again stressed the importance of his books for his work on the *History* as well as his indifference to popular fashion in assembling his collection. Writing in the excellent French in which he had published his early essay on literature, Gibbon declared to Deyverdun, "Les auteurs les moins chers à l'homme de goût, des ecclésiastiques, des Byzantins, des orientaux, sont les plus nécessaires à l'historien de la décadence et de la chute [Authors who are the least appealing to the man of taste—ecclesiastics, Byzantines, Orientals—are the most necessary for the historian of decline and fall]." In planning his move to Lausanne Gibbon contemplated the enormous cost of transporting his entire library and lamented that heaven had not chosen to make Switzerland a maritime nation ("Le ciel n'a pas voulu faire de la Suisse un pays maritime"). He decided to leave several thousand books behind—a collection that has only recently surfaced, after more than two centuries, in the London Athenaeum—because, as he wrote to Deyverdun, he counted on finding the standard works available in Lausanne.

A new catalogue was made of the library in Lausanne, and its survival in New York's Morgan Library became generally known in 1980, although it had been there since 1904. Gibbon's industrious modern bibliographer, Geoffrey Keynes (brother of the great economist), had missed this catalogue when he drew up his own in the late 1930s. The fate of Gibbon's library after his death in 1794 is well known, because he prescribed in his will that it be sold apart from six works in ninety-seven volumes that he bequeathed to the library of the Academy at Lausanne. William Beckford, of all people, bought the library in order, in his own words, "to have something to read when I passed through Lausanne." Read it he did. "I read myself nearly blind," he claimed, and then "I made a present of the library to my physician." The physician, Dr. Frédéric Scholl, who is unfortunately often equipped with an umlaut he does not deserve, ultimately sold off the library in two phases, and the records of those sales provide still further documentation for Gibbon's collection.

Beckford's role in the dispersal of this great eighteenth-century library is heavy with irony. In his own copy of Gibbon's *History* he wrote a jeremiad against its author, which is properly reproduced among the testimonies in the catalogue for the Williamstown exhibition. I cannot refrain from mentioning on this occasion that I possess a fine copy of the original publication of Henry Davis against the fifteenth and sixteenth chapters from the library of Roger Senhouse. Opposite his bookplate and below his signature Senhouse has written in pencil, "See also Wm Beckford's caustic ramblings on Gibbon (Anthony Hobson's lecture quoted [them], Grolier Club, May 1959)." It seems therefore appropriate for me, like Sotheby's Anthony Hobson, to quote Beckford's astonishing words once again to the Grolier members:

> The time is not far distant, Mr. Gibbon, when your almost ludicrous self-complacency, your numerous, and sometimes apparently wilful mistakes, your frequent distortion of historical Truth to provoke a gibe, or excite a sneer at everything most sacred and venerable, your ignorance of the oriental languages, your limited and far from acutely critical knowledge of the Latin and the Greek, and in the midst of all the prurient and obscene gossip of your notes—your affected moral purity perking up every now and then from the corrupt mass like artificial roses shaken off in the dark by some Prostitute on a heap of manure, your heartless scepticism, your unclassical fondness for meretricious ornament, your tumid diction, your monotonous jingle of periods, will be still more exposed and scouted than they have been. Once fairly kicked off from your lofty, bedizened stilts, you will be reduced to your just level and true standard.

It would require the insight of a clinical psychiatrist to explain Beckford's decision to buy Gibbon's Swiss library, but in the end we must be grateful to him for handing it over to Dr. Scholl, who at least put it on the market in a responsible way. Because we are so well informed about the library, it might be both entertaining and instructive first to explore a few titles that Gibbon clearly knew but were not to be found in his library, either in Bentinck Street or in Lausanne, and then to consider some important books that he possessed but clearly ignored. We may thereby learn a little more about his methods of work and his own tastes. At the end I should like to consider Gibbon's vision of himself within the whole literary pantheon as reflected in the selection of busts of great authors that he bought to be displayed among his books at Lausanne when his life was drawing to its close. The six drafts of his *Memoirs* make it poignantly obvious that Gibbon was concerned not only to secure his image in posterity but to establish the lineaments of it.

Let me turn to a large and important work cited by Gibbon but conspicuously absent from his library. This is the great Bollandist compilation published from 1644 onward under the general title of *Acta Sanctorum*. The enterprise had not been completed when Gibbon was writing, but its systematic survey of saints' days had already progressed magisterially from January into October. In a paper contributed to a commemorative symposium in 1976 an eminent Byzantinist, the late Sir Steven Runciman, unfairly rebuked Gibbon for completely ignoring the *Acta Sanctorum*. The fact is that Gibbon does cite the work in a note in chapter 33: "See the Acta Sanctorum of the Bollandists.... This immense calendar of Saints, in one hundred and twenty-six years (1644–1770), and in fifty volumes in folio, has advanced no farther than the 7th day of October. The suppression of the Jesuits has most probably checked an undertaking which, through the medium of fable and superstition, communicates much historical and philosophical instruction."

The unfairness of Runciman's criticism is even more apparent in the notes that Gibbon drafted for his early volumes. These, most of which were published for the first time by Patricia Craddock in 1972, are bound in red morocco and preserved at the Morgan Library. There the *Acta Sanctorum* are invoked four times, and at one of these citations Gibbon states, "The Bollandists by whom I have been guided have laboured the article of St. James with indefatigable diligence." We have to ask where Gibbon could have been reading the great volumes of the Bollandists. The note in chapter 33 provides a terminal date of 1770 for what Gibbon saw with its last day as October 7. This is precisely the day with which the volume published in 1770 ended. Since Gibbon manifestly had no knowledge when he was writing that another volume, for October 8 and 9, had appeared in 1780, it is safe to say that his consultation of the Bollandist volumes took place between 1770 and 1780. Although the single citation of the *Acta* in the *History* was published in 1781, it clearly depends upon investigations in the preceding decade.

Fortunately the *Memoirs* make it possible to establish with near certainty exactly where and when Gibbon consulted the *Acta Sanctorum*. In 1777, in the warm flush of fame after the publication of the first volume of the *Decline and Fall* in the previous year, Gibbon went to Paris for some months at the invitation of his old amour, Mme. Suzanne Necker. Although he had a busy round of social engagements, he found time to read as well. "The fashionable suppers often broke into the morning-hours," he admitted. "Yet I occasionally consulted the Royal library, and that of the Abbey of St. Germain: and in the free use of their books at home I had always reason to praise the liberality of those institutions." There can be little doubt that it was through the generosity of these libraries in 1777 that Gibbon became acquainted with the large tomes of the Bollandists. By contrast his total silence on the subject after 1781 suggests that he never again had or sought access to those large and costly editions.

I take a second example of a major work cited by Gibbon but absent from his library. In Europe in the eighteenth century the most substantial account of late antiquity and early Byzantium was the monumental *Histoire du Bas-Empire* by Charles Lebeau. This Catholic scholar had been born in 1701 and belonged therefore to an older generation than Gibbon. Lebeau's history started appearing in 1757. The man himself died in 1778, but the publication of his work continued until 1787 to produce a grand total of twenty-four volumes. Gibbon's French was as flawless as his German was nonexistent, and he cannot have avoided a history so conspicuously overlapping his own in a language that he could easily read. Yet Gibbon never added Lebeau's *Histoire du Bas-Empire* to his library, and in the first three volumes of his *Decline and Fall* he never even cites the work. But in what might be called the Lausanne triad—the three final volumes all completed in Lausanne and published in 1788—Lebeau appears twice in Gibbon's notes. The first reference occurs in chapter 49 when Gibbon remarks on the restoration of images after the iconoclast struggle of the eighth century. In a bracing conjunction of anticlerical and antifeminist sentiment Gibbon observed, "The idols, for such they were now held, were secretly cherished by the order and the sex most prone to devotion; and the fond alliance of the monks and females obtained a final victory over the reason and authority of man." In a footnote, Gibbon contrasts Protestant and Catholic opinion on the issue and asserts that the Catholics were generally "inflamed by the fury and superstition of the monks." He goes on, almost apologetically, to say, "And even Le Beau (Hist. du Bas Empire), a gentleman and a scholar, is infected by the odious contagion."

This brief but revealing comment allows us to draw a few inferences. Gibbon manifestly found Lebeau uncongenial as a believing Catholic, but equally he had respect for him as a person. The description of him as "a gentleman and a scholar" almost certainly betrays personal contact during one of Gibbon's visits to France, most probably the one in 1777 (the year before Lebeau died). Gibbon's antipathy to Lebeau's religious bias probably accounted for his failure to acquire the *Histoire* for his library, but at least when he was at work on the Lausanne triad he clearly consulted it. Lebeau is invoked on one other occasion, this time in chapter 53, where Gibbon acknowledges that he is using a summary of the Greek text of Theophanes Continuatus as furnished by Lebeau in his fourteenth volume. "See the anonymous continuator of Theophanes," he wrote in a note, "whom I have followed in the neat and concise abstract of Lebeau (Hist. du Bas Empire, tom. xiv, p. 436, 438)." It is no secret that Gibbon's Greek was much less strong than his Latin, and his Latin less strong than his French. One may well imagine his relief at gaining access to a difficult Byzantine source through Lebeau's summary. Furthermore, a neat and concise abstract was much to Gibbon's liking in sorting out the chaos of Byzantine history. He had himself created a similar kind of abstract in the rapid overview that constitutes his chapter 48, a virtuoso summary of Byzantine history much admired by the German classicist Jacob Bernays and the only chapter in the entire *Decline and Fall* without a single footnote (a fact obscured by the later annotations by Bury and the unfortunately named Oliphant Smeaton).

Outside of the *Decline and Fall* Lebeau appears once more in Gibbon, and that is in the fragmentary notes for volumes V and VI from the year 1787. He had found something on Greek fire that caught his attention, and therefore we have to assume that at the time he was reading, at least cursorily, through the *Histoire du Bas Empire*. Where did he do this? The references to Lebeau, inside and outside the *Decline and Fall*, were all written after 1783, when Gibbon returned to Lausanne. The testament of Gibbon may hold a clue. Although he instructed that most of his books be put up for sale at his death, he gave, as we have already noted, a little under one hundred volumes to the library of the Academy of Lausanne. It would be reasonable to assume that this was an expression of gratitude for courtesies accorded to the famous historian by local scholars when he was living among them. It would make sense to see him leafing through Lebeau's fundamentally uncongenial work within the rooms of the Academy.

Through the citations of the *Acta Sanctorum* and Lebeau's *Histoire* we can catch a glimpse of Gibbon as he supplemented the already considerable resources of the personal library he had commended to Mr. Davis as proof of his *bona fides*. It must be said, however, that in both cases Gibbon's anticlerical prejudices perhaps impelled him to pay less attention to these works than they deserved, and it is understandable why he refrained from the large expense he would have incurred in acquiring them for himself. On the other hand, we have to ask now what impelled him to buy books he nowhere cites at all.

From this category I have chosen the editions of the Greek novelists, all of whom figure in Gibbon's library (several in two editions) and none of whom is ever mentioned by him. The authors are Chariton, Xenophon of Ephesus, Longus, Achilles Tatius, and Heliodorus. Their works were all romantic novels in Greek with amatory escapades and hair-raising adventures. This genre of literature was popular in the Roman Empire and once evoked the disapproval of the emperor Julian. Unlike the Latin novelist Petronius, who was also represented in Gibbon's library, these Greek writers (apart from Chariton) wrote in the centuries covered by the first volumes of the *Decline and Fall*. In Gibbon's day they were thought to be even later in date than they are now. They reflect the tastes and styles of their epoch, and they contain some fascinating parallels with Christianity, including resurrection of the dead and the representation of wine as blood. Several of these novels are written with great finesse, notably the *Ethiopian Tale* of Heliodorus, who was a master of Greek style and a formidable storyteller. Since we know from Gibbon's famous admiration of Fielding and *Tom Jones* that he was by no means averse to fiction or unaware of its importance for social history, it seems surprising that he should have acquired these books and not used them in his work. Above all, it is hard to believe that anyone who had read Heliodorus or Achilles Tatius could have penned the notorious judgment that Gibbon rendered on later Greek literature at the end of chapter 2 of his *History*: "If we except the inimitable Lucian, this age of indolence passed away without having produced a single writer of original genius, or who excelled in the arts of elegant composition...cloud of critics, of compilers, of commentators, darkened the face of learning, and the decline of genius was soon followed by the corruption of taste." There is not the slightest hint of the existence of the Greek novels.

Yet the presence of editions of the novelists in Gibbon's library must at least betoken a recognition on his part that these writers deserved to be there. A well-stocked classical library had to have them. At the same time Gibbon's evident neglect of them strongly suggests that he had not read them, or certainly not read them with attention. Because they are all in Greek, some more difficult than others and the best of them—Heliodorus—notably difficult, it is probable that Gibbon simply chose not to make the effort. There was no Lebeau to have provided a neat and concise summary of these authors, and the Latin translations that accompanied the editions of the Greek in all cases were as drab and impenetrable as academic Latin could possibly be. The only work in a comparable genre that Gibbon not only owned but clearly had read was Philostratus's fabulous life of the wonder-worker Apollonius of Tyana. But this had long been a much-discussed text for paganism in the early days of Christianity, and Gibbon naturally invoked the miracles of Apollonius in a famous footnote for comparison with the miracles of Jesus. Had he known the resurrections and pagan eucharists of the novelists, it is hard to believe he would not have made use of them.

The presence of such books in Gibbon's library exposes volumes that evidently served for ostentation rather than use, to borrow his own celebrated language for both a harem of concubines and a library. These unexploited volumes lead us to the larger issue of the image of himself that Gibbon wished to leave with the world and with posterity. His frequent drafting of his autobiography implies a deep concern with establishing an acceptable account of how he became so famous. For his library, on which he had lavished no less care than on his memoirs, he decided in 1788 to order from Wedgwood eight busts of great literary figures as an adornment to his collection. He had taken his twenty-year-old protégé at Lausanne, Wilhelm de Sévery, with him to England in late 1787, and as he and the young man were preparing to return to Switzerland in June of 1788 he instructed him to arrange for the eight busts. This was obviously a well-considered project, since the busts had to be made to order. They survive in the archives of the *pays de Vaud* to this day.

The writers whom Gibbon chose to display were Homer, Plato, Aristotle, Cicero, Shakespeare, Milton, Newton, and Pope—a remarkable assemblage. The classical names are all impeccable, but for none of them did Gibbon have any noticeable affinity. After his youthful explorations he hardly read Homer, and philosophy was never much to his taste. As a passionate admirer of Tacitus, he cannot have felt very close to the windy periods of Cicero's Latinity. Shakespeare and Milton were equally impeccable choices from the modern era. As this exhibition reminds us, he used Shakespeare as a stick with which to beat Samuel Johnson, and he clearly appreciated Shakespeare's humanity. But there is no sign that Gibbon was a frequent reader of either Shakespeare or Milton. For busts of near contemporaries he chose Newton and Pope. He certainly admired the precise chronological investigations of Newton, and he had a copy of the *Optics* in his library. Pope as a satirist must have been congenial to Gibbon, but nearly all of his observations on Pope touch on the translation of Homer, which Gibbon characterized as "a portrait endowed with every merit, except likeness to the original."

Taken as a whole, therefore, the literary eminences selected by Gibbon for display in his library appear to reflect what he considered commonly accepted opinion. They bear small relation to the personal preferences of Gibbon himself. It looks as if he wished his library, with its eight literary busts in black Wedgwood arrayed among his precious books, to constitute a kind of summation of universally acknowledged greatness, whether incorporated by Gibbon into his work or not. Gibbon was transforming his library into an antechamber of immortality. The sequence that began with Homer and ended with Newton and Pope was clearly meant to point forward to the next member of the pantheon, Gibbon himself.

A personal library is not simply a collection of books. It is a mirror of its owner, but a magic mirror that reflects far more than the image that is put before it. It can expose secret aspirations and cut deeper than any scalpel into an unquiet heart. For the genius that Gibbon undoubtedly was, his library is our surest guide into his human frailty and his ambition. He could write and rewrite the pages of his *Memoirs* in quest of a perfect image of the historian of the Roman Empire, but his library was not so easily reworked. In its majesty and authority it reveals both the man that Gibbon was and the man he wanted to be.

## BIBLIOGRAPHICAL NOTE

The catalogue of the exhibition at Williamstown was expertly prepared by George Edwards (New York: Grolier Club, 2000). The second edition of Geoffrey Keynes's catalogue is indispensable: *The Library of Edward Gibbon* (Dorchester: St. Paul's Bibliographies, 1980). For Gibbon's fragmentary notes, see Patricia Craddock, *The English Essays of Edward Gibbon* (Oxford: Oxford University Press, 1972). This invaluable volume contains far more than the English essays. Gibbon's letters have been edited by J. E. Norton in three volumes (London: Macmillan, 1956). Steven Runciman's polemic may be found in his paper, "Gibbon and Byzantium," in G. W. Bowersock, J. Clive, and S. R. Graubard, *Edward Gibbon and the Decline and Fall of the Roman Empire* (Cambridge, Mass.: Harvard University Press, 1977).

The much neglected and exceptionally perceptive drafts for Jacob Bernays's study of Gibbon may be found in his *Gesammelte Abhandlungen*, edited by H. Usener (Berlin: Wilhelm Hertz, 1885), vol. II: *Edward Gibbon's Geschichtswerk*. Documentation for the letter to Sévery and the Wedgwood busts may be found in the catalogue of the Lausanne commemorative exhibition in 1976, *Exposition Gibbon à Lausanne, organisée à l'occasion du Colloque "Gibbon et Rome,"* at the Musée historique de l'ancien Evêché. I owe knowledge of the recent discovery of Gibbon's books at the Athenaeum to John Pocock.

# CHAPTER FOUR

# WATCHMEN

## *Gibbon's Autobiographies*

*Gibbon and the "Watchmen of the Holy City": The Historian and His Reputation* 1776–1815, by David Womersley

IN A LETTER TO HIS PATRON HOLROYD (LORD SHEFFIELD) Gibbon observed that the first volume of the *Decline and Fall of the Roman Empire* would, as he put it, "decline into the World" on February 17, 1776. The next two volumes appeared in 1781, and the final three not until seven years later. In February 1776 Gibbon was, as David Womersley observes at the beginning of his fascinating and pioneering new book, a man "without reputation." He had published his essay on literature and his critique of Warburton on the sixth book of the *Aeneid,* and he had sat in Parliament, but he was by no means a famous man. But in 1788, when the final volumes of his great history were delivered to the public, he was very famous indeed, and so he remained until his death in 1794.

Gibbon was an assiduous and astute custodian of his own reputation as it grew. With scholarship that is both meticulous and imaginative (*res olim dissociabiles*—a rare conjunction), Womersley has succeeded in tracking Gibbon's calculated moves to adjust and enhance the impression he made on his contemporaries, not only in the course of publishing the history but also throughout the six attempts that he made to write his own autobiography. Womersley ends his work with a conclusive demonstration of the arbitrary alterations that Sheffield imposed upon the autobiography as he prepared his composite edition of the manuscripts after Gibbon's death. The title of the book incorporates a quotation from Gibbon's *Vindication* of his fifteenth and sixteenth chapters (on Christianity), but the book itself covers a far larger field. It begins with Gibbon's minute but revealing revisions in the second edition of the first volume of the history, and it concludes with the second edition of the *Memoirs*, which Sheffield brought out in 1814 and 1815.

At the end of his preface, in paragraphs that have an apotropaic character, Womersley describes his study as "methodologically promiscuous." He appears to be shielding himself from what he calls the "unintelligent rigidity" of literary theorists by defending a close contextual analysis of Gibbon's writings, with particular attention to the intellectual and physical environment as it changed during and after Gibbon's lifetime. One can only applaud this doctrine, which Womersley summarizes in a Gibbonian manner as a special kind of Arian trinitarianism: "The father is bibliography, the spirit is context, but close reading is only the son. It is a later, dependent, and subordinate activity which can be practised with safety only within the boundaries marked out for it by its senior colleagues." Womersley's method demands much of his readers, but it is brilliantly justified by the results. The detective work that supports his arguments is exhilarating and leaves us with a much clearer understanding of both Gibbon and Sheffield.

In a detailed study of the alterations that Gibbon introduced into the first volume of the *Decline and Fall* in the second and third editions, Womersley concentrates on the fifteenth and sixteenth chapters because these were to provoke so much fierce controversy. It is clear that Gibbon had expected from the start that there would be clerical resistance to what he had written, but the revisions for the second edition, which followed the first by only three and a half months, reveal that he was already concerned to diminish the force of passages that might show an unacceptable advocacy of deist thought. When he was making his revisions in April and May 1776 he was evidently trying to anticipate the gathering opposition. Womersley has turned up a most important unpublished note in the Sheffield papers at the Beinecke in Yale stating explicitly that Gibbon was even willing to consider excising the two chapters if they were seriously to disrupt the impact of his work. According to Sheffield,

he "asked whether I thought it advisable to withdraw the offensive passages from the second Edition then at the Press." Although Sheffield
advised him against such action, the French edition in three volumes
appeared in 1777 without the fifteenth and sixteenth chapters, which
the translator regretfully noted he had to omit. Even so, a French text
of those chapters turned up that year in a separate fourth volume with a
fictitious London imprint.

Womersley demonstrates that as criticism from the pious began to
mount, Gibbon realized that the public outcry could actually serve to
enlarge his reputation. Accordingly in making revisions for the third
edition of the first volume, published in May 1777, he adopted a conspicuously different strategy from the softened language of the second
edition. His tone became more confident, and his views were bolstered
by a barrage of scholarly references in support of his assertions. This procedure prefigured the strong reply that he was to make to Henry Davis
in the *Vindication* of 1779. Womersley's analysis of Gibbon's creation of
an appropriate polemical style in which to respond to his critics tellingly
invokes the grand precedent of Bentley's celebrated exposure of the
Phalaris letters, but the irony in Gibbon's arrogation of Bentley's style
was, of course, that Bentley himself would have deeply disapproved of
Gibbon's deist tendencies. Bentley's work simply gave Gibbon, as it later
gave A. E. Housman, a model of devastating criticism. Gibbon's proud
defense of his Christian chapters, once he had discovered their potential
for launching his fame, depended for its efficacy on his maintaining the
scholarly high ground. Hence the potentially damaging charges of plagiarism in Davis's book, with its parallel columns documenting alleged
borrowings, roused Gibbon to issue his long riposte. Davis, unlike many
others, aimed directly at Gibbon's scholarship, and that was the high
ground he needed to hold.

With the Bentleian *Vindication* behind him Gibbon could concentrate on the preparation of the two volumes that were destined to appear
in 1781. These included his celebrated treatment of Constantine (an
extraordinary anticipation of Burckhardt's *Constantin* in the next century) and his no less celebrated treatment of Julian and Athanasius.
Drawing fruitfully on a study of Gibbon's Athanasius by Timothy Barnes,
Womersley tries to understand why Gibbon's Julian was less positive
than one might have expected and his Athanasius so much more positive. Gibbon even asserted, reasonably if surprisingly, that Athanasius
would have made a better emperor than any of "the degenerate sons of

Constantine." Obviously his critics would find themselves confounded by this assessment. Here, however, contextual analysis does not uncover the whole story, and it would have been helpful if Womersley had added to his "methodological promiscuity" a modest dose of old-fashioned Teutonic *Quellenforschung*. Gibbon's Julian, admirable in many things but nonetheless a fanatical despot, is nothing more nor less than a faithful reflection of the Julian of Ammianus Marcellinus, whose depiction he had studied at a tender age in Lausanne in the biography by La Bléterie. His juvenile notes on the work survive in the Lausanne Commonplace Book of 1755 and show exactly the same interpretation as the pertinent chapters of the history. In fact, Gibbon's notorious remark about Julian's "populous" beard, with insects living in it, is translated literally from La Bléterie's "barbe peuplée."

Womersley's discussion of the Gibbonian contrast between Athanasius and Julian comments on Julian's "affectation," as expressed repeatedly in Gibbon's text. Yet *affecter* is a favorite word of La Bléterie in describing the emperor. As for Athanasius, La Bléterie had already made the comparison in the archbishop's favor. He called him "ce grand homme," and returned to Julian's treatment of him in his *Life of Jovian*, where he translated the hate-filled letter of Julian to Ecdicius, the prefect of Egypt—a letter quoted at length by Gibbon and followed by words that unmistakably echo La Bléterie's own commentary. Here is Gibbon:

> The death of Athanasius was not *expressly* commanded; but the praefect of Egypt understood, that it was safer for him to exceed, than to neglect, the orders of an irritated master. The archbishop prudently retired to the monasteries of the Desert.

And here is La Bléterie:

> Non content de bannir Athanase, l'empereur donna des ordres peut-être secrets de lui ôter la vie; ou du moins Ecdicius, pour faire sa cour à Julien qu'il voïoit mécontent de sa négligence, prit de soi même la résolution de délivrer pour jamais le paganisme d'un si redoutable ennemi. Quoiq'il en soit Athanase remontoit le Nil pour se retirer dans la Thébaïde.

> [Not content with banishing Athanasius, the emperor gave orders, perhaps secret, to take away his life; or at least Ecdicius, to pay court to Julian whom he saw displeased with his negligence, decided on

his own to deliver paganism from such a formidable enemy. However that may be, Athanasius went up the Nile to retire into the
Thebaid.]

In substance, language, and sequence, Gibbon comes very close to La
Bléterie, whose interpretation he found both congenial and useful for his
purposes, but it is an interpretation that he had lived with and absorbed
for decades.

The last three volumes of the *Decline and Fall*, published in 1788,
occupy Womersley less than the earlier ones, although he has an illuminating chapter on Gibbon's Mohammed. He skillfully explores the eighteenth-century use of the founder of Islam as a code for non-Trinitarian
heresies, and argues that Gibbon's account must be read with that in
mind. Johnson's famous insinuation that Gibbon might once have been
a Mohammedan is plausibly interpreted as an allusion to his theological eccentricities rather than to his youthful interest in Arabic studies,
although his personal interest in that area of scholarship undoubtedly
encouraged and enriched his presentation of it. With the volumes of
1788 Womersley and his reader have already reached the point at which
Gibbon undeniably enjoyed a huge reputation, and he had begun to
contemplate the writing of an autobiography to secure it for posterity.

Gibbon embarked on the first of the six unfinished drafts of his *Memoirs* precisely in 1788, but this was not his first attempt to describe his life.
In 1783 he composed in French and in the third person a brief autobiographical sketch, mentioned by Sheffield in the *Miscellaneous Works* and
preserved in the British Museum. It is odd that with his scrupulous and
impeccable attention to the *Memoirs* Womersley has nothing to say at all
about the French autobiography. The piece is clearly dated by a reference at the end to the recent publication of the 1783 octavo edition of
the history, and Gibbon states that he is at work on a continuation down
to the capture of Constantinople by the Turks. This document mentions
both Oxford and Lausanne, but without any allusion to the religious
conversion that led to Gibbon's translation to Switzerland. His fondness
for the French language and for Parisian society is eloquently expressed,
no doubt honestly but with an eye to Francophone readers. He does,
however, mention with satisfaction the strong criticism of the fifteenth
and sixteenth chapters and asserts that he was reduced "à la tâche facile
mais humiliante de confondre le calomniateur" [to the easy but humiliating task of confounding the calumniator]. Replying to Davis was by no

means an easy task. Even in so slight an autobiographical essay as this Gibbon has made his observations with an eye to his reputation. He was clearly not ready yet to address his adolescent embrace of Catholicism, but he could proclaim unhesitatingly that the society of Paris was "la plus douce et la plus éclairée de la terre" [the sweetest and most enlightened on earth].

Similar expressions of Francophilia occur elsewhere in Gibbon's manuscripts, but the events of 1789 were to change all that and to make the representation of his life a far more complex task than he imagined it to be in 1783. The death of Deyverdun, Gibbon's friend of more than thirty years, on July 4, 1789, was followed by the storming of the Bastille on the 14th. Gibbon's world was shattered almost overnight. The loss of his friend had been anticipated, but the revolution in France forced Gibbon to reassess not only his espousal of French culture but his own political orientation. In the years leading up to his own death in 1794 the revolution drove him to an increasingly conservative outlook, in which he came to defend traditional institutions and manners in a way that would have been unthinkable earlier. In drafts C, D, and E he even reproached himself for his contemptuous treatment of Bishop Warburton long ago in his 1770 essay on Book VI of the *Aeneid.*

Through a systematic analysis of successive drafts of the *Memoirs* Womersley is able to track Gibbon's reassessment of two momentous episodes in his life, the death of his father and the experience he had at Magdalen College, Oxford. The first version of his father's death is cool, almost unfeeling: "Few, perhaps, are the children, who, after the expiration of some months or years, would sincerely rejoyce in the resurrection of their parents" (draft C). But finally in the third version we find the following: "My grief was sincere for the loss of an affectionate parent, an agreeable companion, and a worthy man" (draft E). Similarly Gibbon's withering account of Oxford dons and his own conversion to papism is metamorphosed, in draft F, into a long and generally respectful account of a place full of eccentrics but nonetheless full of ancient wisdom and tradition, where (of all things) the writings of Conyers Middleton impelled the young Gibbon to convert. Here Gibbon openly admits to an influence that had long been surmised, but he attaches it not to the notorious chapters in the history but to his own short-lived conversion.

In a compelling analysis, based on detailed review of the manuscript narratives, Womersley considers Gibbon's disenchantment with the French Revolution in the light of his sympathy with Burke's *Reflections on the Revolution in France*, which appeared in November 1790. Gibbon came to regret the old era that was now gravely threatened and to fear that in some way the world might hold him responsible for inciting the revolutionaries through opinions he had expressed in his history. He now felt the need to assert the primacy of family, old institutions, and traditional government. The Oxford University Press deserves high praise for allowing Womersley to print relevant parallel passages from the drafts of the *Memoirs* in columns, so that the reader can easily confirm the legitimacy of his conclusions. The penultimate draft (E), in annalistic form and dated to March 1791, constitutes a direct reaction to Burke, as we can see from a note that Sheffield purposefully elevated to the main text in his edition: "I beg leave to subscribe my assent to Mr. Burke's creed on the Revolution of France. I admire his eloquence, I approve his politics, I adore his Chivalry, and I can almost excuse his reverence for church establishment." Significantly these words nearly duplicate what Gibbon had written to Sheffield in a letter dated 5 February 1791.

To the rapidly changing political scene in France and Burke's *Reflections* it might be reasonable to add the publication of Boswell's *Life of Johnson* in 1791 as another incentive for Gibbon's efforts to alter his own autobiography. The fullness of the final draft (F) on Gibbon's early years looks like an attempt to achieve Boswellian amplitude. Gibbon's desire in January 1793 to propose, through Sheffield as intermediary, a new biographical project consisting of lives of major British political, military, and ecclesiastical personalities would be hard to explain without the impact of Boswell's biography and renewed attention to Johnson's own biographies. The letter to Sheffield incorporating this curious proposal notes that work on the *Memoirs* "must be postponed till a mature season" and that Gibbon will probably not live to see them in print. Womersley is the first to observe that the character of the drafts changes according to Gibbon's expectation of posthumous or nonposthumous publication. Draft E, with its tribute to Burke, belongs to the latter category, but draft F, which was to be deferred for the biographies, clearly belongs to the former. Womersley's work on the drafts of the *Memoirs* makes even more obvious the terrible inadequacies of the Bonnard edition and the inanity of trying to create a composite text. The situation has recently become more complicated through the emergence of a new fragment of the *Memoirs* that seems independent of any of the six drafts known hitherto. It was unknown to Womersley. In an exhibition of Gibboniana at the Chapin Library of Williams College in Massachusetts there was a small sheet in Gibbon's late handwriting, lent by George Edwards from his personal collection. It is reproduced as the frontispiece to the catalogue of the exhibition (Grolier Club, 2000), and the brief text runs as follows, with cancel lines through the letters given here in square brackets:

> the Emperors of Germany, and Kings of Spain have threatened the liberty of the old, and invaded the treasures of the new, World. The successors of Charles the fifth [h] may disdain their humble kinsmen of England: but the small volumes of Tom Jones, that exquisite picture of human life, will survive the palace of the Escurial [of the ho] and the Imperial eagle of the house of Austria.

This famous passage is known from an isolated sheet among the manuscripts of the *Memoirs*. It has been conventionally associated with the discussion of genealogy near the beginning of draft A, because the two manuscripts show close affinities in their account of the descendants of Confucius. The text of the sheet that is already known is

> the Emperors of Germany and Kings of Spain, have threatened the liberty of the old and invaded the treasures of the new World. The successors of Charles the fifth may disdain their humble brethren of England, but the Romance of Tom Jones, that exquisite picture of human manners, will outlive the palace of the Escurial and the Imperial Eagle of the house of Austria.

Apart from differences in punctuation and capitalization, the Edwards fragment shows three significant variants from the received text. It has "kinsmen" instead of "brethren," "small volumes" instead of "Romance," and "life" instead of "manners." The second cancellation proves that Gibbon was copying a preexisting text, and he was presumably making changes as he went along. The most striking of the variants is the reference to *Tom Jones* in terms of small volumes. This can only allude to the original duodecimo edition of the work in 1749. Gibbon's admiration of Fielding's novel is well known, but when he refers to it elsewhere he calls it a romance. The new scrap, therefore, would appear to postdate the known independent sheet, whenever that was written (perhaps in 1789). The more plain and vigorous language of "kinsmen" and "life" in place of "brethren" and "manners" would also suggest a later redaction. How the scrap escaped the Sheffield papers in the British Museum is as hard to guess as why Gibbon was impelled to think of the size of the original volumes of Fielding's novel. His own library contained the octavo edition, and so it is possible that he saw the duodecimo edition in his final months with Sheffield. This new fragment suggests that Gibbon's drafts of the *Memoirs* were much messier than the majestic parade of six drafts to which we have become accustomed.

The last part of Womersley's book is devoted to a searching examination of Sheffield's ruthless alteration of the drafts of the *Memoirs* as he had received them. It is clear that the objective was to create an image of Gibbon that would be acceptable in the changed world of 1796, to minimize his Francophilia, to soften his anticlericalism, and even to make Gibbon say things he did not say. Womersley is absolutely correct in saying that Sheffield's editing of the drafts of the *Memoirs* is nothing less than scandalous. The point can be well illustrated by one of Womersley's most startling examples, an alteration that was carelessly omitted altogether in Bonnard's edition. In commenting on the much-discussed passage in the *Decline and Fall* about the darkness of the Passion, which no pagan in the ancient world appeared to have noticed, Gibbon had written in draft C, "In an ample dissertation on the miraculous darkness of the passion, I privately drew my conclusions from the silence of an unbelieving age." Sheffield printed these lines in his edition but replaced the verb "drew" with "withdrew," thereby utterly subverting Gibbon's meaning and effectively making him repent of what he had said in his history. The mutilation and manipulation of Gibbon's words extended even to such harmless expressions of Francophilia as "I tore myself from the embraces of Paris" (draft C). Sheffield printed, "I reluctantly left Paris."

Readers of Gibbon are now even more in debt to David Womersley than before. *Gibbon and the "Watchmen of the Holy City"* is an exemplary work of scholarship.

# CHAPTER FIVE

# SUETONIUS IN THE EIGHTEENTH CENTURY

WHEN BOSWELL APPEALED TO AUTHORITY IN introducing his *Life of Johnson*, he invoked Plutarch, "the prince," he declared, "of ancient biographers." There followed a quotation, first (ostentatiously) in Greek and then in translation, of the familiar lines from Plutarch's *Alexander the Great* on the value of apparent trifles in a man's action or conversation for the illumination of his character. Earlier in the eighteenth century the Abbé de la Blèterie in France had similarly invoked the name of Plutarch to sanctify his biography of Julian the Apostate, and he had similarly seen fit to cite exactly the same passage from the life of Alexander.[1] No reader with any knowledge of Plutarch's Lives could have taken the invocations of that ancient master seriously. Neither Boswell nor the Abbé de la Blèterie wrote biographies in the Plutarchean manner. The sole point of contact was the celebrated passage they both quoted to justify the inclusion of superficially insignificant details.

As a result of the famous and often reprinted translations of Plutarch by Amyot, North, and Dryden, Plutarch's name had become almost synonymous with the genre of biography. And if Plutarchean parodies, like the anonymous *Life of John Wilkes, Esq.*, published in 1773, presuppose some acquaintance with the original biographies in the reading public,

---

1. The citation occurs at the end of the preface to La Blèterie's work, first published anonymously with an Amsterdam imprint in 1735.

it would nevertheless be dangerous to assume that Plutarch's *Lives* were read as often as they were placed on bookshelves or mentioned in prefaces. They were a legacy of the sixteenth and seventeenth centuries to the eighteenth, and there was no one to say that they were not the very models of good biography. But Plutarch is like the Bible: you can find an appropriate quotation in support of whatever you are doing. The passage in the Alexander spoke eloquently to the more creative and adventurous biographers of the eighteenth century, even though they must have been perfectly well aware of the great distance between themselves and Plutarch. Their interest, for its own sake, in sordid details of personal life, the abundant record of conversation on all manner of themes, the fascination with bad people as well as good are all far removed from Plutarch's world. When Plutarch undertook to compose the life of Demetrius, whom he judged a person of reprehensible character, he felt obliged to offer his readers an apology and an explanation for doing something that seemed unedifying.[2] Plutarch had no interest in human character on its own, but only as a basis for moral instruction. He had no interest in socially insignificant people, but only in the great. He cared little for the lives of literary figures.[3]

If the most important and original contributions to biography in the eighteenth century came, as most would probably agree, from Samuel Johnson (and through him Boswell) and also from Rousseau, whose *Confessions* are an undoubted masterpiece in the autobiographical genre that Johnson thought the ultimate form of biography, then it was certainly not Plutarch who provided whatever inspiration from antiquity those writers may have had. Of the ancient biographers Suetonius comes much closer to Johnson and Rousseau, and it is surprising that no one has hitherto attempted to trace in any detail the fortunes of his Lives of the Caesars and his Lives of the Poets in the eighteenth century. In his book titled *Samuel Johnson, Biographer* Robert Folkenflik touches very briefly on this subject and leaves it after just two paragraphs.[4] It is clear that Suetonius was not a conspicuous author in the education of the time. In his translation of

---

2. Plut., *Life of Demetrius*, ch. 1.

3. His biography of Pindar, now lost, was probably due more to Plutarch's well-attested devotion to his Boeotian homeland than to any great interest in the poetry of the Boeotian Pindar.

4. R. Folkenflik, *Samuel Johnson, Biographer* (Ithaca: Cornell University Press, 1978), 97–98. I am indebted to my late friend and colleague, W. J. Bate, for drawing my attention to this book.

the Lives of the Caesars of 1732, John Clarke observed, "Notwithstanding this great and apparent usefulness of Suetonius, he has, I think, got but little footing in our schools."[5] But it is equally clear that scholars and superior men of letters both in England and on the continent were at the same time well acquainted with Suetonius and were, in addition, remarkably concordant in their estimate of his qualities and achievement.

To assess the place of Suetonian biography in the eighteenth century it would be well to start with the interest shown by professional classical scholars and then to move on to the influence of this interest on the literary milieu in general. Against the background that emerges men like Johnson and Rousseau, as well as Gibbon and Duclos, will appear in sharper focus. Although no classical author can ever serve wholly to explain works of genius in a later age, he can nevertheless help us to understand them better. I shall attempt to argue that while Plutarch represented the biographical ideals of the past, as seen through Amyot, North, and Dryden, it was Suetonius who represented what was new in the genre as it developed in the eighteenth century.

After the pioneering work on the text of Suetonius by Isaac Casaubon toward the end of the sixteenth century, little was done with this author until he was taken up in the final third of the next century by the Dutch scholar Graevius at Utrecht. Graevius's edition of 1672, and revisions of his work that appeared in 1691, 1697, and 1703, became the foundation for widespread study of Suetonius in England as well as the Netherlands. It is still not well known that Richard Bentley was actively preparing an edition of Suetonius in Cambridge at least between the years 1713 and 1719.[6] He was in touch with both Graevius and Graevius's pupil, Burman. He assembled collations of eight manuscripts of Suetonius and entered annotations for his new text into four separate copies of Suetonius in his possession. Bentley never brought his work to completion, possibly because it was becoming amply apparent that the market was glutted. In addition to Graevius's editions, those by Patinus of 1675, Pitiscus of 1690, and Jacob Gronovius of 1698 were still in circulation; and Graevius's text was the basis of further printings in 1705, 1706, 1707, 1708, 1714, 1715,

---

5. Clarke's *Suetonius*, v. Jabez Hughes, Degory Wheare, and Thomas Blackwell all expressed a similar opinion. See H. D. Weinbrot, *Augustus Caesar in "Augustan" England* (1978), 22.

6. M. Ihm, "Richard Bentley's Suetonkritik," *Sitzungsberichte der königlich preussischen Akademie der Wissenschaften zu Berlin*, phil.-hist. Classe, May 23, 1901; Edmund Hedick, *Studia Bentleiana III: Suetonius Bentleianus* (1902).

1718, and 1722. An English translation of Suetonius by Jabez Hughes, John Hughes's brother, appeared in 1717 and was reprinted in 1726. Bentley perhaps despaired of being heard amid such frantic activity; he was not, in any case, prone to fads.

Among scholars this extraordinary enthusiasm for Suetonius continued deep into the century. Pieter Burman, Graevius's pupil, produced an edition of his own in 1736, to be followed by Ernesti's edition of 1748 and Oudendorp's of 1751. One can readily sympathize with Gibbon's note on the edition of Oudendorp, about which he had read in the *Bibliothèque raisonnée:* "But why make one after Graevius's edition?"[7] Hughes's English translation was replaced in 1732 by John Clarke's which was soon reprinted in 1739. As the century wore on, Oudendorp was reprinted in 1761 and Ernesti, incorporating notes by Oudendorp, in 1775. It is probably fair to say that there was greater professional interest in Suetonius in the eighteenth century than there has ever been before or since.

Perhaps the most influential of those who read Suetonius at the turn of the century, when Graevius's edition was still relatively new, was Pierre Bayle, whose *Dictionnaire* was known and reprinted throughout the eighteenth century. His entry for Suetonius was very full and took open issue with certain seventeenth-century clerical writers who found fault with the biographer's frankness and occasional obscenity. In replying to this ecclesiastical censure, Bayle adopted a view of Suetonius that became commonplace in subsequent decades. He presented Suetonius as a model of candor, sincerity, and impartiality. Suetonius reports without judging, he tells what he knows without fear, and he flatters no one. It may be something of a surprise for a modern reader of the *Lives of the Caesars* to think of their author as a paradigm of objectivity; but that is how the eighteenth century, using Bayle's spectacles, perceived him. Here are Bayle's words (or rather, some of them): "They are an unending tissue of select and curious facts, and told in a succinct manner, without digressions, reflections, and arguments. There is everywhere a character of sincerity which makes one feel, without the slightest difficulty, that the author is afraid of nothing and expects nothing, and that neither hate nor flattery motivates his pen. This provides great charm for readers of good taste.... He is a writer who has found the art of guaranteeing his good faith, and it is notable that he wrote without passion." As to the notoriously indelicate passages, especially in the life of the emperor

---

7. *Le journal de Gibbon à Lausanne*, ed. G. Bonnard (1945), 234.

Tiberius, Bayle observes, "The way in which Suetonius has detailed the debaucheries of emperors does not at all demonstrate that he liked perversity or enjoyed describing it, or that in general he left anything to be desired in his probity and rectitude. It only shows that he was very candid and very sincere."

When one turns from Bayle's *Dictionary* to the preface to John Clarke's translation of Suetonius in 1732, it is hard not to feel that Clarke had been reading Bayle quite recently. In any case, his view of his author is very much that of his time, and I quote it: "The character of Suetonius is that of a plain honest impartial author, that appears to have writ with all possible coolness, and without the least bias upon his mind at all; or any other concern, than that of delivering to the world a faithful and just account of the behaviour and conduct, both public and private, of the several emperors, whose lives he has given us, so far as he himself could come at it....There is nothing in him like flattery, disguise or concealment in the least. He has, as an honest historian should do, given as well the foul, as the fair side of them all...."[8] Far from being corrupting or indecent, Clarke judges Suetonius's work "highly proper to be put into the hands of our youth at school and university."

Throughout his career Edward Gibbon, ironist though he was, consistently maintained a view of Suetonius identical to that of Bayle and Clarke: Suetonius composed his lives truthfully, without passion or prejudice. In 1764 Gibbon noted in his journal that Voltaire had questioned the historical reliability of Suetonius's account of Tiberius's sexual excesses as an old man on the island of Capri.[9] Gibbon, who manifestly understood both Suetonius and old men much better than Voltaire, observed that Tacitus appears to confirm Suetonius in this matter, and furthermore "I perceive no trace of hatred in their writings. They often document what they say, and they distinguish with no less good faith than insight the different phases of the dissimulation, cruelties, and public debaucheries of this emperor....With regard to the exquisite debaucheries that amaze M. de Voltaire, it is precisely in a 70-year-old man that I find them plausible."[10]

Over a decade later, in his celebrated *Vindication* of the chapters on Christianity in the *Decline and Fall*, he took a similar view of Suetonius.

8. Clarke's *Suetonius*, iv.
9. *Le journal de Gibbon à Lausanne*, (n. 7 above), 240.
10. Ibid.

He recalled the "honest complaint" of a sixteenth-century writer "that the lives of the philosophers have been composed by Laertius, and those of the Caesars by Suetonius, with a much stricter and more severe regard for historic truth, than can be found in the lives of saints and martyrs, as they are described by Catholic writers."[11] After this provocative attack on a very special and highly partisan genre of biography, Gibbon went on to say that if Suetonius "had disguised the vices of Augustus, we should have been deprived of the knowledge of some curious and perhaps instructive facts, and our idea of those celebrated men might have been more favourable than they deserved."[12] Finally near the end of his life, as he made notes for the revision he never carried out of the opening chapters of the *Decline and Fall*, Gibbon once again showed his belief in the integrity of Suetonius as a biographer. "I here confused," wrote Gibbon of his account of Augustus's family, "the maternal with the paternal descent of Augustus.... The opposite reports of friends and enemies are honestly and doubtfully stated by Suetonius."[13]

What I am suggesting was the dominant view of Suetonius in the eighteenth century reappears in France explicitly in the preface which Voltaire's disciple, Jean-François de la Harpe, affixed to his translation of Suetonius, published in 1771 (a year in which two translations of the *Lives* were published in French). La Harpe declares, in language again reminiscent of Bayle, "He does not pause in his narrative nor seem to take any interest in anything, nor to give the slightest sign of approval or blame, of sympathy or indignation.... The result of this indifference is a very well founded presupposition in favor of his impartiality: he neither loves nor hates the men of whom he speaks: his readers are left to judge them.... You need read only ten pages of Suetonius to see that he takes no side and writes without emotion."[14] Although La Harpe's translation had taken its origin from a request from the Duc de Choiseul,[15] he was aware of a wider interest in certain places. "The author of Emile," he wrote, "somewhat regrets that there is no longer any Suetonius."[16]

11. E. Gibbon, *Vindication*, ed. P. Craddock in *The English Essays of Edward Gibbon* (1972), 303.

12. Ibid.

13. Craddock (n. 11 above), 342.

14. De la Harpe, *Suétone* (1771), 2–3.

15. Cf. A. Jovicevich, *Jean-François de la Harpe, adepte et renégat des lumières* (South Orange: Seton Hall University Press, 1973), 68.

16. De la Harpe (n.14), 2.

Jean-Jacques Rousseau had indeed said something like that, for in *Émile* he recommends the study of biography as a beginning of the study of the human heart. The biographical historian penetrates to the secret places of his subject and catches him unawares. But it is only in the writings of the ancients that such educational biography can be found. Today, laments Rousseau, decency keeps men from speaking out: "Decency, no less severe in writings as in actions, allows one to say no more in public than what it allows one to do....However many times the lives of kings are written and rewritten, we shall have no more biographers like Suetonius."[17]

Voltaire, who had, we may recall, suspected Suetonius's report of Tiberius's senile pleasures, stood apart, as he often did, from the conventional assessment of Suetonius in the eighteenth century. He had not been at all pleased by La Harpe's plan to translate Suetonius: "I am very annoyed that you would bury your talent in a translation of Suetonius, an arid writer, in my view, and a very suspect anecdotalist....I would far rather have a new tragedy in your style."[18] But even Voltaire warmed to the project in time and eventually told La Harpe how much he looked forward to the translation. He must have been disappointed when it appeared. The scholars of Europe tore it apart.[19] When they had done with exposing all La Harpe's errors, the poor man must have wished he had followed Voltaire's advice and written a tragedy instead.

Voltaire apart, casting (as Gibbon wrote) "a keen and lively glance over the surface of history," we see a remarkable uniformity in the way in which those secular writers who knew Suetonius's work judged him. It is difficult not to believe that the availability of an exceptionally large number of editions, commentaries, and translations sparked the interest, dormant for a century, in this forceful, outspoken, and well-documented biographer, so different from Plutarch. Although there is no reason to think that Suetonius's name was a household word, as Plutarch's was, there is every reason to think that many of the literary leaders of the age found him, on the whole, sympathetic. He seemed to be an honest reporter, who used all the sources he could find to present, without

---

17. J. J. Rousseau, *Émile*, Book 4 (Paris, 1874), 278.
18. Quoted by Jovicevich (n. 15), 68: Voltaire, *Corr.* 71.244.
19. Cf. Jovicevich (n. 15), 68–69; Christopher Todd, *Voltaire's Disciple: Jean-François de la Harpe* (London: Modern Humanities Research Association, 1972), 89.

praise or blame, portraits in the round. His emperors were no paragons; he knew their strengths and their weaknesses. And even in the worst of them he knew their virtues. It is only after a recitation of Caligula's merits that Suetonius makes his renowned transition to the vices: *Hactenus quasi de principe, reliqua ut de monstro narranda sunt* [So much, as it were about an emperor; the rest must be told as of a monster].[20] There is less to go on for Suetonius's biographies of poets and grammarians, but it is of great significance simply that he chose to write them at all; and in the eighteenth century rather more extant biographies of poets were credited to him than now. The works of Suetonius's predecessors in literary biography were not known in the eighteenth century, and his successors in the genre, such as Diogenes Laertius and Philostratus, had a more limited scope. Altogether the new interest in Suetonius, from Graevius and Bayle onward, may be expected to have had some connection with the new doctrines of biography in the same period. For those doctrines, most clearly visible in Johnson and Rousseau, are uncannily close to those ascribed to Suetonius.

Already in 1722 John Hughes had written the lives of Abelard and Heloise, which he prefixed to a translation of their letters: "We find in them surprizing [*sic*] mixtures of devotion and tenderness, of penitence and remaining frailty, and a lively picture of human nature in its contrarieties of passion and reason, its infirmities and its sufferings."[21] In a standard work on the art of biography in eighteenth-century England the author comments on the date of this passage, "an early date for such an observation."[22] But it is not perhaps so early when we recall that it was precisely John Hughes's brother who had published, five years before, the first eighteenth-century translation of Suetonius into English. It is above all in the presentation of contradictory characteristics that the peculiarly Suetonian mark can be distinguished, as Bayle had justly noted. Since attention to personal detail and meaningful trifles is as much Plutarchean as Suetonian, the pronouncements of Roger North, though in many ways anticipating Johnson, do not represent so bold a departure from the

---

20. Suet., *Cal.* 22.

21. John Hughes, Lives of Abelard and Heloise (1722): quotation with comment in D. A. Stauffer, *The Art of Biography in Eighteenth Century England* (Princeton: Princeton University Press, 1941), 343 n. 100. In Stauffer's work of 572 pages Suetonius's name occurs twice.

22. Stauffer (n. 21 above), *loc. cit.*

standard of Plutarch as that of Hughes. North's insistence on the desirability of personal acquaintance with the subject of a biography looks forward to Johnson, of course;[23] but it is, in itself, a doctrine without any clear classical antecedent. As a biographer, Goldsmith, too, is essentially in the Plutarchean tradition, with his emphasis on moral judgements.[24]

Though anticipated here and there, Johnson was in fact the truly original biographer of his age. His formidable genius cannot be explained simply in terms of reading and influences, but it seems increasingly evident that among the ancients Suetonius must have held a special attraction for him. So voracious a reader as Johnson cannot have missed the new interest in Suetonius in England and abroad, and he must have found in him a biographer who exemplified the searching candor he craved in biography.

In writing about the *Lives of the Poets* many a modern critic has been impelled to mention Suetonius if only for comparison—a justifiable comparison. There is a dramatic echo of the Life of Augustus at the end of the Life of Dryden.[25] But one can go further with the Life of Savage, where again the influence of Suetonius has been suspected. I believe it can be proved. In the Lives of the Caesars Suetonius turns regularly at the end of a life to a series of topics that he has evidently reserved in each case for a general treatment in the context of the subject's death. Either before or just after the notice of death he dilates on the physical characteristics, personal manner, and literary tastes of the subject. It will be necessary, and by no means disagreeable, to quote at some length from several representative lives to establish this point. For the present purpose I shall use the translation of John Clarke from 1732. On the emperor Tiberius:

> He was in his person large and robust, of a stature somewhat above the usual size; broad shouldered and chested, and in his other parts proportionable. He used his left hand better than his right.... He was of a fair complexion.... He had a handsome face, but frequently full of pimples, with large eyes.... He walked with his neck stiff and unmoved, commonly with a frowning countenance, being for the most part silent, very seldom talking to those about him; and when he did, it was very slowly, and with an effeminate motion of his fingers.... He had small regard to the gods or matters of

23. Cf., most recently, Folkenflik (n. 4 above), 83 and 185 n. 19.
24. Stauffer (n. 21 above), pp. 380–86; Folkenflik (n. 23 above), 83.
25. Johnson, *Lives of the English Poets*, ed. C. B. Hill (1905), 1: 469.

religion, being mightily addicted to astrology.... Yet he was exceedingly afraid of thunder.... He applied himself very diligently to the liberal arts, both Greek and Latin. In his Latin stile he affected to imitate Corvinus Messala.... But he rendered his stile obscure by an excess of affectation and niceness.... He composed a lyric ode... some poems in Greek in imitation of Euphorion, Rhianus and Parthenius, with which poets he was wonderfully taken....[26]

Next, on the emperor Claudius:

He had a majestic and graceful appearance, either standing or sitting and especially when he was asleep; for he was tall, but not slender. His gray locks became him well, and he had a fat neck. But his hams were feeble, and failed him in walking.... Besides he had a stammering in his speech, and a tremulous motion in his head.... Though in the former part of his life he had but a very crazy constitution, yet upon his advancement to the empire he enjoyed a good state of health.... He was sensible of his being subject to passion and resentment, but excused himself therein by proclamation.... Amongst other things people admired in him his forgetfulness and want of thought.... He frequently appeared so careless in what he said, so regardless of circumstances, that it was believed he never reflected or considered who he himself was, or amongst whom, or at what time, or in what place he spoke.... By the encouragement of T. Livius.... he undertook the writing of a history.... In his reign too he writ a great deal, which he constantly had rehearsed to his friends by a reader.... He compiled too the history of his own life, in eight books, full of impertinence, but in no bad stile.... He likewise applied himself with no less care to the study of the Graecian literature, declaring his love of that language, and the excellency thereof upon all occasions.[27]

Now, on Nero:

His stature was a little below the ordinary size: his body so spotted and marked as to make a vile appearance; his hair somewhat yellow, his countenance fair rather than handsome, his eyes grey and dull, his neck fat, his belly prominent, legs very slender, but

26. Suet., *Tib.* 68–70.
27. Suet., *Claud.* 30, 39–42.

his constitution very healthful.... He was much addicted to poetry and composed verses readily and with a great deal of ease; nor did he, as some think, publish those of other people for his own. I have had in my hands some little pocketbooks of his, with some well known verses, all of his own writing; and writ in such a manner that it was very apparent, they were not transcribed from a copy.... He had likewise a mighty fancy for painting and image making, but above all things, an extravagant affection for popular applause.[28]

With these passages in mind, all written by Suetonius in connection with the notice of death, compare Johnson, in the Life of Savage, immediately after he has recorded his subject's death:

He was of a middle stature, of a thin habit of body, a long visage, coarse features, and melancholy aspect; of a grave and manly deportment, a solemn dignity of mien, but which upon a nearer acquaintance softened into an engaging easiness of manners. His walk was slow, and his voice tremulous and mournful. He was easily excited to smiles, but very seldom provoked to laughter.... He had the art of escaping from his own reflexions and accommodating himself to every new scene. To this quality is to be imputed the extent of his knowledge compared with the small time which he spent in visible endeavours to acquire it.... His method of life particularly qualified him for conversation, of which he knew how to practise all the graces. His temper was in consequence of the dominion of his passions uncertain and capricious; he was easily engaged and easily disgusted; but he is accused of retaining his hatred more tenaciously than his benevolence.... As an author... he has very little to fear from the strictest moral or religious censure.... Of his stile the general fault is harshness, and the general excellence is dignity.[29]

The mark of Suetonius on this concluding part of the Life of Savage is surely unmistakable.

In France Jean-Jacques Rousseau, who had lamented in *Émile* the absence of a contemporary Suetonius, nevertheless acknowledged in a footnote that there was one writer of the time who had, at least in part dared to imitate Suetonius: "Only one of our historians, who has imitated

28. Suet., *Nero* 51–53.
29. S. Johnson, *Life of Savage*, ed. C. Tracy (1971), 135–39.

Tacitus in his main characteristics, has dared to imitate Suetonius...in matters of detail; and that very feature, which adds to the value of his book, has brought him into disrepute among us."[30] Rousseau was referring to that *enfant terrible* of the establishment, Charles Pinot Duclos, whose biography of Louis XI had scandalized the French authorities and who had acquired a large following with the publicity that naturally attaches to moral condemnation.[31] Both Gibbon and Walpole knew Duclos principally as the author of the *Louis XI*; and Rousseau was quite right in signaling, with obvious approval, the Suetonian character of that work. Although Duclos himself survived notoriety to become the perpetual secretary of the French Academy and to enjoy what Gibbon maliciously judged the scorn of colleagues who failed to do him the honor of hating him,[32] the rebel Rousseau had a considerable respect for him. The feeling appears to have been mutual. Rousseau dedicated his opera *Le devin du village* to Duclos in gratitude for his good offices in getting the work produced, and Rousseau kept for more than twenty years his copy of Duclos's *Confessions du Comte de + + +*, a work that he much admired.[33]

Rousseau's appreciation of the biography of Louis XI was therefore part of a larger interest in its author's writings. In view of the bold, unorthodox tastes and opinions of both men, it is scarcely surprising that Suetonius should have constituted one of the links between them. Duclos would certainly not have repudiated Rousseau's assessment of the character of his life of Louis XI, nor would any modern reader of that work. That the king is presented in the round with all of his faults and foibles is remarkable enough. Louis may have sincerely believed that it was the part of a good host not only to share his dinner with a guest but also to share his bed with him; but only a Duclos, a Rousseau, or a Suetonius were likely to report so hospitable an instinct. Duclos knew perfectly well what he was doing, as he makes eloquently clear near the end of the life:

> The principal error that befalls those who want to depict men
> is to suppose that they have a fixed character rather than a life

30. J. J. Rousseau, *Émile* (Paris, 1874), 278, note.
31. See E. Heilmann, *Charles Pinot Duclos: Ein Literat des 18. Jahrhunderts und seine Beziehungen zu Rousseau, d'Alembert, Marmontel und anderen*, Diss. Berlin (1936); P. Meister, *Charles Duclos*, Thèse Bâle (1956); J. Brengues, *Charles Duclos (1704–1772) ou l'obsession de la vertu* (Saint Brieuc: Presses Universitaires de Bretagne, 1971).
32. Gibbon, *Journal* (n. 7 above), 196.
33. Meister (n. 31 above), 43.

that is but a tissue of contradictions: the more deeply one studies them, the less one dares to delineate them. I have recorded several actions of Louis XI that seem not to belong to the same character. I make no claim to reconcile these actions nor to make them consistent. It would even be dangerous to do so: it would mean creating a pattern, and nothing is more opposed to history, and consequently to truth. I have represented Louis XI as devout and superstitious, greedy and generous, enterprising and timid, merciful and harsh, faithful and faithless—just as I have found him in following the various events.[34]

This account of the aims of Duclos's biography could be applied verbatim and with complete accuracy to the Lives of the Caesars.

The resemblance between Duclos and Suetonius is not confined to method and outlook. Both were uncommonly fortunate in having direct and privileged access to documentary material. In May of 1741 Duclos was officially entrusted with the manuscript of the Abbé Legrand, which was to form the core of his biography of Louis XI. This remarkable windfall provided the biographer with far more revealing detail than his sponsors expected. The Legrand manuscript served Duclos much as the inquisition register of Jacques Fournier has served Emmanuel Le Roy Ladurie in his stunning account of Montaillou. Suetonius, by virtue of his post as *ab epistulis* (secretary in charge of correspondence) in the court of the emperor Hadrian, had direct access to the imperial archives; and many of his most illuminating passages depend upon material he found there. He evidently studied with care the documents, letters, and memoirs he uncovered; when he cited them, he did so judiciously and tellingly. The parallel between Duclos and Suetonius becomes even closer when we observe Duclos duly installed as perpetual secretary of the Academy. He emerges as an *ab epistulis* of the eighteenth century, differing from his Roman predecessor in the much longer and more successful tenure of his office.

It was Duclos who particularly urged Rousseau to write an autobiography;[35] and we may well imagine, in view of the relations between the two men, that the insistence of Duclos was taken seriously. When Rousseau resolved to undertake the work, he chose as a title *Confessions*, which naturally evokes above all the self-revelations of Augustine.

34. C. P. Duclos, *Oeuvres* (1820), 4: 331.
35. Cf. Meister (n. 31 above), 42–43.

Yet Rousseau cannot have forgotten Duclos's *Confessions du Comte de + + +,*
which he had admired for so long; and Rousseau rewarded Duclos's
solicitude with a memorable letter in which he formulated the principles of his autobiography: "But I have much to say," he wrote, "and
I will say everything. I will omit none of my faults, not even one of my
bad thoughts. I will portray myself just as I am: the bad will nearly always
obscure the good. In spite of that I have difficulty in believing that any
of my readers would dare say to themselves, I am better than that man
was."[36] These words, written to Duclos from Môtiers in January 1765,
are more Suetonian than Augustinian in spirit; and they anticipate very
closely the words of the second and definitive introduction which Rousseau eventually placed at the beginning of the *Confessions.*

Rousseau's emphasis on the importance of domestic and superficially
trifling details in biography had led him to what he considered a new
and unique kind of autobiography. Like Johnson, Rousseau had pushed
his views on biography to their inevitable conclusion: as he put it in the
original preface to the *Confessions,* "Nul ne peut écrire la vie d'un homme
que lui-même [No one can write a man's life but himself]." Johnson likewise declared, "No one is so fit to be a man's biographer as the man himself." Both men had arrived at this position from a concept of biography
that demonstrably owed more to Suetonius than to any other antecedent
biographer. Obviously the temperament and genius of both predisposed
them in this direction, and it is perhaps safer to say that they found in
Suetonius an echo of their own sentiments rather than a model.

But there can be no denying that the fortunes of Suetonius in the eighteenth century were closely bound up with all that was most original in
the biographical writing of that time. If he was not so familiar an author as
Plutarch to the public at large, he was certainly well known to those scholars and biographers who were at the forefront of their profession. By the
middle of the eighteenth century the works of Plutarch had acquired that
universal and uncontested respectability which effectively precludes any
fertilization of creative minds. The energetic work of editors and critics
on Suetonius's Lives in the late seventeenth and early eighteenth century
heralded a new era in biography. Suetonius's works became widely available. They were controversial and exciting. Neither the anathema of the
church nor even the disdain of Voltaire could prevent them from having
an impact on some of the greatest writers of the age.

36. J. J. Rousseau, *Corr. complète,* (1975), 23: 100, letter no. 3875.

# CHAPTER SIX

# THE REDISCOVERY OF HERCULANEUM AND POMPEII

FOR JUST OVER TWO CENTURIES THE BURIED CITIES of Herculaneum and Pompeii have excited the imagination of writers and travelers of the Western world, and it was almost two thousand years ago that Mount Vesuvius destroyed those cities. When Goethe and Tischbein visited Italy in 1787, the twin sites had already become an integral part of the Grand Tour, but fame came slowly. The first systematic excavations were soon halted and not renewed for over twenty years; and when they were renewed, the digging was inept and sporadic. Most tourists were more interested in the volcano itself than in the ancient settlements it had extinguished so many centuries before. The story of the rediscovery of Herculaneum and Pompeii is a lesson in the operations of chance in history and a disquieting illustration of the ways in which the treasures of our past have been restored to us.

[ 1 ]

The coastal region of Campania on the Bay of Naples, at the foot of Vesuvius, was known to the ancients as the Campi Phlegraei, the blazing fields. Although no traditions of devastation survived in classical times among the residents, it is obvious that in some remote age there had been flames, together with an eruption that carried burning rocks and lava down the mountainside. Current speculation puts that event in the sixth century B.C. In any case, by A.D. 79 Vesuvius seemed utterly benign, and not even a severe earthquake in A.D. 62 persuaded the Italians otherwise. When the eruption occurred, the Campanian cities were still busy rebuilding after the earthquake of the preceding decade. Not all cities suffered annihilation like Herculaneum and Pompeii; Naples, for example, had a flourishing future in store. But the cities that were buried, whether under mud, as at Herculaneum, or under ash, as at Pompeii, were soon abandoned. A great fire at Rome in A.D. 80 put an end to an official government rescue team that was obliged to go home hurriedly, and the survivors who returned to retrieve their property competed with robbers in burrowing into some twelve feet of debris. Two Latin poets, Martial and Statius, both writing soon after the disaster, singled out Herculaneum and Pompeii as the principal losses in the eruption of Vesuvius; and if these are the cities we think of today as the Vesuvian cities, we are at one with the ancients.

Thanks to Martial and Statius, whose observations were later augmented by Pliny, Plutarch, and the historian Dio, the memory of the buried cities lived on. Their appearance on a medieval copy of an antique map was a further protection against oblivion. The original of that map was probably done in the third century A.D. on the basis, at least as far as Campania was concerned, of indications from a still earlier time. The copy, scrupulously executed in the thirteenth century, passed into the hands of Konrad Peutinger at Augsburg in the early sixteenth century. Scholars and humanists were therefore not short of evidence for the existence of the lost cities of Campania, and Boccaccio's transient allusion to *la già grande Pompea* in *L'ameto* suggests how much they were part of the common heritage of cultivated people.

Precisely when Peutinger was corresponding with interested friends about the desirability of publishing the important map that had recently come into his possession, an Italian scholar of remarkable energy and assiduity was making a careful record of every classical inscription he encountered. Theodor Mommsen first drew the attention of modern classical scholars to the significance of Mariangelo Accursio, better known by his Latin name of Mariangelus Accursius, in the history of Latin epigraphy. His work provided the foundation later for the more celebrated and influential Muratori in the eighteenth century. At Scafati, close to the site of Pompeii, Accursio had observed in the altar steps of the Church of the Madonna an ancient inscription (now published in the *Corpus Inscriptionum Latinarum* X as number 938). It contained the words *Cuspius T. f. M. Loreius M. f.*, which represent the names of a certain Cuspius, son of Titus, and of a certain Marcus Loreius, son of Marcus. These names were evidently a part of some sort of list; beyond that little could be said. But Accursio's record acquired a special importance long afterward, for in 1862 the excavators at Pompeii published five fragments of an inscription from the so-called House of Mars and Venus: the text was a list of local magistrates, and it included the names *Cuspius T. f. M. Loreius M. f.* (now published as *CIL* X. 937). The new fragments thus proved that the inscription Accursio had seen in the steps of the church at Scafati had come from Pompeii. The conclusion is inescapable and has been generally acknowledged.

There is clearly no way of telling how the stone from Pompeii reached Scafati nearby, but it cannot have left its original place before the destruction of A.D. 79. Nor is it the kind of prize a robber would have labored to extract and carry away. Once available, of course, it was a useful building block; and travelers in classical lands are all too familiar with the sight of ancient inscriptions walled up in relatively modern buildings. But how did the stone ascend through the ash and topsoil to present itself to the builders of Scafati? It can only have been brought up. At some unknown time in the Middle Ages, in some unknown digging—which, to judge from what happened later, may have been connected with the construction of canals for watering the land—this inscription from Pompeii was uncovered. With an insouciance that was, until the twentieth century, characteristic of nations whose soil was rich in antiquities, the Pompeian inscription was simply abandoned to the first person who needed a solid block of stone.

That was, as far as can be told, the beginning of excavation at Pompeii, and without the scholarly diligence of Accursio in the sixteenth century and an accidental discovery in the nineteenth we should never have known about it. Nothing further occurred in the vicinity of the buried cities until the end of the sixteenth century, when another unexpected discovery took place.

Between the years 1594 and 1600, during the installation of irrigation canals in the area of Pompeii, excavators accidentally brought up two more Latin inscriptions from the city. One (*CIL* X. 952) commemorated a local senator, and the other (*CIL* X. 928) appeared to contain the text of a dedication to Jupiter at the behest of *Venus fisica*. Of these the second turned out to be of great scholarly interest. The epithet *fisica* attached

to Venus cannot mean what it might at first seem to anyone uniniti-
ated in Latin philology, and it remains unexplained to this day. More
remarkable, however, was the incontrovertible proof that an ancient
settlement lay beneath the soil. The discovery caused little excitement
and aroused the curiosity of only a few. In his *History of Naples*, issued
in 1607, Giulio Cesare Capaccio took note of the excavation. Although
he was perfectly familiar with the ancient testimony on Herculaneum
and Pompeii, the recent digging did not deter him from believing that
both cities lay beneath sites farther to the north, at Torre del Greco and
Torre dell'Annunziata, respectively. Not only did the work at the end of
the sixteenth century lead to no progress at all in identifying the city,
from which by then at least three inscriptions had been unearthed, but
it also failed to generate any interest in excavating further. Inscriptions
have rarely captured the imagination of the general public. In 1637 the
expatriate German scholar Luc Holste, known as Lucas Holstenius, the
distinguished librarian of Cardinal Barberini and later of the Vatican,
correctly divined the location of Pompeii from the two texts brought up
at the end of the previous century; but those scholars who noticed his
conjecture refused to believe it.

In the *Guida de' Forastieri (Guide for Foreigners)*, as published in 1685,
on the eve of significant new discoveries at Pompeii, tourists were coolly
informed that Herculaneum was at Torre del Greco, where Hercules
was said to have built a city that was subsequently *dal Vesuvio assorbita*. In
a handsomely illustrated chapter near the end of the guidebook, with
the title "Del Monte Vesuvio," tourists could read all eight lines of Martial's poem on Herculaneum and Pompeii as well as a summary of the
younger Pliny's narrative of his uncle's death during the eruption of A.D.
79 (dated in the guide to 81). Nowhere in this charming little book was
there a hint that the cities of the past had already begun to disgorge their
secrets.

In 1689 more canals were dug, and two more inscribed stones
emerged. Unfortunately both of these texts are now lost, but it is apparent from a lively academic controversy of the period that one of them
actually bore the name of the city of Pompeii. The architect Picchetti
immediately and unhesitatingly drew the wrong conclusion. The workmen had accidentally penetrated, he declared, a villa of Pompey the
Great. Although such obtuseness does small credit to the history of scholarship, it is refreshing to observe that at least Francesco Bianchini, in
his *Storia universale* of 1697, attacked Picchetti for missing the obvious

implication of his finds. But even so, in the world at large no one really cared whether or not the name of Pompeii or Pompey stood on an old stone from a Campanian canal.

[ I I I ]

In the early years of the eighteenth century, some workmen had uncovered pieces of marble in the process of digging a well near Resina. An Austrian cavalry officer, Prince d'Elboeuf, appointed to the court of Naples at the time, heard of this surprising source of marble just as he was planning a pleasure dome for himself by the seaside. He had envisaged, it appears, a floor constructed of pulverized marble, and therefore naturally undertook to investigate the supply available at Resina. As work began in 1711 at the site of the well, d'Elboeuf confronted the first works of art to emerge from the cities of Vesuvius. A statue of Hercules was soon followed by three magnificent statues of women, who were promptly called, for no very obvious reason, Vestal Virgins. D'Elboeuf recognized the quality and importance of his discoveries and eagerly continued his excavations. He chose to present the statues to his cousin in Vienna, Prince Eugen, in the hope of gaining funds for the enterprise. D'Elboeuf had become, without realizing it, the first excavator of the theater at Herculaneum.

Although the project ground to a halt a few years later, largely because of complaints from the Vatican about the illicit smuggling of the newly found statuary out of Italy, the enthusiasm of d'Elboeuf had important consequences. What had moved him was evidently the art he uncovered, and it was the art he exported. His excavation in Campania was the first in search of ancient remains. The impact of works of art was of a very different order from that of inscriptions. The Vestal Virgins could be enjoyed at once without any special expertise; they could adorn a salon or a garden. The whole rediscovery of Herculaneum and Pompeii turned, as we shall see, on those statues; and as the eighteenth century wore on, it was the art from those cities—the sculpture and paintings especially—that came to fascinate Europeans of wealth and taste.

In 1736 the three ladies from Herculaneum passed into the possession of Friedrich Augustus II, king of Poland and elector of Saxony. Prince Eugen had died, and his collection was sold by the family. The so-called Vestal Virgins were transferred to Dresden, where they could be admired by, among others, Friedrich Augustus's daughter, Maria Amalia.

This young woman was destined to become the bride of the Spanish king of the Two Sicilies, Carlo III, who had been reigning at Naples since 1734. In the first four years of his rule, this Bourbon monarch had shown no particular interest in the antiquities of Campania. He made no explorations of the canals that had yielded the inscriptions of Pompeii; he did nothing to resume the excavation of d'Elboeuf. Yet he has often been credited with the initiative for reviving the buried cities of Vesuvius because in late 1738 the work at Herculaneum was renewed at his order. But the initiative was in no way his; earlier that year he had gone to Dresden to marry Maria Amalia. When he then took her back to Naples with him, she carried with her the memory of those three statues. She knew there must be more where they came from. She was no sooner in Italy than the digging began.

The excavation was conducted in the least scientific way imaginable; and although the era of professional archaeology lay in the distant future, there was little excuse for the carelessness and confusion of Carlo's Spanish engineers. The work at Herculaneum was a completely subterranean operation and motivated solely by the desire for art objects. The architecture and plan of the city were of no concern. When one area had been cleared, the earth removed from the next was simply transferred into it, and more than one contemporary observer commented wryly on this perpetual shifting of the earth underground. Visitors were viewed with suspicion and were generally refused authorization to draw or transcribe anything they saw. Charles de Brosses went to Herculaneum in 1739, and heard from a visitor ten years later that nothing had improved. "I have learned with displeasure that the work, which was so badly conducted in my time, is no better today. The underground regions are as dark and poorly excavated as they were ten years ago. As far as the new discoveries are concerned, the authorities are so jealous that they scarcely allow the curious any time to look at them while passing by, without giving any opportunity to study them closely, still less to copy them or to make a detailed description on the spot." De Brosses recalled with disgust his descent into the excavation "as if into a mine," and the dark tunnels illuminated only by torches which infected the stifling air and forced him to retreat to the entry shaft just to catch his breath. Horace Walpole, Thomas Gray, and the tireless Lady Mary Wortley Montagu, who all visited Herculaneum in the year after de Brosses, formed no more favorable an impression than his.

Apart from the few who had been to Naples and a small number of scholars, Europe paid little attention to what had been going on at

Herculaneum for a decade. In 1749 de Brosses was astonished to hear people in Paris talking about the discoveries as if they were quite new. When at about the same time the Marquis Venuti, librarian and consultant to the Neapolitan court, published the first scholarly report on the finds at Herculaneum, the author of the two long review articles on Venuti in the *Bibliothèque raisonnée*, volumes 47 and 48 (1751 and 1752), was moved to express his surprise that, despite the great interest of the new material, so little had appeared about it in the journals. Meanwhile, just as Venuti had been completing his publication on Herculaneum, Carlo's workmen had accidentally discovered some columns and paintings on the site of Pompeii. No doubt at the urging of Maria Amalia, the excavation of Pompeii was started at once, exactly ten years after her arrival in Naples. There followed six years of unheralded and unproductive rummaging in the deep ash. In 1754, in a spirit of boredom, the whole project was dropped for a short while. Neither Herculaneum nor Pompeii had made much of an impact on Europe.

[ I I I ]

In the middle fifties of the eighteenth century, the work on the Vesuvian cities began to gather momentum. The amazing discovery of hundreds of papyrus rolls, all baked into something resembling charcoal briquettes, together with the luxurious villa in which they were found, brought fresh excitement to Herculaneum. And the renewal of excavation at Pompeii in 1755 uncovered the substantial house of Julia Felix. The newly established Academy of Herculaneum undertook to publish all the objects discovered; the first volume of the *Antichità di Ercolano esposte* appeared in 1757. But tourists were no more welcome than before. Designers like Robert Adam and Charles-Louis Clérisseau were hurried through the excavations with unseemly speed. Meanwhile, in the year of their visit, 1755, Johann Joachim Winckelmann arrived in Rome.

The great German art historian, whose gaze was always turned toward Greece, nevertheless passed most of the last thirteen years of his life in Rome. He served as contact and guide for many of the most distinguished visitors to the city. Although Roman antiquities were hardly his principal interest, he explored the excavations near Naples on three occasions: in 1758, 1762, and 1764. He received the same frigid reception as others, but his sharp eyes and retentive memory allowed him to fill his letters with fascinating details about what he saw. He inspected the Herculaneum papyri, and recorded inscriptions at Pompeii. He marked the absurdity of the excavation methods; at Pompeii the old system of redistributing the earth continued to be applied even though the work was not underground. In two celebrated open letters (*Sendschreiben*) Winckelmann condemned the procedures he observed; and when at last these letters were translated and brought to the attention of the local authorities, they had an effect. Anger at the eminent art historian gradually gave way to placation. No archaeologist, however incompetent, cares to be exposed in front of the whole learned world. Winckelmann had performed a most important service. He gave publicity to Herculaneum and Pompeii and, at the same time, improved the quality of work on the sites.

The letters he wrote from Naples during his three trips are proof of Winckelmann's interest in the finds from the area. He kept in touch over the years through the friends and clients of his who went there. The painter Angelica Kauffmann, one of the first to depict a scene from A.D. 79, spent the winter of 1763–64 in Naples, and at Rome she was in the circle of Winckelmann. So was the renegade English politician John Wilkes, as well as Johnson's biographer Boswell (*ein junger Schottländer, den ich sehr wohl kenne*, "a young Scotsman, whom I know very well"). Another of the more eccentric antiquarians of Winckelmann's acquaintance was the Englishman Lord Baltimore (*welcher Herr von ganz Maryland in Virginien ist*, "who is lord of all Maryland in Virginia"). When Sir William Hamilton arrived in 1764 to represent England at the court of Naples, he, too, promptly became an acquaintance of Winckelmann.

Hamilton, who remained in Italy into the beginning of the nineteenth century, witnessed—and indeed contributed to—the end of the general indifference to the discoveries at Herculaneum and Pompeii. He was even more of a social magnet than Winckelmann, and he was devoted to the antiquities and geology of Campania. His cultivation of the ridiculous boy-king, Ferdinand IV, who at the age of eight had replaced Carlo in 1759, ensured some influence over the policies of the court. His close observation of Vesuvius both at rest and in eruption led to the volumes he published under the title *Campi Phlegraei*, and his own collection of local antiquities led to a major accession for the British Museum. Sir William Hamilton dominates the emergence of the cities of Vesuvius from obscurity into splendor. Without his patronage, all the efforts of Winckelmann might have been in vain. When he assumed his post in 1764, he presided over Naples's two greatest tourist attractions, Mount Vesuvius and the infant king of the Two Sicilies. By the time Goethe and Tischbein called on him in 1787, Herculaneum and Pompeii had become at least equally interesting.

As an illustration of the relative neglect of the sites when Hamilton was first at his post, despite the major publications by Winckelmann and the Academy of Herculaneum, let us consider the rather improbable presence of three notable British tourists at Naples in early March 1765. They are John Wilkes, James Boswell, and Edward Gibbon.

Wilkes, who had been traveling in Italy in the company of Mlle. Corradini, a dancer from Bologna whom he picked up in Paris, proposed in late February to see the antiquities of Naples. Winckelmann provided him with an introduction. After an excruciating five-day journey from Rome, during which he spent part of one night in the coach because the local accommodations were so appalling, he arrived in Naples on February 26. Writing one of his typically chaste letters to his daughter Polly, he declared, "This is in my opinion the pleasantest place in Europe." In Naples, Wilkes spent considerable time with Boswell, who arrived there just four days later and took great pleasure in sharing observations on the sensual delights of the city. If Wilkes actually visited Herculaneum or Pompeii, he left no record of it. The only thing he thought worth reporting to his Polly in any detail was his ascent of Vesuvius on March 18: "It is with difficulty you ascend: I had five men to get me up;—two before, whose girdles I laid hold of; and three behind, who pushed me by the back. I approached quite to the opening...but could see very little." Wilkes remained at Naples until the end of June.

Boswell noted that he called on Hamilton, which Wilkes may have thought it wiser not to do, in view of his political position. Boswell also made the traditional ascent of Vesuvius, four days before Wilkes. His report: "smoke; saw hardly anything." We know that sometime during his three weeks at Naples, given over to seeing "Classical Places," he actually did visit Pompeii and Herculaneum, not to mention a grotto alleged to be Virgil's tomb and the royal palace at Portici, near Resina. But if the antiquities made any great impression on him, nothing so far published has shown it. On the contrary, it was the natural beauty and licentious atmosphere of Naples that most captivated him. "Naples is indeed a delicious spot....But, my dear friend, modern Naples has nothing of the ancient Parthenope except its heat and its idleness. The people are the most shocking race, eaters of garlic and catchers of vermin—an exercise which they scruple not to perform on the public streets. Swift's Dermot and Sheelah would make a true Naples Eclogue...."

Into this world came Edward Gibbon near the end of that Italian tour, which seemed to him in later life to have provided the precise moment at which he was inspired to write the *Decline and Fall*. He spent six weeks in Naples, from the end of January to the middle of March 1765, but he left no account whatever in his journal. His *Memoirs* suggest that what had most impressed him were Mount Vesuvius and the king of the Two Sicilies: "Six weeks were borrowed for my tour of Naples, the most populous of cities relative to its size, whose luxurious inhabitants seem to dwell on the confines of paradise and hell-fire. I was presented to the boy-King by our new Envoy Sir William Hamilton...." There was not a word of Campanian antiquities, nothing on Herculaneum or Pompeii, even though his journal has revealed that at Lausanne in the previous year he had read through the second part of the review of Venuti in volume 48 of the *Bibliothèque raisonnée*. It is remarkable that Gibbon evidently had no contact with Winckelmann in Rome, despite their common acquaintance, the Scottish antiquarian James Byres, and a common enthusiasm for the ancient world. Nor, in Naples, did his path cross that of Winckelmann's friends, Wilkes and Boswell.

In fact, one wonders what Gibbon was doing for those six weeks. The warm climate and sensuous character that Boswell so much savored in Naples appear to have unnerved the future historian of the Roman Empire. He wrote to his stepmother Dorothea, "I cannot say whether you will find me improved in anything else, but at least I think I am become a better Englishman....I am reconciled to my own Country, that I see many of its advantages better than I did." By July, when he was back in England, he again declared himself a better Englishman and observed, "What a mixture of pride, vice, slavery and poverty have I seen in the short time I passed at Naples." It seems clear that Gibbon's sojourn in Naples was in some way disturbing for him; but if there is anything peculiar about his total silence on the discoveries at Herculaneum and Pompeii, it is only because he was to become in time so great a master of the history of the Roman Empire. One might have expected him, more than others, to share Winckelmann's curiosity and indignation. In six weeks Gibbon was surely taken to the excavations, however hurriedly, by Hamilton or an associate, just as Boswell was. But not even in the *Memoirs* was he moved to mention those places.

## [ I V ]

Almost as if to oblige Sir William Hamilton and to usher in the wide-spread fame that the buried cities have enjoyed ever since, Mount Vesuvius erupted in 1766, with several encores throughout the remainder of the century. Under Hamilton's leadership and with the successive publications of the *Antichità di Ercolano*, the art of Herculaneum and Pompeii took hold of European taste; beginning with Goethe's Italian journey, literature fell under the cities' spell. But there had been nothing inevitable about the rediscovery. On the contrary, the earliest indications of what lay buried were largely ignored; it was not until art supplemented epigraphy that anyone took action. And when that happened, the mentality of treasure hunters dominated the work. Local authorities put impediments in the way of scientific research. Recognition was slow in coming from the cultivated public. The resurrection of the past is more systematic now than it was then, but much of the old indifference and many of the old obstacles remain. Inscriptions are still being built into churches (or mosques), or left to be broken up in some vacant lot. Collectors and dealers are still willing to sacrifice a site for instant reward. Herculaneum and Pompeii can teach us more than Roman history.

PART II

# THE NINETEENTH CENTURY

# CHAPTER SEVEN

# SIGN LANGUAGE

*Gesture in Naples and Gesture in Classical Antiquity,* by Andrea de Jorio, translated and with an introduction by Adam Kendon

NEAR THE END OF *THE BIRDS,* ARISTOPHANES' COMIC fantasy, one character, concealing himself under a parasol from the watchful gaze of all-seeing Zeus, asks an interlocutor to take his parasol and to hold it over him so that he can report the latest news. This delicious piece of stage business beautifully demonstrates the fundamental truth that without two free hands an ancient Greek would have been tongue-tied. And the Romans were no different, as we can see from a long discussion by the rhetorician Quintilian in the early empire on how to gesture when speaking to a courtroom. Sometimes the entire body could be manipulated in ways that were no less eloquent than movements of the hands. In fact, the external appearance of the body could be as significant as the way it moved. Philosophers were traditionally grubby, with long and filthy hair, whereas sophists were well groomed and perfumed.

Nonverbal expression was developed to a high art in antiquity, and it has long been clear to anyone who has traveled in the Mediterranean countries that gestures are as natural and as important there today as they were then. Andrea de Jorio, a canon of the Cathedral of Naples and a curator at the city's Royal Museum in the early decades of the nineteenth century, became convinced that the entire repertoire of gestures that he observed every day in the streets of Naples had survived unaltered from antiquity. Thus was a bold inference for a city unusually rich in its history as well as its gestural vocabulary. Confronted with the astonishing paintings and sculptures from the recently excavated sites of Herculaneum and Pompeii, as well as the collection of images on southern Italian vases in the Naples museum, de Jorio decided to make a systematic inventory of Neapolitan gestures in the hope of putting forward authoritative interpretations of those ancient scenes. His book was published in 1832, and it enjoyed a legendary reputation in the nineteenth century among those who believed, as de Jorio did not, that gestures constituted a kind of language.

The twentieth century found little time for de Jorio's pioneering work until recently, when the rise of semiotics combined with an interest among art historians in gesture to invest his achievement with an importance that not even he could have imagined. Even so, this book has been more often cited than read. In view of its immense relevance to contemporary studies of gesture in the context of language and culture, it is surprising that we have had to wait so long for a translation into English.

Adam Kendon has now given us the first complete, annotated rendering of *La mimica degli antichi investigata nel gestire napoletano*. Kendon himself is an established leader in the new scientific approach to the study of gesture. He is the author of a work on the sign language of Australian Aborigines, as well as of numerous articles in semiotic and anthropological journals. Although, as he has often remarked, gestural activity has for centuries attracted the attention of travelers, philosophers, and linguists, it has become a serious academic industry only in the last two decades.

Gesture is obviously not the same as speech. It may have a translatable vocabulary, but it certainly lacks syntax. Yet, as Aristophanes shows, in many cultures speech cannot happen without gesture, though gesture can undoubtedly happen without speech. This appears to be nowhere more true than in Naples. Hence the renewal of interest in a work published two centuries ago, a work that could easily be called ponderous were it not for the astonishing revelations that it provides. In a drab and clinical style worthy of Masters and Johnson, it describes a world of pullulating impropriety.

De Jorio came from a leading family of the island of Procida in the Bay of Naples. He aspired from childhood to a life in the church, and, no doubt with help from family contacts, he became canon at the tender age of thirty-six. A farmer's accidental discovery of an ancient tomb near Cumae, in the area of Pozzuoli, led to de Jorio's being called in to prevent pillaging, and the bas-reliefs that were found there ignited a passion for antiquities that consumed the cleric for the rest of his life. In trying to explain the meaning of dancing figures on the reliefs, de Jorio began a gradual transformation into an archaeologist and a gesture analyst.

De Jorio immersed himself in the volumes of the Herculaneum Academy, where much of the material from the excavations in the previous century had been published with learned commentary. He occupied himself with writing guidebooks for visitors to the Royal Museum. As time passed, he concentrated more and more on the gestures that he observed in the ancient works of art. As a trained classical scholar, de Jorio already had a good knowledge of the ancient texts, which he undertook to mine for references to gestures. Fortified with all this erudition, de Jorio set about his great task of cataloguing what he observed in the Naples of his own day.

His presumption that Neapolitan gestures were a survival of classical ones was no more than a hypothesis. Despite his optimism, de Jorio was never able to prove it. Besides, his knowledge of Latin was considerably more profound than his knowledge of Greek, and it is disconcerting to see him ignore so much important Greek evidence (including that episode in *The Birds*). Yet the enterprise was both audacious and original. More than a century and a half later, the book is a sheer delight to read. Kendon's translation is not elegant, but it is serviceable, which is what he intended it to be. It must be said that occasionally he falters in his mother tongue ("foreigners are always asking we Neapolitans"), and the proofreading of texts quoted in Latin has been very badly done. Any reader keen enough to examine the passages cited in Kendon's notes would be well advised to consult an edition of the original. The references at least are invariably correct.

De Jorio is not a theorist of gesture. He is an observer and an interpreter. In his introductory pages he comments wryly on the reaction of visitors from the buttoned-up cultures to the north. In the Naples museum, which was a part of the Grand Tour, he had many an occasion to offer explanations of the gestures depicted on ancient vases "in the same way as we would explain our own." Still, says de Jorio, "to those who had been born in distant regions and who, on account of their cool and sluggish temperament are rather unsuited to gesturing, these explanations seemed cold and without meaning."

To instruct such souls, de Jorio prepared his elaborate account of gestures as he saw and understood them in Naples. His book is nothing less than an encyclopedia of gestures, with comprehensive headings organized alphabetically beginning with *abbracciare* ("embrace"). Kendon has wisely retained the Italian original at the start of each entry, so that the movement from one cluster of gestures to another is exactly as de Jorio created it. After *abbracciare* comes *additure* ("pointing, indicating"), and onward through such delights as *bacio* ("kiss"), *dormire* ("sleep"), *grattarsi* ("scratching oneself"), *mano in fianco* ("hands on hips"), and *schiopetto* ("snapping the fingers"). The entry titled *perfetto* ("perfect") announces gravely that it is not a treatise on metaphysics but merely a complement to the earlier discussion of *giusto* ("just").

De Jorio commissioned a local artist named Gaetano Gigante, who specialized in Neapolitan scenes for the tourist market, to create a series of images that were, in de Jorio's opinion, more lifelike and more reliable than those snapped up by the foreigners. These images, charmingly called *bambocciate* (from a word for simpleton that is meant to evoke the life of plain folk), became an integral part of de Jorio's book. He equipped them with explanatory commentary and placed them alongside a few ancient images on which he offered comment. He added to these some famous drawings of hands performing various gestures (some untranslatable into polite language), and of heads with hands at various positions. These images have been, until now, the best-known part of de Jorio's work.

It is difficult to know what a gesture is. Kendon insists that a bodily expression must be willful to count as a gesture, although he acknowledges that gesture is a concept "with fuzzy boundaries." Involuntary reactions, such as laughing, crying, or blushing, are not to be taken as gestures unless they are feigned, and yet we all know that in the Mediterranean world many a recognizable gesture occurs as involuntarily as a laugh or a blush. When today's Greek silently answers a question in the negative, he does not shake his head from side to side, as we do; he tips his head back, sometimes with a concomitant closing of the eyelids. This was an act already known to Homer and familiar to Athenians in the age of Pericles. The Greek verb is *ananeuein*, "to tip one's head upward." De Jorio duly lists this act under the heading of *negativo*, and he characteristically provides Latin parallels (though no Greek ones). But he does not inquire—nor does Kendon, for that matter—whether this act is willful in the same sense that holding out the index and little fingers of the hand certainly is, in one of the most potent and menacing of gestures (*fare le corna*, or "horns").

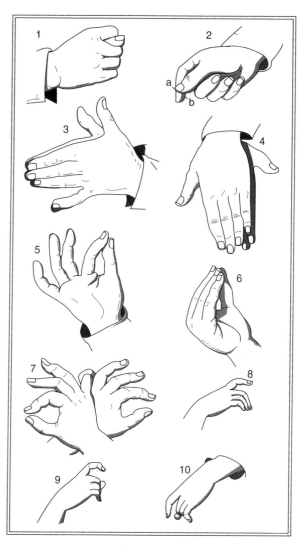

FIGURE 7.1.

De Jorio is simply interested in documenting what he notices people doing with their hands and bodies. He is persuaded that archaeological scholarship will benefit; and he declares, in Kendon's less than felicitous prose, that "among the objectives of this work, then, one of the main ones has been to prepare for archaeologists new methods for the understanding of antiquity." Yet he is well aware that eighteenth-century and early-nineteenth-century archaeology, which delivered those paintings and sculptures that first captivated him, had to concern itself with gross obscenity. Representations of copulation of various kinds, fellatio, cunnilingus, bestiality, and the gestures that accompany such lubricious conduct all fell squarely within de Jorio's investigation.

Some of the gestures on which he finds it necessary to dilate at length involve configurations of the fingers that would be readily understood—and resented—on the streets of any American city today. (We need hardly assume that this gestural lingua franca was imported by immigrants from Naples.) This obviously posed a terrible problem for the canon of a cathedral. What de Jorio called "obscene signs" he acknowledged to be a stumbling block, "particularly for us." In a work intended only for the eyes of professional scholars, anything could be said—and indeed was said, as in the volumes of the Herculaneum Academy. De Jorio realized that he could have chosen to omit offensive material, but he decided otherwise. As he rightly asked, "How would it be possible to cite the ancients in support of our discoveries, especially their monuments, if four-fifths of them are felt as an affront to delicacy?"

And so, in a remarkable effort of self-abnegation, de Jorio announced that he would always use "the necessary discretion in expression and modesty in words," but invoke from the rich store of Neapolitan gestures those that every reader would know to be obscene in order to explain the ancient gestures. Hence, says de Jorio with evident satisfaction, "with such an innocent expedient, that which was not decent was successfully concealed." How he imagined that ignorant northerners of sluggish temperament would be helped by this ruse is not immediately apparent.

In handling obscene texts, as opposed to obscene images, de Jorio undertook for the edification of archaeologists to provide cross-references that would illuminate the indelicate parts of his inquiry without actually spelling out what was going on. In some cases, he compels a serious reader to make an extensive romp through the sources in order to find out what a given gesture is really about. The reader who embarks

upon his apparently inoffensive rubric of *salutare* ("greeting") begins
with an undoubtedly benign gesture solemnly described as "palm of the
hand raised towards the face and oscillated in the direction of the interlocutor." De Jorio knows that in northern Europe this indicates a summons but in the south indicates "welcome" or "goodbye." He moves on
to other gestures of greeting:

1. Mano in fica ("fig") 2. Danaro (money) 3. and 4. Stupido (stu-
pid) 5. Amore (love) 6. Bacio (kiss) 7. Condotta versipelle (dis-
sembling conduct) 8. Schiopetto (snapping the fingers) 9. and
10. Disprezzo (scorn)

But he has to cope with antiquity. Because he knows his Petronius well,
he can invoke a funny moment when Lichas (whom he erroneously calls
Lycas) greets the rogue hero Encolpius: "Lycas politely moved his hand
and said, 'Greetings, Encolpius.'"

About this, de Jorio coyly remarks:, "We will say with some certainty
that he makes one of the gestures of salutation that we have described.
However, the question is: Which one? Who can know?" In fact, de Jorio
knew perfectly well, as anyone who follows up his "cross-reference" will
quickly discover. What Petronius says in the full text, of which de Jorio
cites only part, is that Lichas took one look at Encolpius's genitals, politely
put his hand there, and said, "Greetings, Encolpius."

There are many instances of cloistered humor of this kind, in which
de Jorio seems to wink at readers in the know, and one cannot help
wondering whether these juicy little items, both visual and textual, did
not provide an impetus for his sociological research. On the extended
middle finger, which the ancients already recognized as unchaste (*impu-
dicus*), de Jorio allows himself more of those rhetorical questions that
invariably show him on the borders of decency. Yet he summons up the
pertinent texts in Persius and Martial for those who care to consult them,
and presumably he also counts on those who already know what this very
common gesture means.

Likewise, in his treatment of a comparably infamous configuration of
the hand, de Jorio is overtly reticent but covertly revealing. This is the
*fica*, or *mano in fica*, or "fig," of which there is an uncompromising representation in one of the plates of hand gestures. It is explicitly described as
"hand as a fist with the point of the thumb interposed between the middle finger and the index finger so that it sticks out." We are then given
a variety of interpretations of this ugly gesture: apotropaic, insulting,

inviting (for obscene purposes). De Jorio expatiates most implausibly on some ancient paintings in which he detects the "fig." Although women figure in those images, de Jorio is betrayed by his lack of Greek. If he had known his Aristophanes, he would surely have added a "cross-reference" to line 1,350 of *Peace*, where it is clear that the word for "fig" (*sukon*) stands for the female genitals. Thanks to Kendon's note, the reader will at least discover that the Italian *fica*, a very rude word, "is defined as a vulgar term for 'vulva' and, by extension, a vulgar term for 'woman.'" Proper Italian for "fig" is *fico*, not *fica*.

Fans of Fellini's *Satyricon* will be pleased to find in these pages an explanation of that grotesque actor in the opening sequence who farts onstage. He is named Vernacchio, and, in the words of the screenplay, "emits a rapid and quasi-musical series of farts." In a lengthy account of gestures for derision or ridicule (*beffeggiare*), de Jorio describes a gesture called *vernacchio*, in which a farting sound is produced through the application of the hand to the mouth when filled with air. "Such behavior is so insulting," declares de Jorio, "that it is scarcely used in Naples except by those who belong to the lowest classes of the population." Whether the *vernacchio* was known to Augustus's Rome as well as to Fellini's Rome is not clear, but de Jorio thinks that it was, and he bases his view on a text of Horace, which he characteristically invokes with a rhetorical question and an incomplete citation.

Poor de Jorio! He is so often let down when he tries to relate his Neapolitans to the ancients. The primary justification for his work is flawed at best. Certain gestures, such as tipping the head upward or raising the middle finger, do indeed appear to have survived through the ages, as if they represent some kind of fundamental repertory of gesture peculiar to the human animal. But much of what de Jorio records is only marginally relevant to antiquity, and as a result his own interpretations of ancient images are far less compelling than his interpretations of the contemporary scenes, the *bambocciate*, that he commissioned.

Two of his case studies will be sufficient to illustrate the poverty of de Jorio's method. He attempts to explain a famous image of a nude dancing woman, seen from behind, as known to him from the publications of the Herculaneum Academy. He quotes from the learned commentary of the academicians while censoring the more indelicate of their citations. The woman seems quite obviously to be dancing, as the academicians claimed; but de Jorio is much taken by the exposure of her buttocks to the viewer and the open circle created by the thumb and forefinger of the left hand that she holds over her head. The canon of Naples Cathedral wishes us to believe that this is an erotic invitation (or insult), issued by the display of the backside (a form of mooning, it seems) and the representation of the female genitals by the fingers of the left hand. Of course he cannot say this outright, but he refers the reader to his detailed description of the gesture under his rubric *disprezzo*, or "scorn."

For a second example of de Jorio's misguided method of interpreting the ancients, consider his Plate XVIII, a drawing of a vase painting. The drawing is defective in its transcription of two of the four Greek words, but never mind. There are four figures, from left to right: a female called Euodia ("Sweet Smell") gesturing to the right; a seated satyr named Komos ("Revelry") facing right and playing long pipes; a female called Galene ("Relaxation") facing left and holding a tambourine; and finally at right the figure of Dionysus facing left, looking at the two women with the satyr between them. We hardly need a hierophant to tell us that this is a Dionysiac scene, with music and revelry. For de Jorio, however, this is a picture of a quarrel, because the two women are looking at each other and the one on the left is pointing a finger at the other. "It seems natural and clear," he writes, "that the first woman is reproaching the other woman with something, and that the other is surprised about this and she also denies it." As for the musical satyr between the two women, "This is because in such scenes the person playing this sort of role [of the jealous woman] usually does it from behind someone." De Jorio assures his reader that a true Neapolitan would have grasped all this the moment he saw the picture.

It is sad to find such nonsense in the pages of a work that the author compiled so meticulously and so lovingly. In truth, the book is almost useless for the archaeologists and the art historians whom de Jorio thought it would benefit. And yet he opened up the systematic study of gesture in ways that he could never anticipate, for generations long after him. This is a great work built on a false premise, which is ultimately a far better thing than a poor work built on a sound premise. It would have helped if de Jorio had been able to cast his net far wider than the streets of Naples and the collections of the Royal Museum. But all its silliness notwithstanding, the book commands respect.

After reading de Jorio's book, no one will ever again be able to read Clement Moore's immortal verses on St. Nicholas in quite the same way: "He spoke not a word, but went straight to his work, / And fill'd all the stockings; then turned with a jerk, / And laying his finger aside of his nose, / And giving a nod, up the chimney he rose." The tomb of St. Nicholas can be seen today at Myra in southwestern Turkey, and so his gestures ought perhaps to have fallen within the classical purview of de Jorio. But Moore's St. Nicholas is Santa Claus, and he comes from those northern climes where de Jorio thought that temperaments were naturally sluggish. What a mistake! We need a de Jorio of the North Pole.

# CHAPTER EIGHT

# BERLIOZ, VIRGIL,
# AND ROME

*Presented, with sound illustrations, at a symposium on Les Troyens,*
February 3, 2003, Metropolitan Opera, New York City

FROM THE AGE OF MONTEVERDI IN THE EARLY
seventeenth century down to the early nineteenth century the myths and
history of ancient Rome provided a rich storehouse of plots for librettists.
The Roman theme across those three centuries enjoyed its popularity as
a vehicle both for special effects and for strong emotions. Busenello, who
wrote the libretto for Monteverdi's *Coronation of Poppaea*, also wrote the
text for an opera on Dido, set by Cavalli in 1641. Other great themes
were Julius Caesar, Scipio Africanus, and the emperor Claudius. Händel's
*Agrippina* and *Julius Caesar* were products of this operatic taste for Roman
subjects. The prolific librettist Metastasio provided numerous texts on

*Note*: The only systematic attempt to address this subject, as far as I am aware,
is David Cairns's paper, "Berlioz and Virgil: A Consideration of 'Les Troyens' as
a Virgilian Opera," *Proceedings of the Royal Musical Association 1968–69* (published
1969), pp. 97–110. Cairns addressed this topic as a musicologist, I as a classicist.
I hope that our approaches may be seen as complementary. Quotations from
Berlioz's *Memoirs* in the present essay are in Cairns's admirable translation, as
published by Knopf in 2002.

ancient Rome including, once again, a *Dido* that was set by literally dozens of composers in the eighteenth and early nineteenth centuries.

But by the late eighteenth century interest in Roman mythological figures was declining in favor of Greek ones. To use Edgar Allen Poe's famous terminology, the grandeur that was Rome was yielding to the glory that was Greece. Some of this change was inspired by the Greek War of Independence and the celebrated exploits of Lord Byron, who was much admired all over Europe. But there were other reasons. Greek myth and tragedy spoke more eloquently to romantic sensibilities. Gluck's two Iphigeneias, Alcestis, and Orpheus enjoyed great popularity, and Medea became a familiar heroine in settings by Cherubini and later Pacini. By the 1820s Rome had nearly disappeared as an operatic subject. Pacini wrote a work in 1825 on the final moments of ancient Pompeii but more to provide special stage effects for the eruption of Vesuvius than to accommodate a taste for things Roman.

The French Revolution and the tumultuous career of Napoleon awakened a new interest in modern, as opposed to ancient, history and contributed, in music at least, to putting ancient Rome out of style even as it left space for Greece. The strong new taste for historical dramas in opera, is reflected in Rossini's *William Tell*, the majority of Donizetti's operas, Meyerbeer's *Huguenots, Robert le Diable,* or *L'Africaine* (about Vasco da Gama). Early Verdi likewise chose subjects from relatively modern history, with the exception of Nabucco and Attila, which provided ancient but not Roman subjects. Even the early Wagner chose his topics from renaissance Rome (*Rienzi*) and Shakespeare (*Liebesverbot*). Apart from Bellini's Norma, a kind of Druid Medea who thinks of killing her own children to spite her lover, Spontini's francophone masterpiece of 1807 on a vestal virgin (*La Vestale*) was the last important work on a wholly Roman theme until Berlioz produced his opera on the Trojans a half-century later.

Berlioz much admired Spontini's opera, but that was by no means the principal reason he chose to write an opera on what was in fact the primal foundation legend of Rome—the fall of Troy and the flight of Aeneas to Italy by way of Carthage. He was swimming very much against the stream in writing a huge opera in the middle of the nineteenth century on the foundation of ancient Rome, and the reason he turned to this subject was that he loved Virgil's epic poem, the *Aeneid*. As a boy he had not only mastered this work but memorized it at the hands of an exacting teacher, his father. In his *Memoirs* Berlioz wrote, "It was Virgil who first found the way to my heart and fired my nascent imagination, by speaking to me of epic passions for which instinct had prepared me." He describes his emotional response to the powerful lines in Book IV of the poem when Dido, whose great love for Aeneas was thwarted by his divine mission, took her own life.

Berlioz wrote his own libretto for *Les Troyens*. It is clear that his constant point of reference was the *Aeneid*. His borrowings are unmistakable. Even his deviations, which reflect a keen sense of theater based largely upon a deep knowledge of Shakespeare, show unflagging respect for Virgil's narrative. Berlioz's biographer, David Cairns, correctly observed, "Not only the characters' passions...but the Virgilian ambience itself, the whole environment of the epic, have been absorbed by the composer into his being, and given back in his own language." Few, if any, opera composers have ever known a classical author as Berlioz knew Virgil. The Virgilian template for *Troyens* is fundamental, even more so than the evident influence of Shakespeare in the love duet of Act IV.

The *Aeneid* begins with a quarrel among the gods that propels Aeneas, who has fled with his son and shipmates from the collapse of Troy, into a terrible storm at sea. He comes ashore at Carthage on the North African coast and discovers a great city founded by another exile, the queen Dido, a Phoenician by origin. Aeneas meets Dido, and she persuades him to tell the story of the fall of Troy, which he does across two entire books of the poem (Books II and III). Dido falls in love with Aeneas as she hears his dreadful story.

Obviously Berlioz could have started his opera effectively with a big storm, in the style of Bellini's *Pirata* or Rossini's *Italiana* (or Verdi's *Otello* later), but he could hardly have done much with the immensely long narrative that Aeneas addresses to Dido. So he chose to begin his work with the fall of Troy itself, presented on stage in a preliminary opera of two acts. *La Prise de Troie* is both dramatic and programmatic. The details of the action are largely drawn from Aeneas's narration to Dido and are therefore Virgilian in substance. The direct representation of Troy's collapse defines and explains Aeneas's mission, and of course it can be told without any of the divine squabbling over mortal affairs that seems so alien to modern readers of the poem. In fact, Berlioz decided to banish all the individual gods from his libretto with the sole exception of Mercury, who makes a brief but powerful appearance not far from the end in order to summon Aeneas on from Carthage to Italy.

So Berlioz begins with two great acts on the fall of Troy. He has structured them, in a bold but utterly Virgilian way, around the figure of Cassandra, who was fated to know and to foretell what was to come without anyone ever believing her. Although she appears in precisely this role in Virgil, she is less prominent there, and it is probably no accident that for Berlioz she is a pendant to Dido in his operatic structure. In Virgil she is said to be in love with a certain Coroebus, whom Berlioz's good theatrical instincts impelled to put on stage. The opera opens artfully at the moment when the Greeks have lifted their siege of the city, leaving behind only a large wooden horse. The Trojans rejoice, but Cassandra knows better. There is a marvelous moment of stillness in all of this jubilant hubbub when Hector's widow, Andromache, suddenly appears on the stage with her little son Astyanax. Neither sings a note. Berlioz took this moment of mournful and ominous repose, in which he introduced a memorable solo for English horn, directly from Virgil's lines about Andromache before the kingdom had collapsed:

II. 455–57:
*infelix qua se, dum regna manebant,*
*saepius Andromache ferre incomitata solebat*
*ad soceros et avo puerum Astyanacta trahebat*

[...where poor Andromache often used to go alone in the old days to see her father-in-law or to take Astyanax to his grandfather]

Aeneas himself is now brought into the action and delivers the Virgilian account of the priest Laocoon. This percipient but ill-fated man had immediately suspected that the huge wooden horse outside the city was some kind of trick on the part of the Greeks. Laocoon threw a spear at the horse. After that he and his two sons were destroyed by two enormous serpents that came out of the sea. The innocent Trojans are unwilling to believe Cassandra, according to Virgil:

II. 246–47:
*tunc etiam fatis aperit Cassandra futuris*
*ora dei iussu non umquam credita Teucris.*

[Then Cassandra revealed the doom to come in words that a god ordained the Trojans never to believe.]

The Trojans simply assume that Laocoon was impious and justly punished. They therefore command the horse to be brought into the city to the music of a sonorous march with rhythms that any ear accustomed to the meter of Virgil's dactylic hexameters will immediately recognize. Berlioz's Trojan March is a musical refashioning of Latin lines that had reverberated in the composer's head for a lifetime.

The second part of the Trojan component of the opera opens with the ghost of Hector appearing before Aeneas. Berlioz has crafted this almost word for word from Aeneas's first-person narrative in Virgil:

II. 282–90:

> quibus Hector ab oris
> exspectate venis? …
> quae causa indigna serenos
> foedavit vultus? Aut cur haec vulnera cerno?
> heu fuge, nate dea, teque his, ait, eripe flammis.
> hostis habet muros; ruit alto a culmine Troia.

[From what shores, Hector, do you come,
long awaited?
What unworthy cause has fouled your
serene face? Why do I behold these
wounds?
Alas flee, son of a goddess. Take yourself
away from these flames. The enemy holds
the walls. Troy is collapsing from its lofty
peak.]

> De quels bords inconnus reviens-tu?
> Quel nuage semble voiler tes yeux sereins?
> Hector, quelles douleurs ont flétri ton
> visage?
> Ah! fuis, fils de Vénus! L'ennemi tient nos
> murs! De son faîte élevé Troie entière
> s'écroule.

[From what unknown shores do you come
back? What cloud seems to veil your
serene eyes? Hector, what griefs have
defiled your face?
Flee, son of Venus! The enemy holds our
walls. From its high peak all Troy is
collapsing.]

Finally Cassandra huddles with the other Trojan women against the onslaught of Greek soldiers who have poured out of the interior of the wooden horse. She calls the women "frightened doves," in an evocation of one of Virgil's most exquisite similes, describing Cassandra's mother Hecuba and her daughters:

*Mais vous, colombes effarées, pouvez-vous consentir à l'horrible esclavage?*
But you, frightened doves, can you agree to dreadful slavery?

II. 515–17:
*hic Hecuba et natae nequiquam altaria circum,*
*praecipites atra ceu tempestate columbae,*
*condensae.*

[Here Hecuba and her daughters huddled in vain around the altar like doves buffeted in a dark storm.]

The Trojan part of the opera ends with the suicide of the women of Troy, a dramatic but conspicuously un-Virgilian element in the story, introduced to create a powerful finale to Act II. Berlioz must have been aware of the legend of the mass suicide of the Trojan women, although I know of no reason to believe that he was acquainted with Euripides' tragedy about them. In this climactic moment of despair Berlioz brings in the cry *Italie*, proclaiming Aeneas's mission to go to Italy and to found the city of Rome. This cry, which recurs later, is totally Virgilian and derives from a *Leitmotiv* in the poem:

I. 2–3: *Italiam fato profugus Laviniaque venit / litora*
I. 553–54: *si datur Italiam sociis et rege recepto*
*tendere, ut Italiam laeti Latiumque petamus*
IV. 361: *Italiam non sponte sequor.*
IV. 381: *i, sequere Italiam ventis, pete regna per undas*

The opera moves to Carthage, where the queen Dido is seen to be enthroned in prosperity and splendor. Aeneas and his crew arrive, but obviously he cannot tell his story to the queen as he does in Virgil because we have already seen it onstage. What follows in the first of the three Carthage acts has almost nothing to do with Virgil and everything to do with the expectations of Parisian audiences of the time. There are ballets, ceremonies, and spectacles. Berlioz even invents a war for Dido with a local enemy, Iarbas, so that Aeneas's willingness to be her ally can serve as the basis for the growing infatuation of the queen.

But the inspiration of Virgil returns powerfully in the two final acts of Aeneas at Carthage. Dido and Aeneas enjoy a hunt together in a mountain wilderness, where a fierce storm drives them into a cave in which, quite obviously, their love is consummated. Virgil leaves us no doubt about what happened:

IV. 167–68:...*fulsere ignes et conscius aether*
*conubiis summoque ulularunt vertice Nymphae*
IV. 172: *coniugium vocat*

[Fires gleamed, the sky was complicitous in the union, and
Nymphs wailed from the top of the height...
...calls it a marriage...]

Berlioz setting of this episode is voiceless apart from the now disembodied and reiterated cries of *Italie*. The composer wanted the scene to be fully staged and withdrew it from the 1863 premiere because he was so dissatisfied with the way it was presented. The ferocity of the hunt scene then gives way to more un-Virgilian ballet. Yet even here we have the first of two minor but very significant tenor songs, both of which are thoroughly rooted in Virgil's poem. These two songs effectively frame Berlioz's magical scoring for the passion of Dido and Aeneas. Iopas sings of the earth, just as he does at the end of Book I of the *Aeneid*:

I. 740–43:
        *cithara crinitus Iopas*
*personat aurata, docuit quem maximus Atlas.*
*hic canit errantem lunam solisque labores,*
*unde hominum genus et pecudes, unde imber et ignes...*

[Long-haired Iopas, whom mighty Atlas taught, plays his golden
lyre. He sings of the wandering moon and the labors of the sun,
whence come the race of men and beasts, whence rain and fire...]

Later the sailor boy Hylas sings of homesickness on board ship. Hylas is Virgil's Palinurus from the end of Book V but under another and more singable name, evoking a narcissistic youth in Greek myth. Virgil's boy, Palinurus, unlike Berlioz's Hylas, accidentally falls off the boat into a watery grave. Because Berlioz's son Louis was also a professional sailor and we know that he wrote this song with Louis in mind, it is hardly surprising that he chose to suppress Palinurus's sad fate for the no less melancholy but less ill-starred Hylas.

Between Iopas and Hylas come those tremendous scenes of love that mirror Virgil's description of Dido and Aeneas in Book IV of the *Aeneid*:

IV. 395:
*multa gemens magnoque animum labefactus amore*

[...with many a groan and crazed in his mind with a great love]

For the ensemble, *nuit d'ivresse et d'extase infinie* [night of intoxication and infinite ecstasy], Berlioz turned to his beloved Shakespeare in *The Merchant of Venice*, where Jessica and Lorenzo recall earlier legendary lovers (among them Dido and Aeneas). But the rapture is abruptly and ominously terminated by another invocation of *Italie*, this time in the single divine epiphany of the opera—the appearance of Mercury, taken directly from Virgil: *Aen.* IV. 554–70, where the god appears to Aeneas in a dream and tells him not to delay (*rumpe moras*).

The departure of Aeneas is fated, and Dido knows it:

*Inutiles regrets!...je dois quitter*
*Carthage! Didon le sait...*

[Useless regrets...I must leave Carthage.
Dido knows it.]

The overwhelming scene of Dido's death stays as close to Virgil as Berlioz could possibly manage:

IV. 657–60:
*"felix, heu nimium felix, si litora tantum*
*numquam Dardaniae tetigissent nostra carinae."*
*dixit, et os impressa toro "moriemur inultae,*
*sed moriamur," ait. "sic, sic iuvat ire sub umbras."*

["Lucky, alas too lucky if only the Trojan ships had never touched our shores," she said, and pressing her face to the couch went on, "We shall die unavenged, but let us die. Thus, thus is it best to join the dead."]

*Je vais mourir, dans ma douleur immense submergée, et mourir non vengée.*
*Mourons pourtant!*

[I am going to die, overwhelmed by my immense grief, and die unavenged. But let us die nonetheless.]

Berlioz was particularly proud of Dido's wordless cries in the score. "Strange," he wrote, "that none of my yapping critics should have blamed me for daring to produce such a vocal effect. I think it deserved their anger." These cries are developed from Virgil's description of Dido's frenzy:

IV. 589–90:
*terque quaterque manu pectus percussa decorum*
*flaventisque abscissa comas*

[Striking her comely breast three and four times with her hand and tearing her blond hair]

*Didon parcourt la scène en s'arrachant les cheveux, se frappant la poitrine et poussant des cris inarticulés.*

[Dido runs across the stage while tearing her hair, striking her breast and uttering inarticulate cries.]

Even when a boy Berlioz had been moved, as he tells us in the *Memoirs*,[1] by Virgil's matchless lines on Dido's final moment. In his opera he did them full justice:

IV. 691–92:
*ter revoluta toro est oculisque errantibus alto*
*quaesivit caelo lucem ingemuitque reperta.*

[She turned over three times on the couch. With her wandering eyes she sought the light in the high heaven and groaned when she found it.]

Berlioz's masterpiece can be called a thoroughly Virgilian work. It is never crudely imitative. The music of Virgil's Latin—its dactylic rhythms and its sonority—so long and so deeply embedded in Berlioz's brain, perhaps even contributed, as suggested earlier, to his musical ideas as he brought the Trojans to the stage. Any experience of this opera creates an impact that feels uncannily like the experience of reading—and hearing—Virgil's poem.

---

1. In Cairns's translation, "When I came to the scene where Dido dies on the pyre... my lips trembled and the mumbled words would hardly come. At last, at the line *quaesivit... repertam* I was seized with a nervous shuddering and, in the impossibility of continuing, stopped in my tracks." Clearly Berlioz's text had the variant reading *repertam*, which the best modern editor of Virgil (Mynors) has replaced with *reperta*.

# CHAPTER NINE

# EDWARD LEAR IN PETRA

*It seems no work of Man's creative hand,*
*By labor wrought as wavering fancy planned;*
*But from the rock as if by magic grown,*
*Eternal, silent, beautiful, alone!*

*Match me such marvel save in Eastern clime,*
*A rose-red city half as old as Time.*

—J. W. Burgon, "Petra,"
Newdigate Prize Poem, 1840

THE ANCIENT ROCK-BOUND CITY OF PETRA CAPTURED
the imagination of the Victorians. Dean Burgon's famous prize poem
about a place he had never seen has made the city rose-red for generations of armchair travelers. Although the Crusaders had built castles in
the vicinity of Petra, the city, which lies today in the southern part of
the kingdom of Jordan, disappeared completely from the books and
itineraries of Europeans. Petra was known from the ancient Greek and
Latin texts to have been the capital of the Nabataean Arabs, famed for
their commercial activity in transporting the spices and incense of south

Arabia to the Mediterranean Sea.[1] But until 1812 no one in the West had ever seen the city or even knew where it was located.

Posing as a Muslim, Swiss traveler Johann Ludwig Burckhardt managed to persuade the suspicious Arabs of Transjordan to convey him to an ancient site of which he had heard fabulous reports. He was led into Petra in August of 1812 through the narrow defile that is called the Siq and remains today the principal access to the city. Burckhardt penetrated far enough into Petra to see the great tombs of the eastern cliffs. In his account of his journey he said modestly and correctly, "It appears very probable that the ruins...are those of the ancient Petra."[2]

Burckhardt's discovery incited a succession of scholars and adventurers to make the dangerous journey into the Nabataean capital. Most travelers went there from Jerusalem by way of Hebron and the northern Negev, on across the steamy Wadi Araba south of the Dead Sea and into the mountains of Edom. Important images of the city created by Léon de Laborde were widely disseminated and widely admired;[3] but, as the excellent American traveler Edward Robinson, from the Union Theological Seminary in New York, observed when he made his visit in 1838,[4] Laborde's drawings were often seriously inaccurate. For example, of Laborde's depiction of the great theater at Petra, Robinson wrote, "This Laborde has given with a good general effect, though not with great exactness."[5] It was not until 1860 that Francis Frith took the first photographs of Petra, and they show eloquently how right Edward Robinson was in censuring Laborde.[6]

1. For overviews of the city and its people, see I. Browning, *Petra* (London: Chatto and Windus, 1973); *Die Nabatäer,* Erträge einer Ausstellung im Rheinischen Landesmuseum, Bonn, May 24–July 9, 1978 (Bonn: Habelt, 1981); G. W. Bowersock, *Roman Arabia* (Cambridge, Mass.: Harvard University Press, 1983); M. Lindner (ed.), *Petra und das Königreich der Nabatäer,* 4th ed. (Munich: Delp, 1983).

2. J. L. Burckhardt, *Travels in Syria and the Holy Land* (London: J. Murray, 1822), 431.

3. Léon de Laborde, *Voyage de l'Arabie Pétrée* (Paris: Girard, 1830), recording a journey made in 1828. For Laborde's view of the Siq, with a magnificent high arch (now lost) over the defile, see most conveniently Browning, *Petra* (n. 1), 114.

4. E. Robinson, *Biblical Researches in Palestine and Adjacent Regions: A Journal of Travels in the Years 1838 and 1852,* 2nd ed. (London: J. Murray 1856).

5. Ibid., (n. 4), 134.

6. A Frith photograph of the theater may be seen in Bowersock, *Roman Arabia,* (n. 1), plate 5.

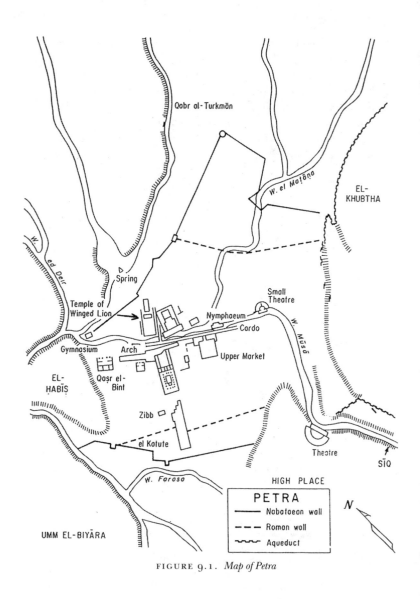

FIGURE 9.1. *Map of Petra*

Over the years reports of visits to Petra in the nineteenth century have been systematically collated and studied in order to recover features, remains, and vegetation that have long since disappeared.[7] Yet curiously, one visitor to the city, who not only described his experiences in detail but also made drawings of several parts of the city, has been completely neglected by students of Nabataean civilization. In a register of all visitors to Petra that was made in the early part of this century—a register that includes every known graffito scratched before 1902—one name is conspicuously absent: Edward Lear.[8]

Best known as the incomparable writer of nonsense verse but also a serious artist and world traveler, Lear went to Petra in 1858.[9] For this amiable but sad man, who suffered throughout his life from epileptic seizures, the journey into Petra was anything but easy. And once he was there his visit was cut short by local tribesmen who importuned him for money and robbed him of much of what he had brought with him. In a letter written to a patron a little over a month after he left the city, Lear remarked rather testily, "Of my own mishaps at Petra you perhaps have heard how above two hundred of them came down on me, and everything which could be divided they took. My watch they returned to me—but all money, handkerchiefs, knives, etc. were confiscated.... English people must submit to these things *because we have no influence in Syria or Palestine nor in the East generally*. I should like to hear of a French party being stopped or murdered—the Arabs (and Turks) know too well that neither French nor Austrians can be touched with impunity."[10]

Nonetheless Lear was able to bring back a collection of drawings and to write subsequently an enchanting account of his journey to the Nabataean capital, an account that was not published until April of 1897, nearly a decade after his death.[11] Lear's narration of his journey is very

7. The first collations of the travelers' reports and still perhaps the most valuable are those of R. Brünnow and A. von Domaszewski in each of the three volumes of their pioneering work, *Die Provincia Arabia* (Strasbourg: K. J. Trübner, 1904, 1905, 1909).

8. Ibid. (n. 7), 3: 192–94 ("Verzeichnis der Besucher von Petra").

9. For the general context of Lear's visit, see the authoritative biography by Vivien Noakes, *Edward Lear: The Life of a Wanderer* (London: BBC, 1985), 125–29.

10. Edward Lear, *Selected Letters*, ed. Vivien Noakes (Oxford: Oxford University Press, 1988), 154.

11. "A Leaf from the Journals of a Landscape Painter," *Macmillan's Magazine*, April 1897, 410–30. Lear died in January 1888.

precise in its topographical detail. It allows one to follow him step by step in the course of his progress through Petra and to identify exactly the places in which he did the drawings that survive today. Biographers of Lear, unacquainted with the site, have understandably failed to recognize the scholarly value of this document. We can see nineteenth-century Petra through Lear's own eyes, and that in itself is an uncommon privilege. Furthermore, what we see is a Petra that is no more.

Lear prepared himself for his journey through a careful study of Edward Robinson's travel narrative, and in Hebron he actually succeeded in engaging the same Arab guide to Petra that had led Robinson twenty years before.[12] Because the local tribes were known to take advantage of travelers who tried to enter the city through the narrow entrance of the Siq, Robinson's guide and Lear's brought him in over the mountains from the southwest. On April 13, 1858, he had his first glimpse of the city from its western extremity. In his journal he wrote, "Reaching the open space whence the whole area of the old city and the vast eastern cliff are fully seen, I own to having been more delighted and astonished than I had ever been by any spectacle."[13] There were far more ancient remains on the surface of the city in its central part than there are now. Lear, like other travelers, reported that he saw "innumerable stones, ruined temples, broken pillars and capitals," and so on.[14]

From the west he moved eastward toward the great rockhewn tombs. He was stunned, as all visitors are, not only by the architectural magnificence of these tombs but by the colors of the stone. Lear wrote,

> Wonderful is the effect of the east cliff as we approach it with its colours and carved architecture, the tint of the stone being brilliant and gay beyond my anticipation. "Oh master," said Giorgio

12. Lear, ibid., 411: "In came my dragoman Abdel with various Arabs, and lastly no less a person than the Sheikh of the Jehaleen himself, no other than Abou Daouk or Defr Alla, the guide to Petra of Robinson in 1838." Cf. Robinson, *Biblical Researches*, 95: "The following morning, Friday, as we were sitting after breakfast in our tent, we were somewhat surprised to see the head Sheikh of the Jehâlîn, Defá Allah. . . . We now made a bargain with him in the presence of Elias."

13. Lear, "A Leaf from the Journals," 421. He passed by way of "the solitary column which stands sentinel-like over the heaps of ruins around": this is the object known locally by the rude name of Zibb Fir'awn.

14. Lear, ibid., 421. These remains appear to be those registered by Brünnow-von Domaszewski, *Die Provincia*, vol. I, as nos. 407 and 421.

(who is prone to culinary similes) [he was, after all, Lear's cook on the journey], "we have come into a world where everything is made of chocolate, ham, curry powder, and salmon."[15]

Lear and his little party pressed on still farther to the east, approaching the point at which the Siq opens out into the city. Lear went a little way into the interior of the narrow passage and then turned around to come out again and face the magnificent monument which all visitors behold with amazement on emerging from the narrow ravine, the so-called treasury, or Khazneh. "I turned round," he wrote, "to see the effect of the far-famed Khazne or rock fane which is opposite this end of the ravine, a rose-coloured temple cut out in the side of the mountain, its lower part half hidden in scarlet blossom, and the whole fabric gleaming with intense splendour within the narrow cleft of the dark gorge."[16] Lear's drawing of the Khazneh from just inside the aperture of the Siq conveys the enchantment of the place, even if it does not accurately represent what one can see from inside the Siq. This is one of three drawings from Petra that are now in the Lear collection at the Houghton Library of Harvard University.

The Houghton drawings, together with one other, of which the whereabouts are now unknown, document perfectly Lear's own account of his artistic activity on that first day in Petra. From the Khazneh he went back westward to work on what he called "the whole view of the valley looking eastward to the great cliff." He describes himself as drawing "in the bed of the stream among its flowering shrubs."[17] Another of the Harvard drawings shows this location quite precisely. It is now known to scholars as the Nymphaeum. A second version of this picture was exhibited in London at the Royal Academy in 1985.[18] Both pictures show an astonishingly rich vegetation that has unfortunately disappeared almost entirely from Petra today. What Lear called "the bed of the stream" was the course of the Wadi Musa, which many visitors see when it is completely dry but which carries torrents of water in periods of rain, particularly in the spring. Lear's images were made, as we have seen, on April 13.

15. Lear, "A Leaf from the Journals," 422.
16. Loc. cit. The printed text gives Khasme, rather than Khazne.
17. Loc. cit.
18. *Edward Lear, 1812–1888*, at the Royal Academy of Arts, ed. Vivien Noakes (London, 1985), 110–11, cat. no. 25a.

The artist then moved up to what he described as "one of the higher terraces where a mass of fallen columns lies in profuse confusion."[19] His drawing at this point is clearly documented by a picture that had once been in the collection of Philip Hofer. We see an admirably accurate representation of the eastern cliffs together with some figures in the foreground. Lear was never very good at drawing figures, and it is therefore not surprising that, when he refashioned this drawing into a substantial oil painting some years later, he marginalized the figures.[20] It is clear that Lear was sitting on the northern side of the wadi where the ground slopes upward and where today modern archaeologists have uncovered a Nabataean temple, the so-called Temple of the Winged Lion. The rising ground on the other side of the stream is the site of Petra's marketplace and several additional temples. The "mass of fallen columns" that Lear describes in his journal are clearly represented in both the drawing and the oil painting. They have long since disappeared.

Finally, as the sun was setting, Lear turned to draw the cliffs in the opposite direction. In his own words, "And lastly at sunset I turned to draw the downward stream running to the dark jaws of the western cliff."[21] Another of the Harvard drawings was clearly done at this moment. It shows the familiar elevations of the rocks just to the north of what used to be known as the acropolis, on the top of which a small crusader fort still remains.

It was a good thing that Lear managed to do so much on his very first day in Petra, because once the word got round that he and his party were there, all of the local tribes decided to press their claims for compensation, called either pleasantly a tax or simply bakshish. All through the night crowds of Arabs kept gathering round Lear's tent. And yet, with admirable *sang froid*, he picked himself up before dawn and went with three guides to make the ascent of the western cliffs in order to see a monument that he undoubtedly knew about from his reading of Robinson's journals.[22] It takes an hour, more or less, to reach the

19. Lear, "A Leaf from the Journals," 422.

20. I am profoundly grateful to the owner of this picture, who wishes to remain anonymous.

21. Lear, ibid., 422.

22. Lear, ibid., 424: "I therefore order Giorgio to close and watch my tent, while I try a visit to Ed Deir." Cf. Robinson, *Biblical Researches*, 140: "Thus the Deir lies high up among the cliffs of the western ridge, more than half an hour distant from the area of the city."

FIGURE 9.2. *Lear, drawing of the Khazneh (by permission of the Department of Printing and Graphic Arts, Houghton Library, Harvard University)*

FIGURE 9·3. *Lear, drawing of the Nymphaeum (by permission of the Department of Printing and Graphic Arts, Houghton Library, Harvard University)*

FIGURE 9.4. *Lear, oil painting of Petra (courtesy of the owner)*

rockhewn monument known as the Deir, or monastery. The ascent is arduous, but Lear enjoyed every moment of it. Although he found the scenery astonishing and admired the colors of rock and vegetation, he concluded, as many other travelers have, that the Deir itself is somewhat disappointing in comparison with the Khazneh, "neither so beautiful in colour nor so attractive in situation, yet a fit crown to the marvels of the ascent."[23] From that lofty eminence Lear was able to look far away to the east, back to the tombs he had drawn the day before.

It seems as if Lear did no drawing at all on his ascent to the Deir. At least he mentions nothing of the kind in his journal, and I know of no drawing that represents this region. Lear could not have been gone for more than three hours altogether. He returned to his camp in time for breakfast and an uproarious squabble with the importunate Arab tribesmen. As the situation around his tent became increasingly alarming, Lear gave the signal for his party to retreat. Even so, before they saved themselves from serious harm, Lear scrambled back up to the top of the theater and for half an hour made another sketch, or at least so he tells us—I have not yet discovered that any drawing from that half-hour survives.[24] The entire party withdrew in the late morning of April 14, with rather fewer personal belongings than they had had when they arrived but otherwise in reasonably sound condition.

Lear's account of his visit to Petra was written in a good-humored tone and with the wit and humanity that characterized everything he did. His text, his exquisite drawings, and his magnificent painting constitute a record of Petra in the mid-nineteenth century that is without parallel. At the same time they tell us a little more about the curiosity and courage of one of the most attractive of the Victorians.

23. Lear, "A Leaf from the Journals," 425.
24. Lear, ibid., 426: "I had not long to devote to my drawing from the upper part of the theatre."

# CHAPTER TEN

# BURCKHARDT ON LATE ANTIQUITY FROM THE *CONSTANTIN* TO THE *GRIECHISCHE KULTURGESCHICHTE*

THE FOUR VOLUMES OF THE POSTHUMOUSLY PUBLISHED
*Griechische Kulturgeschichte* [Greek Cultural History] of Jacob Burckhardt
enjoy the unenviable reputation of having been condemned unani-
mously and without reservation by the most eminent classical scholars
of the time. These were men of unimpeachable authority—Theodor
Mommsen, Ulrich von Wilamowitz-Moellendorff, Karl Julius Beloch,
Eduard Meyer, men who often disagreed brutally with each other but
were united in judging Burckhardt's work utterly useless. Wilamowitz
famously declared that he would be a coward if he did not say straight
out, "The *Griechische Kulturgeschichte* of Burckhardt does not exist as far
as scholarship is concerned." Eduard Meyer's comment was, if anything,
even more insulting: "It is as if someone wanted to write a book about
mathematics without knowing the most basic principles of the discipline." Burckhardt himself had been apprehensive about the reception
his *Kulturgeschichte* would receive at the hands of his professional colleagues, and although at his death he had revised about half the work
for publication he seemed to be disinclined ultimately to offer it to the

public. To friends who had been aware of the cultural history and had urged him to publish it, Burckhardt had once expressed his reservations with characteristically pungent insight: "No sir, such a poor outsider, who doesn't belong to the professional guild, may not venture anything of the sort; I'm a heretic and an ignoramus and, with my questionable opinions, would be viciously torn apart by the *Viri eruditissimi* [learned men]. Ah yes, believe me, I know these people."

The work was not translated into English until the 1950s. An Italian translation published in 1955 is best known for the preface that Arnaldo Momigliano wrote for it. A few books in recent time have addressed the *Kulturgeschichte* in the context of Burckhardt's own thought. Such are Janssen's book on Burckhardt and the Greeks, and the eccentric interpretations of Egon Flaig. The work has had almost no impact on the professional study of ancient history in Europe and North America (to say nothing of anywhere else). This is a pity, because, despite the unfinished form of a good half of the *Kulturgeschichte*, it contains much that anticipates and reinforces current views of the ancient world and the way in which it should be studied. By contrast, Burckhardt's early book of 1853 on the emperor Constantine, *Die Zeit Constantins des Grossen*, went into a second edition in its author's lifetime (1880) and has enjoyed influence and renown throughout the twentieth century. Its cynical interpretation of Constantine's religious policy, which is profoundly indebted to Gibbon's portrait of that emperor, has often evoked disagreement. But its wide-ranging assessment of the age and its eponym, bringing to a sharp analysis of politics and religion a sensitive appreciation of provincial culture and its art, has continued to impress readers. An Italian scholar, writing in 1971, linked Gibbon and Burckhardt together as "these two colossi of modern historiography on the Constantinian age."

Since the study of late antiquity has become such a fertile field of research for both classical and medieval historians in the last thirty years or so, it might be interesting to attempt to trace the growth of Burckhardt's understanding of the late Roman and early Byzantine periods from the *Constantin* to the treasures of methodology and substance that lie within the *Kulturgeschichte*. Viewed superficially, that long posthumous work does not appear to take the reader into late antiquity at all but to confine its inquiry to the archaic, classical, and Hellenistic epochs of Greece. But Burckhardt's deliberate attempt to break free from chronological narrative in his history led him to invoke material from widely disparate periods. He was in search of what he perhaps naively called "the eternal Greek": "Wir lernen hier den ewigen Griechen kennen [Here we get to know the eternal Greek]," as he wrote programmatically in his preface to the *Kulturgeschichte*. This drove him to an account that we would now call synchronic, and it meant inevitably that Burckhardt brought in witnesses from late antiquity at numerous points. Burckhardt had never given up reading the sources for the post-Hellenistic history of the Greeks, and that is why it is not so foolish as it might seem to look to the *Kulturgeschichte* for this subject. His superb and pioneering lecture on Dio Chrysostom from 1864 shows what he could do with the later Greeks in the middle of his career, and his ruminations on the late antique world in the so-called *Weltgeschichtliche Betrachtungen* [*Observations on World History*] prove that his engagement with later classical culture was an integral part of his thinking about the whole course of European history. Fragments of the major lecture he delivered three times in the 1880s on the medieval culture contain much reflection on both Roman imperial and late antique history. The theme was clearly important for him.

Burckhardt's interest in the Greek culture of the Roman and early Byzantine worlds had deep roots. August Boeckh's course on Greek antiquities at Berlin in 1839–40 must certainly have encouraged a wide vision in Burckhardt's approach to the classical world, and as early as 1847, in the midst of his studies of art history, he wrote to his friend Eduard Schauenburg, "I'm reading a lot in the old writers, including the trashy classics; Apuleius is quite wonderful, Lucian too, whom I'm now reading right through, in order to get back into Greek. The *Scriptores Historiae Augustae* are asses, but interesting.... Now for the first time I'm really working with enthusiasm on antiquity." The history and the authors of this period were scarcely in high favor in the middle of the nineteenth century. Not even Mommsen was ever able to bring his published history of Rome forward into the imperial age or beyond, and the recent publication of notes on Mommsen's lectures on this late period demonstrate how uncomfortable he was with the extant evidence and how crudely he interpreted it. Burckhardt's kind of history was, as Burckhardt himself must have recognized, ideally suited to the exposition and interpretation of late antique culture. Although he never projected a work devoted entirely to this theme, its importance did not escape him. Karl Christ emphasized this point fifteen years ago when he published for the first time the full text of Burckhardt's outline notes on late antiquity, which Kaegi had only excerpted in his chapter on the *Kultur des Mittelalters* in the sixth volume of his sprawling biography.

As the excellent teacher that he was, Burckhardt thought about ancient history as a student would. In his extended discussion of research on classical sources in the *Weltgeschichtliche Betrachtungen*, Burckhardt repeatedly looked to the dilemma faced by a beginner. So much scholarly work had already been done that one might reasonably imagine all that was left for a student to do was to consult learned handbooks and dissertations. Burckhardt's comments express in stark language what he said in a more nuanced form in the preface to the *Kulturgeschichte*. Here are his notes from the *Betrachtungen*: "Huge activity—collecting and constructing—in the study of classical antiquity. A beginner discovers, on every imaginable topic, large learned works already available—handbooks, or at least dissertations and monographs—thesauruses, collections of this and that. Doubts if one can do anything new. In fact independent works seem largely pointless in comparison with the mass of handbooks (on the state, law, religion, morality, law, art, etc.). Everything has long since been excerpted from every side."

It is staggering to find a man whose enormous erudition did not keep him from understanding the despair of an initiate into classical studies, especially in the German-speaking universities of the nineteenth century. The scholars who were busy creating all those handbooks and collections, who were toiling tirelessly in the excerpting of texts on one subject or another, or in the hope of reconstructing, fragment by fragment, a lost work from antiquity, thought that they were doing something worthwhile. Mommsen, one of the greatest of the classical scholarly entrepreneurs certainly thought so. Burckhardt's poor opinion of the collectors and excerptors was a reflection of his ostentatious repudiation of the name of philologist. As a disciple of Boeckh, Droysen, and Ranke, he stood far away from the philological terrain of Gottfried Hermann. Although the youthful Mommsen had a passion for history, as the work that won him the Nobel Prize at the end of his life amply demonstrates, much of his mature work was devoted to editing, collecting, excerpting, tinkering, and browbeating. The most original minds he encountered, those of Beloch or Burckhardt, were not to his liking. When Burckhardt proclaimed at the beginning of his *Kulturgeschichte* that he was a *Nichtphilologe* [nonphilologist], from whom the reader could expect from time to time a philological slip (*ein philologisches Versehen*), he was proclaiming his liberation and adjuring his students and readers to join him in his freedom.

Burckhardt wanted to escape from the tyranny of historical events, particularly political events: "Auch sind die 'Ereignisse' das, was am ehesten durch Bücher zu erlernen [Events are what are most easily learned from books]." Burckhardt wanted to step aside from all that. He declared that his task, as he saw it, was this: "To give the history of Greek thought and outlook, and to evoke, on the basis of an understanding of the living forces that brought growth and destruction, what made Greek life work." What a breath of fresh air this must have seemed in 1872, when Burckhardt first offered his course on Greek cultural history. Even today it is challenging and exciting. The *Constantin* of nearly twenty years before showed Burckhardt practicing his style of ancient history without explicitly theorizing about it, and he must have realized that the early fourth century of the common era provided a perfect stage for bringing on the "living forces" that gave vitality to the life of the Greeks.

The book hardly neglected the political elements in Constantine's success, but its evocation of religion and society was spectacularly fresh. The chapter on "Das Heidentum und sein Göttermischung" [Paganism and the Intermingling of Gods] ranges across the Mediterranean world with observations on cults and myths, in both text and image, that in its pointillist brilliance anticipates by more than a century the similar technique of evocative exposition from a multitude of telling details in Peter Brown's *The World of Late Antiquity*. It is obvious from the lecture notes of the 1880s that Burckhardt had lost none of his fascination with this material. His prompts to himself are still arresting: for example, "The press of other religions, the Near East as a vagina of religions…millennialism, ecstasy, prophecies, and strong asceticism."

In the *Betrachtungen* Burckhardt discussed in detail the handling of sources for the kind of history he thought should be written. He hammers again at the philologists: "It depends on the designation: the professional philologist is altogether different from the person who is only interested in history and the one who is only interested in general stimulation." Burckhardt accorded an unusually high priority to poetry. He thought that Hesiod's *Works and Days* should be learned by heart. Tragedy, comedy, and lyric poetry all were instructive. Far in advance of his time, Burckhardt singled out the epigram as vital for comprehending the Greeks, and this is especially true of late antiquity in relation to the *Greek Anthology*. Again with extraordinary prescience, Burckhardt turned to the ancient novels for writing later Greek history—Longus, Xenophon of Ephesus, Heliodorus. Only after I had completed my book of 1994 titled *Fiction as History* did I realize what an eloquent supporter of this approach I might have summoned in Burckhardt. He went on to discover other valuable witnesses in the mathematical, geographical,

and medical literature of the ancient world. And, above all, he emphasized rhetoric.

Burckhardt's realization that rhetoric was absolutely fundamental to
understanding Greek culture put him once again far in advance of his
time. The current revival of interest in rhetoric among historians of the
last quarter-century coheres perfectly with his vision. For the history of
late antiquity he identified, with extraordinary foresight, the importance
of the sophists. In the *Betrachtungen* he had noted, "The modern universal historian should know precisely everything: no independent description of ancient time is altogether empty and fruitless.... An example: the
caricature and copying of old Platonic dialectic in the post-classical sophists." Later in the *Betrachtungen* Burckhardt explicitly discussed the transformation of Greek institutions and religion in the post-classical period
through the fifth century A.D., and he singled out the "The continuation
of rationalism and exploitation of the language and rhetorical-dialectical
capability.... This capability survives the polis, public life in the gymnasia
and theaters, and all art; the tongue is the last to survive" In a striking
reaffirmation of this view of the late antique Greeks at the end of his
chapter on *Die Redekunst* in the third volume of the *Kulturgeschichte* Burckhardt wrote, "Dialectic and rhetoric above all, alongside the epigram, are
the last to live on from antiquity. When the state, gymnastics, art, and the
residue of philosophy have undergone decline or total transformation,
the Greek tongue still keeps going."

Nearly thirty years ago I thought I was doing something new in argu-
ing for the historical importance of sophists in my book *Greek Sophists
in the Roman Empire*, because the classical profession was imbued with
Wilamowitz's opinion that the later sophists were insignificant figures
inflated out of proportion by their biographer, Philostratus. But the study
of sophists caught on, and relatively recently we have had the latest in a
succession of long monographs on the subject—the excellent German
*Habilitationschrift* by Thomas Schmitz titled *Bildung und Macht*, a book
that would have warmed Burckhardt's heart. Averil Cameron has written
on *Christianity and the Rhetoric of Empire*, and Peter Brown has given us
*Persuasion and Rhetoric in Late Antiquity*.

Burckhardt understood, as none of the nineteenth-century scholars
did (including Boeckh, Droysen, and Mommsen), that Rome had fostered the continuation of Greek culture. As he wrote in the *Betrachtungen*
and echoed several times in the *Kulturgeschichte*, "The unexpected good
luck of world culture lay in the philhellenism of the Romans, to which

we exclusively owe the continuity of the intellectual legacy." In a sense, therefore, Burckhardt could hardly have undertaken his *Kulturgeschichte* without a thorough acquaintance with late antiquity. Paradoxically the *Constantin* was the best and most natural way to proceed to the Greeks of the classical and Hellenistic periods. Burckhardt's approach was never so synchronic at any point that he lost sight of change over time, and although he ostentatiously eschewed narrative history he identified large epochs, each with a distinctively different character. They were distinguished by broad general categories such as the heroic man, the colonial and agonistic man, and the Hellenistic man. Today no one would rest content with terms such as these, but the means by which they were constructed provide a model for writing cultural history.

Burckhardt believed, as he elaborated in his preface to the *Kulturgeschichte* and expressed pithily in the *Betrachtungen*, that nothing was too poor or trifling to illuminate Greek culture: "The stamp of the rich Greek spirit penetrates even the most worn-out reproduction." This doctrine, worthy of the disciples of *Annales* historiography, exposed areas of ancient life that none of Burckhardt's contemporaries had seen fit to investigate. Momigliano had erroneously taxed Burckhardt with neglecting such well-worn topics as finance, family, and love among the Greeks. In fact these subjects are all addressed in the *Kulturgeschichte*, the first (finance) in a relatively limited way for the simple reason that cultural history is not economic history. But what marks Burckhardt's work as distinctive is his attention to the irrational side of Greek life nearly a century before E. R. Dodds wrote his pioneering book, *The Greeks and the Irrational.*

Burckhardt's treatment of ghosts and demons, of vampires and werewolves in the Greek popular tradition was precisely an area in which his deep knowledge of the later periods served him well. He drew heavily for this material on the second-century A.D. traveler Pausanias and the third-century chronicler and novelist Philostratus. In a brilliant stroke he compared the supernatural figures in pagan popular belief with the heavenly army that Constantine believed was fighting on his side. The link between Burckhardt's first and last works on antiquity have this common denominator in late antiquity. In the cultural history he wrote, "The spiritual multitudes of Constantine are also, at least insofar as they can be made perceptible to Christians and pagans, the copy of earthly multitudes." In his detailed exposition of dream interpretation among the Greeks Burckhardt goes far beyond the usual citation of the classic tragedies. Although surprisingly he makes no use of the bizarre dream diaries of Aelius Aristides, he cites knowingly the surviving handbook of dream interpretation by Artemidorus from the second century A.D., a work that, even in a bowdlerized translation, had an important influence on Freud. It is a work that has assumed massive importance in modern studies on sexuality and the unconscious in the ancient world.

Furthermore, on the subject of dreams, as elsewhere, Burckhardt points up the conspicuous differences from the perspectives of his own day. He was well aware of the fashionable assimilation of nineteenth-century Germans with the Greeks, but he would have none of it. The cultural history was not an exercise in national self-congratulation, and in his preface he mocked the emphasis on classical training in the schools as producing learning that evaporated as soon as the examinations were over. He had no illusions that the Greeks were more important than the rest of world history, and in this respect he again speaks to the late twentieth century. After citing the flamboyant classicism of Winckelmann, Lessing, Goethe, and Schiller, and the dominance of classical *Altertumswissenschaft*, he drily observed that the monuments of Egypt and Assur, the prehistoric remains of Europe, the new studies of ethnographers on remote tribes and places, the investigations into the origin of language in human society show the Greeks as occupying only a small place in the history of peoples. One may well imagine the outrage of a Wilamowitz or a Mommsen. Eduard Meyer might have been more sympathetic.

But Burckhardt would lose the good opinion of even so wide ranging a scholar as Meyer by refusing to play the academic game of scholarly citation. He would invoke only the ancient evidence and not enter into debates over the hypotheses and conjectures of modern scholars. In this matter he tried to reach a broad audience, and to keep his own vision clear. The great professional scholars found this altogether unacceptable. Some lesser souls saw merit in what Burckhardt was doing, and the admiring description from one of them, Gustav Billeter, deserves to be remembered in this context. It, too, has a strangely familiar ring at the beginning of a new millennium: "Is it not ridiculous to think that the image that we have of the Greeks from such a person could be essentially false because he has not read a certain mish-mash of nonsense and is unacquainted with the most recent hypothesis?"

In many ways the pivotal work of Burckhardt as an ancient historian is his lecture on Dio Chrysostom, also known as Dio of Prusa, from May 1864: "Über den Wert des Dio Chrysostomus für die Kenntnis seiner Zeit." This piece remains among his most enduring achievements in classical scholarship and was characterized as recently as 1978, in the standard English study of Dio, as "still the best general appreciation." Burckhardt rightly saw the eighty surviving speeches of Dio as a precious point of entry into the culture of the reign of Trajan, for whom no narrative history or even biography exists. Characteristically Burckhardt was not interested in facts but in the life of that remote but important period of the Roman Empire. His lecture begins with a programmatic statement of what history should be—History as observation and representation not merely of past facts, but also of past life. Dio is introduced, with good reason, as marking a turning point in history, away from the clarity and order of the Roman imperium created by Augustus and noisily revived by Trajan, to a world of mysticism, middle and late Platonism, wonder workers, artificial archaisms, and brilliant rhetoricians of immense learning and subtlety. For Burckhardt the transition from Trajan to Hadrian marked a major change, and arguably he was right.

What is so interesting here is Burckhardt's explicit locating of the late antique mentality in the second century A.D. Similarly, in his course on the Middle Ages from twenty years later, which reached as far as the year 1000, he went all the way back to the second century to expound the nature of the Constantinian empire. This is exactly the interpretation of the period that Peter Brown presented in his Harvard Jackson Lectures about a century later under the title *The Making of Late Antiquity*. Late antiquity was made, he argued, in the second and third centuries. His title was an obvious riposte to Richard Southern's *The Making of the Middle Ages*. Burckhardt already saw the course of Mediterranean history much as Brown did. But his special and unmatched distinction was his recognition of Dio Chrysostom as a kind of symbol of the transition. Burckhardt's account of Dio's renunciation of wealth and worldly glitter is sympathetically done. Burckhardt clearly warms to Dio's scorn for fancy rhetoricians, fashionable philosophers, and other purveyors of intellectual snake oil. Dio's humble appearance put him in the great tradition of Socrates and Diogenes, and although some philosophers aped their appearance, Dio had the vision to detect their fraud. He preferred to be seen as a *Popularphilosoph*. Diogenes as a prototype of the popular philosopher was to reappear later in a memorable page of the *Kulturgeschichte*, in which Burckhardt said of the famous Cynic, "He is the truly cheerful pessimist, who renounces the immeasurably greater part of life that is threatened by misery and loss, in order to accept the rest with moderation, health, and freedom."

Dio Chrysostom had no tolerance at all for the new breed of rhetorical performers, the imperial rhetors and sophists. Their fanciful and contorted orations constructed to win public acclaim by their inventiveness and erudition were not a part of the Hellenism with which Dio identified himself. More than once, as Burckhardt noted explicitly, Dio proclaimed with emphasis, "I am not a rhetor." Burckhardt's translation of these words, "Denn ich bin kein Rhetor," sound very much like his own proud declaration of himself in the preface to the *Kulturgeschichte* as a *Nichtphilologe*. He was a professor for the people: we acknowledge, he said in that preface, "that the teacher here is continually and will remain a learner and a fellow-student." It seems reasonable to recognize in Burckhardt's Dio Chrysostom a prefiguration of himself, and in his presentation of all those rhetors and sophists the *Philologen vom Fach* that he so mightily scorned. The lecture of 1864 looks both backward to classical and Hellenistic Greece and forward to Constantine. That it does so in the form of a tribute to man so conspicuously like Burckhardt himself is proof enough of the powerful influence of Burckhardt's thinking about late antiquity.

But Burckhardt remained, despite his desire to be a Diogenes of his age, a creature of his time. Although much of his commentary on the late antique world was extraordinarily farsighted and fresh, some parts of it were not and remain unsatisfactory today. Let us look a little more closely at Moses Finley's praise of Burckhardt for what he called the "brilliant discovery" of the central place of the *agon* in Greek life, a discovery that passed unnoticed because, as Finley observed, "Hardly any professional ancient historians today read the *Griechische Kulturgeschichte* (or if they do, they fail to acknowledge it)." Frankly Boeckh, Droysen, and Karl Otfried Müller would have been surprised to hear that Burckhardt discovered the importance of the *agon*, and Burckhardt himself would have been surprised to learn that he had accorded it the central place in Greek life. He thought it was highly important at one stage in the evolution of Greek culture, but he saw it transformed into an individualism that negated the communal aspect of competition and presaged the decline of the polis. Modesty and the subordination of the self to the identity of a community disappeared with the rise of a Themistocles, a Pericles, or an Alcibiades, who entirely by themselves could work so much good or evil: "Now we are confronted with the image of a multiplicity of states, which are variously personified through their leading individuals." Momigliano, perhaps influenced by Finley, went so far as to identify Burckhardt's individualism in the time of the disintegrating polis with the classical agonistic spirit, whereas he clearly sees the individual as a deformation of agonistic man.

The problem is that Burckhardt's diachronic account of Hellenism in the last volume of the *Kulturgeschichte* is couched, as we have seen, in terms of different manifestations of Greek man: in Burckhardt's language, the Hellenic man in his chronological development. Thus we are introduced to the colonial and agonistic man, followed next in order by the fifth and fourth century man, who give way to Hellenistic man. Such formulations, which would make any modern reader wince, imply a national character divided into subcategories. These are obviously subcategories of "the eternal Greek" that Burckhardt declared he was seeking from the start. Historical analysis of this kind belongs more to the context of nineteenth-century philosophy than it does to historiography, but it was doubtless this very feature of Burckhardt's approach that made his work so palatable to the high priests of the Third Humanism. It was probably not accidental that the first English language version of the *Kulturgeschichte* came at a time when Werner Jaeger's *Paideia* was enjoying great renown in the English translation made by Gilbert Highet. In the Princeton University library Janssen's *Jacob Burckhardt und die Griechen* stands literally next to Highet's translation of *Paideia*. The Third Humanism moved to America with Jaeger and lasted here for a full generation longer than it did in Germany. The eternal Greek is as alien to us today as he was to the Greeks themselves.

More unacceptable nineteenth-century baggage in Burckhardt lurks in his account of the health and beauty of the Greeks, baggage that the National Socialists would have found no less attractive than the eternal Greek. There can be few pages in the *Kulturgeschichte* that leave a reader so uncomfortable as the introduction to the last volume of the work. The author relates the physical qualities of Greek man to representations in art, which naturally convey the ideal forms: "Art is also a strong witness to the beauty of a race. An ugly people would not have been able to produce it merely by wanting to do so, and what stands as beautiful must also have often existed in reality." The discussion becomes steadily more embarrassing. The Greeks valued beauty more highly than we do, and consequently they all cultivated much better health. The conjunction of beauty and health was an absurdly simplistic vision for an historian who prided himself on expounding ancient life as it really was lived. The long shadow of Winckelmann's rhapsodic account of Greek bodies, still popular in Burckhardt's day, seems to have fallen across these pages.

But perhaps the most completely unacceptable notion in the *Kulturgeschichte*, the *Betrachtungen*, and even the fragments from the 1880s lectures is the consistent representation of late antiquity as a decline or *Untergang*. In the lecture on Dio Chrysostom Burckhardt had referred to the world that came after Dio as *die sinkende alte Welt* (the declining old world). For him the transformation of the polis together with the rise of the individual (who was no longer a socially competitive spirit) was a descent into the conglomerate world of the Christian empire. The lecture fragments hammer home the extraordinary unity and stability of the Christian church, even in the face of heresies, revolts, and barbarian invasions: "The life of the church depended on its unity.... The church could remain one, even if the empire was divided or fell in pieces to the barbarians." In one sense Burckhardt was addressing the problem that Momigliano raised in one of his important later articles on the relation between monotheism and a unified empire. This was a problem for him because the Roman Empire, although polytheist, was obviously as unified as the Christian empire, arguably more so. Garth Fowden took up the issue more broadly in his recent book on Universalism and Commonwealth. But Burckhardt's approach to this interesting issue presupposes some kind of weakening of national strength in the process of creating a Christian empire. His impassioned notes on the Arianism of the German peoples betray his resistance to the enforced uniformity he sees as the protector of orthodox authority.

Such a perspective could not be further from current thinking, which sees in the old declining world the birth of a new and vigorous one. This new world of late antiquity is not to be judged inferior to the old, only different. One of its most powerful forces, however, did not escape Burckhardt's sharp eye, and that was the growing importance of asceticism and renunciation. Here, in his account of *Weltflucht*, or flight from the world, he is on solid ground, and he goes straight to its impact on the traditional Greek values of pagan times: *Verdammung der antiken Ruhmliebe, amor laudis humanae* (condemnation of the ancient love of fame, the love of human praise). There cannot be the slightest doubt that Burckhardt is thinking here of the collapse of what the Greeks called *philotimia*, an insatiable thirst for worldly recognition and renown (normally in return for benefactions and services rendered). In the fourth volume of the *Kulturgeschichte* Burckhardt had introduced *philotimia* as the direct consequence of the rise of individualism: "With the arrival of great individuals comes the growth in thirst for fame (*philotimia*)." The force of worldly *philotimia* and its replacement with spiritual incentives on both the Christian and the pagan sides in late antiquity have only lately been addressed in modern scholarship, and usually with indebtedness to anthropological studies of social organization. The recent book by J. Lendon, *Empire of Honour*, goes so far as to depict *philotimia* as the linchpin of the whole Roman Empire. But Burckhardt had long ago found his way to it, even if by traversing paths that would appear to be pointing in the wrong direction.

Burckhardt's willful abstention from the scholarly debates of his time and his refusal even to keep up with the scholarly literature allowed him to reach places that academic doxography had blocked up for everyone else. The only area in which a modern reader might fault him on his own terms is his excessive reliance on literary sources. In the *Betrachtungen* he rightly lists inscriptions and ruins as important witnesses to the ancient world he wants to evoke, but the regrettable truth is that, despite his convictions, he hardly ever used such evidence. He does not even mention coins, even though a little rummaging in Eckhel's numismatic work would have revealed how immensely important Constantine's *Konsekrationsmünzen* were for the interpretation he instinctively favored. Burckhardt died too soon to see the avalanche of new evidence from papyri that so excited Beloch. But he could certainly have used inscriptions as generously and as innovatively as he used works of art. Yet he did not. One cannot help but wonder whether the domination of epigraphy by Mommsen and his pupils may not have frightened him away from this potentially fertile terrain. After all, he knew those people.

It must be admitted that unfettered originality will always suffer from the lack of those supportive details that fetters inevitably bring. But the sheer scope and power of Burckhardt's reflections on late antiquity over a span of nearly fifty years, from the *Constantin* in 1853 to the year of his death, prove how far he had gone in interpreting that long-scorned world. He pointed the way for historians of the present, even though, as it turned out, they preferred to get there on their own.

## BIBLIOGRAPHICAL NOTE

I have cited, for the *Griechische Kulturgeschichte* and the lecture on Dio Chrysostom, from the *Gesamtausbe* containing the *GK* edited by Felix Stähelin in vols. 8–11 (Stuttgart: Deutsche Verlags-Anstalt, 1930–31) and the lecture in vol. 14 edited by Emil Dürr (1933). Stähelin's introduction in volume 8 of the *Gesamtausgabe* includes a detailed account of Burckhardt's revision of the *GK* and his reluctance to publish. My quotations from the correspondence, as well as the excerpt from the notice by Gustav Billeter, may all be located through that introduction. A drastically abridged translation of the *GK* by Sheila Stern, with an introduction by Oswyn Murray, has recently appeared in English under the title *The Greeks and Greek Civilization* (London: Harper, 1998). For the so-called *Weltgeschichtliche Betrachtungen* I have cited from the edition of Peter Ganz, *Über das Studium der Geschichte* (Munich: Beck, 1982). For the early criticism of the *GK* and related problems in the treatment of Greek history see E. M. Janssen, *Jacob Burckhardt und die Griechen* (Assen: Van Gorcum, 1979). For the notes on late antiquity included in the materials for Burckhardt's lectures in the 1880s on the Middle Ages, see the valuable presentation by Karl Christ, "Burckhardt-Fragmente," in the *Festschrift für Eberhard Kessel zum 75. Geburtstag*, ed H. Duchhardt and M. Schlenke (Munich: Fink, 1982), 25–37. This paper provides much more than the summary account in W. Kaegi's chapter on the *Kultur des Mittelalters* in *Jacob Burckhardt: eine Biographie* (Basel: Schwabe, 1977), 6: 147–272. A.D. Momigliano's introduction to the Italian translation of the *GK* (Florence: Sansoni, 1955) remains important: it is reprinted in *Secondo Contributo alla storia degli studi classici e del mondo antico* (Rome: Edizioni di storia e letteratura, 1960), 283–98 and is available in a revised English translation in *A.D. Momigliano: Studies on Modern Scholarship*, ed. G. W. Bowersock and T. J. Cornell (Berkeley: University of California Press 1994), 44–53. Mommsen's lectures on the Roman Empire are now accessible through the detailed notes of the Hensels: *Römische Kaisergeschichte*, ed. B. and A. Demandt (Munich: Beck, 1992), translated into English as *A History of Rome under the Emperors* (London: Routledge, 1996). Moses Finley's comment on Burckhardt may be found in his *Ancient History: Evidence and Models* (New York: Viking, 1986), 1–3. For S. Calderone's assessment of Gibbon and Burckhardt as *due colossi*, see *Le culte des souverains dans l'empire romain*, ed. W. den Boer, *Entretiens Hardt* vol. 19 (Vandoeuvres–Geneva: Fondation Hardt, 1973), 242. On the enduring value of the lecture on Dio Chrysostom: C. P. Jones, *The Roman World of Dio Chrysostom* (Cambridge Mass.: Harvard University Press, 1978), v. Thomas Schmitz's book on the Second Sophistic is titled in full *Bildung und Macht: Zur sozialen und politschen Funktion der zweiten Sophistik in der griechischen Welt der Kaiserzeit*, Zetemata Heft 97 (Munich: Beck, 1997). The recent work on *philotimia* is J. E. Lendon, *Empire of Honour* (Oxford: Clarendon Press, 1997). For a wide-ranging appreciation of Peter Brown's influence on the study of late antiquity, see the debate ("The *World of Late Antiquity* Revisited") published in *Symbolae Osloenses* 72 (1997): 5–90. I am grateful to Tony Grafton for drawing my attention to the popularity of Winckelmann's *Gedanken über die Nachahmung der griechischen Werke in der Malerei und Bildhauerkunst* in the Wilhelmine period.

PART III

# The Twentieth Century

# CHAPTER ELEVEN

# THE NEW OLD WORLD

*The Culture of Classicism: Ancient Greece and Rome in American
Intellectual Life, 1780–1910,* by Caroline Winterer

IN 1881, AT HARVARD'S SANDERS THEATER, A
glittering academic company presented a performance of Sophocles'
*Oedipus the King* in an edition of the Greek text that had been scrupulously prepared for the occasion. Critics arrived from London and
Chicago to sit together with Longfellow, Whittier, Emerson, and Henry
James. George Riddle, who had acted with Edwin Booth, took the leading role. Among the younger performers were the future novelist Owen
Wister, the future Shakespearean scholar George Lyman Kittredge, and
the future composer John Knowles Paine. Although many critics raved,
one Boston newspaper carried a letter that characterized the plot of the
play as "foul and revolting." But the Reverend Edward Everett Hale rose
to proclaim from the pulpit that Sophocles' drama was wholly compat-
ible with the Christian faith.

This memorable patronage of classical culture fired an enthusiasm
for Greek and Latin plays at universities across the nation. It erupted
within the context of a dedication to the classics that had long been
a powerful stimulus to art, politics, and morality in the United States.
That dedication had taken various forms from the seventeenth century
onward, but its intensity had never cooled. From the education of young

ministers in the early days of Harvard College, which had been founded in 1636, to the civic ideals of the Founding Fathers and the deep classical learning of Thomas Jefferson and John Quincy Adams, authors such as Demosthenes, Cicero, and Virgil inspired Americans. Their new republic considered the old Roman republic its prototype, but as the nation matured and plunged into a savage internecine struggle, Greece emerged as the more potent model. The democracy of Athens inspired the North, and the slavery upon which it depended inspired the South. The Greek play at Harvard in 1881 emerged from a rich domestic heritage of classicism.

In her book on this fascinating subject, Caroline Winterer interprets the Greek play and its successors as "a vivid illustration of classicism's transformation from preparation for civic duty to platform for private self-culture." That is far too simple. The artificial terminus of 1910 that Winterer imposed on herself only obscures what is going on. The growth of Hellenism in the United States closely paralleled a similar evolution on the other side of the Atlantic. In Europe, as in America, the Greek revolution of the 1820s had powerful repercussions. It caught the imagination of such poets as the British Shelley ("we are all Greeks") and the American Poe ("the glory that was Greece").

Travel in the Mediterranean countries fostered this new spirit and gradually moved both European and American thought away from "the grandeur that was Rome" (the other half of Poe's evocation). In Europe, Droysen's *Geschichte des Hellenismus* (1877–1888) and Grote's *History of Greece* (1846–1856) were among the many works that opened up a new world of Greek history and culture to replace the Rome of the eighteenth century. After all, the Grand Tour had included Italy, but not Greece or the Holy Land. Even the great eighteenth-century German art historian J. J. Winckelmann, who profoundly admired the sculpture of the Greeks and pointed the way for future study of classical art, never went to Greece. He worked and died in Italy. But the nineteenth century discovered the eastern Mediterranean. In 1812, the Swiss Johann Ludwig Burckhardt was the first Westerner in modern times to see Petra, and the American Edward Everett went to Athens and elsewhere in Greece in 1819. German Karl Otfried Müller went to Delphi to copy inscriptions in 1839.

The linkage of classicism in America with classicism in Europe is fundamental to understanding the whole phenomenon. Americans felt a combination of rivalry and envy toward their European contemporaries.

This comes through eloquently in the reaction of the famous lexicographer Noah Webster to the last phase of the eighteenth century's obsession with Rome. Of the huge success of Gibbon's *Decline and Fall of the Roman Empire*, Webster wrote in 1794 that "in no particular is the false taste of the English more obvious than in the promiscuous encomiums they have bestowed on Gibbon as a historian.... Let a man read his volumes with the most laborious attention, and he will find at the close that he can give very little account of the Roman empire; but he will remember perfectly that Gibbon is a most elegant writer."

The nineteenth century saw this uneasy relationship between the old world and the new reinforced through the discovery of German scholarship, or *Wissenschaft*, which was gradually imported to America through translations of German textbooks and the teaching of professors who had been trained in Germany. George Martin Lane of Harvard took his doctorate at Göttingen with a thesis on ancient Smyrna, although he is best known today for lines of doggerel titled "One Fish Ball" (the antecedent of the mid-twentieth-century pop tune "One Meat Ball"). If Lane failed to sustain the high level of German classicism when he returned to the States, another American scholar, who studied in Berlin and took his doctorate at Göttingen, succeeded. This was Southerner Basil Lanneau Gildersleeve, arguably the greatest of all American classicists and, significantly, an ardent supporter of the Confederacy.

Gildersleeve's deep knowledge of Greek had nothing to do with the American educational system. He learned Greek from his father, a Presbyterian minister, and he could read the Gospel of St. John in the original at the age of five. He acquired other languages with equal facility, falling in love with Goethe before traveling to the poet's homeland to sit at the feet of some of the greatest classical scholars of the century. When he returned to America, he embarked upon a luminous career, first at the University of Virginia and then at Johns Hopkins University, where he founded the first major classical journal to be published in North America. His commentary on Pindar's Olympian and Pythian Odes is still important today.

Gildersleeve always considered himself a man of the South, and during the Civil War he wrote an extraordinary series of fiery editorials for the *Richmond Examiner*. His voice, from inside the Confederacy, betrays a rare combination of zealous patriotism and deep erudition. His comparison, in 1863, of the Greeks' Peloponnesian War with the American struggle is still incisive. It ends with a chilling vision of a Southern victory:

"As the walls of Athens were razed to the ground with the music of the flute, so the marble fronts of the Fifth avenue are to be levelled with the street with the notes of the banjo and the rattle of the bones." (Winterer lists Ward Brigg's superb publication of the *Examiner* pieces in her bibliography, but she has missed their power and their relevance for American classicism.)

America's embrace of nineteenth-century Hellenism took many forms, ranging from high gentlemanly culture to tough philological analysis. According to Winterer, Greek tragedy had not been much in vogue until the Harvard play of 1881: "The most frequently performed Greek tragedy in nineteenth-century New York City, for example, was Euripides' *Medea*, staged at least fourteen times between 1845 and 1881, both in Puccini's operatic form and in English translation." Opera plots are another matter altogether, and Winterer's tantalizing attribution of a *Medea* to Puccini is a delectable error for a work by Pacini. Harvard's play was something totally new. It was performed in Greek, and with a text and a staging that at least purported to be authentic.

Above all, the Harvard production was a response to a challenge from abroad. In 1880, Balliol College at Oxford had mounted a production of Aeschylus's *Agamemnon* in Greek. This production was itself a part of a growing interest in classical theatricals at the time, and it was the explicit inspiration for the Harvard *Oedipus*. The American play was not only a great social success. It also raised the banner of international scholarship through its newly edited text and the authenticity of its production. Private self-culture had nothing to do with it, but public self-representation certainly did, not only within America but with reference to Europe.

The Greek play was to have a long history. After the architectural firm of McKim, Mead and White designed the Harvard Stadium, the rounded classical proportions of its closed end were soon pressed into service as an amphitheater for an elaborate production of the *Agamemnon* in June 1906. This grandiose affair, somewhat damped by drizzly weather, attracted almost as much attention as the *Oedipus* of 1881. It deeply moved Paul Elmer More, who, along with Irving Babbitt, championed something called New Humanism, which tried to stem the rising tide of the social sciences. In 1915, More wrote, "I have seen a band of young amateurs present the *Agamemnon* in the Stadium at Harvard, and through the crudeness of their acting and the helplessness of the chorus and the disadvantage of a language I could scarcely follow, I still knew that here was a higher form of drama than anything on the modern stage, and that the art of Aeschylus was profounder and more everlasting in its emotional appeal than Shakespeare's even."

In 1933, the Greek play returned triumphantly with a young Harry Levin, the future literary critic, as Odysseus in the *Philoctetes* of Sophocles, and in 1939 a young Leonard Bernstein composed a score for a production of Aristophanes's *The Birds* that a contemporary critic compared to Barnum and Bailey minus the elephants. Then, in April 1956, on the diamond anniversary of *Oedipus the King*, Sophocles' *Oedipus at Colonus* was presented in Greek in the courtyard of the Fogg Art Museum, with Erich Segal as Creon and myself as the Messenger. Seated in the front row were an array of eminent personages, including Harvard's president, who was himself a classicist, and two renowned classical scholars, Herbert Bloch and Werner Jaeger, who had left Germany in the 1930s. The power of Greek drama, performed in a language that few could understand and probably no ancient Greek would have recognized, could still move an audience through its Aristotelian mixture of pity and fear. And the presence of Bloch and Jaeger symbolized, in a way that did not go unnoticed, the fusion of American Hellenism with German.

The roots of the Harvard Greek play can thus be seen to extend far down into the nineteenth century, and into the momentous shift in international classicism from Rome to Greece. What happened to classics in America was part of a transformation that was taking place in Europe. The change from purely philological study to a more contextual approach that emphasized culture and civilization had started in Germany and reached the States through Americans who had studied there. Of these, Harvard's Edward Everett, who took his doctorate at Göttingen in 1817, and George Bancroft, who took his doctorate at the same university in 1820, were the most influential at the start. Everett's travels in Greece vastly enriched his teaching with firsthand knowledge of the landscape and the monuments of the ancient Greeks. Cornelius Felton, who held Everett's chair in the middle of the century, also traveled extensively in Greece. Both men felt an obligation to transmit their classical learning to a broader audience than their own students. As Winterer shows, the popular dissemination of the classics in the mid-nineteenth century made the field increasingly accessible to those who had formerly been excluded from university education. Classics became an effective vehicle for upward mobility, particularly for women.

It is almost misleading to speak of classicism in America. There were many classicisms, just as there had been many enlightenments in Europe (as J. G. A. Pocock has argued). American classicism of the eighteenth century, with its emphasis on Rome and its unremitting attention to the construing of original texts, was utterly different from the more broadly based and distinctly Germanic classicism of the nineteenth century. There was a sense that Americans could compete with the best of the Europeans, and the Greek play was emblematic of that. The scholarship of Basil Gildersleeve was proof of it. The next generation, at the end of the century, produced still more Americans who pursued Greek studies successfully in Germany and returned to make contributions of international importance. Such were Princeton's David Magie (Ph.D. Halle, 1904) and Illinois's William Abbott Oldfather (Ph.D. Munich, 1908).

The rise of the social sciences was not, as the New Humanists thought and as Winterer appears at times still to believe, the enemy of the classics. Karl Otfried Müller's bold and fruitful speculations about the psychological implications of Greek mythology dated from 1825. Karl Marx and Max Weber were both thoroughly professional classical scholars, whose new perspectives in political science and economics remain important today. If the number of university students enrolled for degrees in classics can be seen to decline, it is essential to recognize that classics became at the same time an integral part of several emerging disciplines, especially anthropology, politics, economics, comparative religion, and the history of science. Classics also took up its natural abode in the older disciplines of history and philosophy. This was part of the shift from translating ill understood texts in the classroom to the thoughtful interpretation of them. It was by no means a retrograde step.

At the end of her book Winterer records the birth of American archaeology and the establishment of American centers abroad. The conspicuous markers in this process are the foundings of the Archaeological Institute of America in 1879, the American School of Classical Studies in Athens in 1881, and the more broadly based cultural enterprise, including painting, sculpture, and architecture, known as the American Academy in Rome in 1894. All three institutions flourish today, and they represent a natural evolution from the exploratory travels of Everett, Felton, and others earlier in the nineteenth century. But once again America was participating in developments that were thoroughly international in character, and once again America was scurrying to catch up with the overseas competition. The French School at Athens came into existence in 1846, although its presence there was not fully stabilized until 1870, the same year Schliemann started his excavation of Troy. The German

Archaeological Institute opened its Athens section in 1872 and launched its excavation of Olympia in 1875. The Germans began work at Tiryns the following year, and in 1878 they began the excavation of the Turkish site of Pergamum, which continues to this day.

In the rush to send classics students abroad, the Americans at least managed to get to Athens before the British, who set up their school in 1886. The new interest in artifacts and excavation inevitably tended to eclipse the kind of classicism that was exclusively based on texts and textual criticism. For some this seemed a decline or a loss, but for others it was a liberation. Archaeology brought modern scholars and travelers into immediate contact with the past in a way that texts never had, and it could be pursued by enthusiasts without the arduous training in Greek and Latin that had been the prerequisite for the old classicism. The implications for classicism in visual terms were enormous.

Classical architecture had an old and honorable tradition in America, but the rise of professional archaeology gave new impetus to the appreciation of sculpture, painting, pottery, coins, and various small objects. It encouraged private collecting and museum acquisition. Winterer devotes five interesting pages to the establishment of the museum at the University of Michigan on the initiative of Henry Frieze, but there is so much more to be told about museums and collecting in later nineteenth-century America. A few lines are given to Luigi Palma di Cesnola, the eccentric and irresponsible collector of the Cypriote antiquities now in the Metropolitan Museum in New York, but nothing is said of the no less eccentric but considerably more responsible Edward Perry Warren, to whom the Museum of Fine Arts in Boston is indebted for a substantial part of its classical collection. Warren, the son of a wealthy paper manufacturer in Massachusetts, embodied a form of classicism that was rare in the United States, although not abroad. He looked to the Greeks as models of enlightened homosexuality (Uranianism, as it was called in Britain). So Warren moved to Oxford and proceeded to buy important pieces of ancient art, many of which were shocking by late-nineteenth-century standards. In his passion for classical erotica Warren was about a century ahead of his time, particularly in the puritanical America he left behind but so generously adorned.

Of course the old ways of the philologists held on. Many professors were undoubtedly boring (many still are), but they did not kill their subject. Attacks leveled at the dry-as-dust professors whose classes concentrated on grammar and translation were nothing new. Winterer writes of the early-nineteenth-century Yale professor James Luce Kingsley that after slogging resolutely through the *Agricola* of Tacitus he told his students to their astonishment that they had been reading "one of the noblest productions of the human mind." Yet this sad remark hardly differs from A. E. Housman's startling observation a century later, when he abruptly declared, just before exiting smartly from his classroom, that Horace's Ode IV. 7, *diffugere nives*, was "the most beautiful poem in ancient literature." At least we have *A Shropshire Lad* and other poems to show that there really was more to Housman than textual criticism. That could hardly be said of a distinguished professor at Harvard who declared in the late 1950s that the principal value of the fragments of Sappho lay in the rare forms they preserved. One should never judge the meaning of the classics in American culture or European culture on the basis of scholars such as that. Theirs was not a classicism that had a broad impact, even if it occasionally served scholarship brilliantly (as, in the case of Housman, it did).

The transformation of classical taste that is so obvious in the late nineteenth century continued unimpeded well into the twentieth century, and that is why it is such a pity that Winterer chose to end with 1910. Classicisms did not end in that year. Not only did their migration to other burgeoning fields continue, particularly with the support of archaeology and anthropology, but the strictly classical disciplines themselves proliferated dramatically far beyond 1910. The discovery of papyri in Egypt opened a huge new field of research, with vast implications for social and economic history. Although reading and interpreting these documents from the daily life of ancient Egypt demanded formidable linguistic and historical skills, the excitement they generated galvanized the study of the ancient Greco-Roman world. It is not surprising that William Westermann, an American classicist who had taken a Berlin degree in 1902, returned to Germany in 1912 as a young professor to sit at the feet of Ulrich Wilcken, the pioneering master of papyrology. Westermann determined to introduce the new field to America and to encourage American universities to follow the example of the European ones in building up collections of these new documents.

It was Westermann who encouraged the University of Wisconsin to bring Mikhail Rostovtzeff, a dazzlingly erudite and energetic Russian scholar who had fled the Russian Revolution, to teach in Madison, and from Wisconsin Rostovtzeff went to Yale, where he towered among the historians of his time. He was a classicist by training but in practice a historian who was equally at home in archaeology and papyrology. He concentrated on the social and economic history of antiquity. As president of the American Historical Association, he brought enormous prestige to American classical studies, and he fostered a generation of eminent disciples. The achievement of Westermann and Rostovtzeff lies totally outside Winterer's research, even though both men rose to prominence before 1910. They embody the twentieth-century metamorphosis of American classics through its continued participation in international scholarship. And these were not merely classroom professors: Westermann was sent by Woodrow Wilson to be a participant in the Versailles peace conference. His still unpublished diary is a precious document for classicism in the public life of the period. Rostovtzeff spent hot months year after year in unbelievable squalor along the banks of the Euphrates, where he excavated the Parthian town of Dura-Europus.

Winterer's bleak tale of classicism gradually grinding to a halt in the process of academic curricular change misses what really happened. She ends on an elegiac note, with the Harvard report on general education after World War II. Neither she nor John Finley, who wrote much of that report, comprehended that classics had moved outward from the old curriculum and taken up residence in many departments other than classical ones. We have seen that in tracking classicism it is necessary to look hard at the growth of economics, political science, history, religious studies, anthropology, art history, archaeology, the history of science, philosophy, and comparative literature. If fewer people have a perfect command of Greek and Latin than was once the case, that is regrettable, but it is not disastrous as long as some people continue to have that command. We ought not to deceive ourselves. In the early days of the American nation, the miserable excerpts that students had to translate for their professors from such hoary books as the *Graeca Majora* did not produce proficient classicists. It was not this training that enriched the mind of Thomas Jefferson or John Quincy Adams. It was their own curiosity and their own deep reading that convinced them of the rewards of the classics.

What happened in the nineteenth century, with the shift from Rome to Greece in the popular and professional imagination, allowed the classics to acquire a deeper meaning and a broader relevance for more readers than before. The concentration on Hellenism paradoxically fertilized Roman studies, because, although (as the Roman poet Horace taught us long ago) the Romans conquered the Greeks, ultimately, in cultural terms, the vanquished Greeks conquered the Romans. The great swing of the pendulum back to Rome occurred outside Winterer's purview, but it is of the greatest significance. Both Hitler and Mussolini looked to the Roman imperial state, not to Greece, as models for their evil work. The Roman republic, which had inspired America's founders, no longer mattered. What mattered was the Roman Empire. The first classicist to understand what was happening and to describe it in vivid prose was Ronald Syme, whose book *The Roman Revolution* appeared in 1939. It clearly portrayed the rise of the first emperor, Caesar Augustus, in the light of the two great fascist states of the time. The classics had by no means lost their contemporaneity.

The aftermath of World War II called forth yet another classicism, bred in the shadow of the fascists. The ruthless exposure of human power and greed in pursuit of conquest and empire led to a return to the more philosophic Greeks. At the same time it engendered a less historical and more comparative humanistic study. These were the years of New Criticism, cultural anthropology, and comparative religion. They were the years in which a Center for Hellenic Studies was conceived expressly "to rediscover the humanism of the Hellenic Greeks," who were presumably to be distinguished from the modern Greeks. The location of the center in Washington, D.C., was deliberately chosen to give the nation's capital "direction." Jacques Barzun commented tartly that the whole undertaking had "all the aspects of founding a church." Another manifestation of this transcendent postwar Hellenism was the timeless serenity of the *Oedipus at Colonus* at Harvard.

It would have been worthwhile for Winterer to see what has become of the classics in the closing decades of the twentieth century, because the great pendulum of change has swung once again. The chaos of the 1960s spawned a new attention to times of chaos in Greece and Rome—to the Hellenistic period (between Alexander the Great and Augustus) and to the turbulent formation of the Byzantine state in late antiquity. There has never been so much study of the Hellenistic kingdoms as in the last thirty years. At the same time late antiquity has emerged not as a decadent afterglow of the classical past but as a vibrant world of its own. It calls into question the entire concept of decline and fall. Peter Brown, whose first great work was a biography of Augustine of Hippo, has concentrated particularly on the spiritual life of late antiquity. He has thereby renewed the close links between classicists and students of religion. But more than that: he and many others have looked farther and farther afield, from the centers of power (Rome, Athens, Byzantium, Jerusalem) to the remote peripheries in search of indigenous cultures and their interactions with traditional classical cultures. Whole new worlds have opened up from India to Scandinavia.

The many forms of classicism did not come to an end in America in 1910. Just as in earlier centuries, classics in the twentieth century revealed an amazing ability to reinvent itself. Naturally this reinvention has caused consternation among those who prefer to remain as they were. The classical profession has been subjected in recent years to a fierce assault from within its own ranks by Victor Hanson, whose books *Who Killed Homer?* and *The Bonfire of the Humanities* proclaim their apocalyptic outlook in their shrill titles. Hanson and his collaborators want us all to become Greeks again, whatever that may entail. But we can no more return to the Romantic Hellenism of Byron and Shelley than to Gildersleeve's principled but inadmissible advocacy of Southern slavery.

The main reason that classicism survives in America and elsewhere is precisely that it is so porous and so multiform. It can instruct and delight according to many different moral and political systems. It can equally accommodate an eighteenth-century divine and Basil Gildersleeve and E. P. Warren. It has a capacity for growth and change that is almost unexampled in the history of Western intellectual life. If certain professors live in fear of jobs lost and departments closed, the public at large is just as stunned and inspired by ancient Greece and Rome as it ever was. The great difference today is that Greece and Rome contribute only some of the world's classicisms. But if Plato and Cicero must stand alongside Confucius, Maimonides, and Ibn Khaldun, that has to be judged an enrichment of us all.

# CHAPTER TWELVE

# THE JULIAN POEMS OF C. P. CAVAFY

THE PUBLICATION OF FIVE POEMS, HITHERTO UNKNOWN, by the poet Cavafy—all on the theme of Julian the Apostate—and the edition of his reading notes on Gibbon's *Decline and Fall* illuminate not only the poet's obsession with Julian but also the principles of his craft.[1] It is perhaps not too presumptuous for a historian to attempt an assessment of Cavafy's work on Julian in the light of the rich new material, for

1. The five new poems may now be consulted in the complete edition of Cavafy's *Ateli Poiïmata* (Unfinished Poems) prepared by Renata Lavagnini and published by Ikaros in Athens in 1994. In that edition these poems are nos. 6, 7, 13, 22, and appendix 4. Also of great help to me was Diana Haas's article, "Cavafy's Reading Notes on Gibbon's *Decline and Fall*" in *Folia Neohellenica* 4 (1982): 25–96. I am grateful to both these scholars for their generosity in showing me their work before publication, and I am likewise grateful to my friend and former colleague George Savidis for first drawing my attention to the new poems in the Cavafy archive. Savidis and I gave them their world premiere at a talk to the Shop Club of Harvard University on Dec. 20, 1979. Savidis's son, Manolis Savidis, undertook, with his father's permission and mine, to offer a study of the Julian poems as his term paper in my last Harvard course, Historical Studies B-11 ("The Christianization of the Roman World"), in the spring of 1980. His paper was full of valuable observations and citations, proving that a mastery of Cavafy's work continues in the Savidis family. I am glad to acknowledge my debt to this paper. Finally I owe thanks to Edmund Keeley for his helpful comments on the present study as well as for more wide-ranging discussion of Cavafy.

he is said himself to have declared that he was a historical poet: "Many poets are only poets...I am an historical poet."[2] This remark finds confirmation in a critique from May 1927, written earlier by the poet or by a sympathetic associate, with a threefold categorization of Cavafy's oeuvre into sensual, historical, and philosophical.[3] Of the sensual and historical categories it is said that there is sometimes so great a degree of overlapping that classification becomes difficult but not impossible.[4] Several of the Julian poems prove this point.

The new poems may now be added to the group of Julianic pieces already known, seven in number. The grand total of Cavafy's poems on the apostate emperor is therefore twelve. It becomes evident that no other historical topic preoccupied this writer to such as extent as Julian, and any interpreter is bound to ask why that emperor held so great a fascination. The question is particularly important because it has long been clear from the previously published poems that Cavafy did not much care for Julian. He shared none of the late romantic admiration for the last of the pagan rulers. Cavafy appears to have been obsessed with removing the glamour and exposing the fraud of this hero of latter-day pagans. There seems to be a paradox in so hostile a treatment from a Greek who was among the first in modern times to write brilliant poetry on sensuality and sexual encounters. At issue here is precisely the blending of sensual and historical matter.

Most of the Julian poems can be dated, although only five of them were actually published in the poet's lifetime. The dates are revealing:[5]

1 Ὁ Ἰουλιανὸς ἐν τοῖς Μυστηρίοις [Julian at the Mysteries], written November 1896, published posthumously

2 Μεγάλη συνοδεία ἐξ ἱερέων καὶ λαϊκῶν [A Great Procession of Priests

---

2. G. Lechonitis, Καβαφικὰ αὐτοσχόλια, 2nd ed. (Athens: D. Charvey, 1977), 19–20.

3. G. P. Savidis, Οἱ Καβαφικὲς ἐκδόσεις (Athens: Tachydromos, 1966), 209–10. Cf. the translation of this critique in Edmund Keeley, *Cavafy's Alexandria* (Cambridge, Mass.: Harvard University Press, 1976), 186–87.

4. Ibid.

5. For the dates of the published poems, see the annotations by G. P. Savidis ad loc. in *C. P. Cavafy: Collected Poems* (Princeton: Princeton University Press, 1975), translated by E. Keeley and P. Sherrard, edited by G. P. Savidis. For the dates of the new poems, see R. Lavagnini's edition of the poems in the publication cited in note 1 of *BMGS*.

and Laity], probably written March 1917 as a revision of a poem from September 1892, published August 1926

3  Ἀθανάσιος [Athanasios], written April 1920, unfinished and unpublished hitherto

4  Ὁ ἐπίσκοπος Πηγάσιος [Bishop Pegasios], written May 1920, unfinished and unpublished hitherto

5  Ὁ Ἰουλιανός, ὁρῶν ὀλιγωρίαν [Julian, Seeing Neglect], published September 1923, no exact date of composition

6  Ἡ διάσωσις τοῦ Ἰουλιανοῦ [The Salvation of Julian], written December 1923, unfinished and unpublished hitherto

7  Ὁ Ἰουλιανὸς ἐν Νικομηδείᾳ [Julian at Nicomedia], published January 1924, no exact date of composition

8  Hunc deorum templa reparaturum [He Would Repair the Gods' Temples], written March 1926, unfinished and unpublished hitherto

9  Ὁ Ἰουλιανὸς καὶ οἱ Ἀντιοχεῖς [Julian and the Antiochenes], published November 1926, no exact date of composition

10  Οὐκ ἔγνως [You Didn't Know], published January 1928, no exact date of composition

11  Untitled poem beginning Εἶχαν περάσει δέκα πέντε χρόνια [Fifteen Years Had Passed], no exact date of composition, unfinished and unpublished hitherto

12  Εἰς τὰ περίχωρα τῆς Ἀντιοχείας [On the Outskirts of Antioch] written c. November 1932 and April 1933, published posthumously

It is clear from the foregoing list that only two of the twelve poems on Julian can be dated before 1920; of these two, one was probably reworked as late as 1917, and even this was kept from publication until 1926. As far as can be told, all of the other poems were composed between 1920 and the poet's death in April 1933. It would scarcely be an exaggeration to say that the last decade and a quarter of his life were the period of his greatest involvement with the life of Julian.

And yet the interest had surfaced early. The satirical account of Julian's fright at the mysteries and the potent sign of the cross that Julian made by reflex is anchored to November 1896, the very time in which Cavafy was engaged in his critical reading of Gibbon's Decline and Fall. As Diana Haas has admirably shown in her examination of Cavafy's annotations to

Gibbon,[6] the decade of the 1890s was important for Cavafy's mastery of Greek history in the Roman and Byzantine ages. She has shown how carefully he compared points in Gibbon with parallel discussions in Paparrigopoulos's history of the Greek people, and she has drawn attention to his particular concern with the early Christian church. His repudiation of Gibbon's snide remark on Gregory of Nazianzus evokes his positive judgment of Gregory in an article on Byzantine poets, published in 1892.[7] Moreover, it seems likely from the extended citations of Gregory and Theodoret in the annotations to Gibbon, now that these can be seen in full, that Cavafy had access to original texts of at least both ecclesiastical writers at that time.

Cavafy must have found that his researches into the early Church spoke to some degree to his own personal needs. He was drawn to Christianity but found his greatest solace in the 1890s not so much in the Church itself as an institution as in the solitary struggles of its pioneers. Few could read his annotation in Gibbon on Simeon Stylites without appreciating the deep feeling with which he wrote it: "This great, this wonderful saint is surely an object to be singled out in ecclesiastical history for admiration and study. He has been, perhaps, the only man who has dared to be really *alone*."[8] The impress of this figure can be seen in the poem on Simeon from July 1917. From a thematic list of his early poems Cavafy's interest in the early Church can be readily inferred. Under the rubric *Αἱ Ἀρχαὶ τοῦ Χριστιανισμοῦ* [The Beginnings of Christianity] he lists a group of poems, largely lost, but including the extant works on Julian at the mysteries and Simeon.[9] The lost poems all date from the 1890s.[10]

6. See note 1 above.

7. Gibbon had referred to "the loose invectives of Gregory," on which Cavafy responded, with accompanying quotations, "No artist—the word is not misplaced here—had spoken so boldly before." For the article of 1892, see C. P. Cavafy, *Πεζά* (Athens: Ikaros, 2003), 62, as noted by Haas in her article.

8. Cited by Haas.

9. G. P. Savidis, ed., *Κ. Π. Καβάφη: Ἀνέκδοτα Ποιήματα 1882–1923* (Athens: Ikaros, 1968), 172. On Cavafy's Christianity, see R. Liddell, *Cavafy* (London: Duckworth, 1974), 205–6 (wearing a cross around his neck, waiting for the patriarchal procession on Good Friday, the last sacraments) as well as Keeley, op. cit. (n. 3 above), 184. Savidis's paper on Cavafy's Christianity is fundamental, *Πάνω νερά* (Athens: Hermes, 1973), 115–20.

10. E.g., *Ἡ ἐπιστροφή τοῦ Κνός* (1892), *Ὁ πειρασμ ός τοῦ Σύρου ἀσκητοῦ Θαδδαίου* or variants of this title (1892), *Πορφύριος* (1892), *Ὁ Ἅγιος Στέφανος* (1898).

In these years and on into the first decade of the twentieth century Cavafy's experience of Christianity was complicated by feelings of guilt and distress over his sexual nature, which he did his best to confront alone. He wrote a series of private confessions about his "solitary erotic passion." There is material, still unpublished, that confirms that Cavafy was genuinely tormented by what was apparently frequent masturbation.[11] By 1911, however, he seems to have reconciled himself to his homosexuality, to have sought partners in fulfilling it, and to have resolved not only to write about it in his poetry but actually to publish the poems.[12] It is with Τὰ ἐπικίνδυνα [Dangerous Thoughts], published in November 1911, that Cavafy publicly declared himself a sensualist. Although the poem is not yet explicitly homosexual as later poems were to be, it is nonetheless a striking departure for Cavafy. It is especially notable for the conjunction of his historical interests with his advocacy of sensuality. The speaker is a young Syrian in the reign of Constans and Constantius, therefore precisely between A.D. 340 and 350, the years of Julian's adolescence. These were the years in which Julian was raised a Christian and became a pagan, the years to which Cavafy devoted three of his later Julian poems (nos. 4, 6, and 7 in the foregoing list). The young Syrian of this epoch is described as partly pagan and partly Christianized. He proclaims that he will not fear his passions; he will satisfy his most daring erotic proclivities. He repeats that he will not be afraid because he is confident that if he is called upon to be ascetic he will have the power to be so. The appearance of this poem and the end of the confessional notes mark a new stage in Cavafy's life and oeuvre. He is moving, with the help of historical analogues, toward a reconciliation

11. Οἱ Καβαφικὲς ἐκδόσεις (n. 3 above), 195. On the confessional notes, see also Liddell (n. 9 above), 72–73. The unpublished material, in the possession of George Savidis, is cited by his son Manolis in stressing the importance of late 1911 as a turning point in Cavafy's life. In April 1913, Cavafy turned 50. This seems to have been a midlife crisis with liberating results.

12. On the nature of Cavafy's work and sexual life from 1911, see Liddell (n. 9), 155–71. The importance of the change in 1911–12 seems to be generally recognized. Cf. G. Seferis, A Poet's Journal: Days of 1945–1951 (Cambridge, Mass.: Harvard University Press, 1974), 139: "Up to a fairly advanced age (maturity), Cavafy seems to remain at a very low level; he seems to be unable to rise above a certain very mediocre ceiling (as it is called in aviation, ceiling, plafond). What happens at and beyond a certain point? How does he cross that threshold? Here's a question that interests me—not only about Cavafy but in general." Cf. Seferis's Δοκιμές, 3rd ed. (Athens: Ikaros, 1974), I: 328, on Cavafy's work after 1910 as one and the same poem in progress.

of his sexuality and his Christianity. The Syrian in "Dangerous Thoughts" was partly Christian but still sensual, just as the Christian Myris in a poem of 1929 set in Alexandria of the year A.D. 340 had rejoiced in the love of a pagan. Inevitably Cavafy would have asked himself what impact Julian would have had on the Greek world of that Syrian youth or of Myris's lover. This was a world in which pagans and Christians could associate easily with one another in unhindered pursuit of the sensual life. It was the avowed aim of Julian, the ascetic pagan, to put an end to all that.[13]

It may be argued, therefore, that Cavafy's return to his historical interests of the 1890s was an important part of his adjustment to his homosexual nature as well as to his Christian sympathies. The adjustment, which began in 1911, led to the elaboration of the erotic category of his work and its conspicuous overlapping with the historical category. The newly published poems contribute substantially to enlarging our understanding of the way in which Cavafy worked on his historical poetry, and it will be helpful to proceed to a close look at these unfinished pieces for what they reveal about both Cavafy's preoccupations and his methods. What is learned can serve in turn to provide a more profound interpretation of the Julian poems already known.

Cavafy's remarkable note on the Athanasius poem is a major addition to our knowledge. Here, on the drafts of a work of April 1920, he appended a note over nine full years later to the effect that he could not find the ancient source for the incident on which his poem was based.[14] He had found in Butcher's history of the Egyptian church the story of the two monks who learned of Julian's death by extrasensory perception while they were in a boat with Athanasius on the Nile.[15] It was a good story, well suited to Cavafy's manner; but when after nine years he had not located it in the *Patrologia* of Migne, either in volume 67 or in volume 82 (to which he obviously had access by 1929), he declared that unless the source could be traced somewhere else the poem could not stand.[16]

13. Cf. Seferis, *A Poet's Journal* (n. 12 above), 137: "Julian represents a problem for Cavafy, he is a splinter on the horizon.... He is worse than a problem; he is a sort of illegal competitor."

14. Στόν Migne 67 (Σωζομενός καί Σωκράτης) καί 82 (Θεοδώρητος) δέν ὑπάρχει ἡ παράδωσις τῆς Butcher. Ἐάν δέν εὑρεθεῖ ἀλλοῦ, σέ κανέναν Βίο τοῦ Ἁγ. Ἀθανασίου, τό ποίημα δέν στέκεται.

15. E. L. Butcher, *The Story of the Church in Egypt* (London: Smith Elder, 1897), I: 185.

16. In fact, the story is in *MPG*, XXVI, cols. 980C–81C.

So firm a commitment to a historical source must be rare indeed in the annals of poetry.

There are other examples of similarly scrupulous scholarship in Cavafy. Among the new poems is one on the saving of the infant Julian during the massacre of his family after the death of Constantine the Great. As Renata Lavagnini has perceptively pointed out, the kernel of this poem is the confrontation of Julian's salvation at the hands of Christians with his own later ingratitude as expressed in the remark λήθη δὲ ἔστω τοῦ σκότους ἐκείνου "Let there be oblivion for that darkness" (from Julian's oration to Helios the King).[17] Cavafy first drafted a poem involving the salvation of Julian together with his half-brother Gallus. He may, as Lavagnini suggests, have worked under the influence of the wording in Gregory of Nazianzus, but he may equally have read hastily in Allard's *Julien l'Apostat*, "But this protection [against Constantius's soldiers] would not perhaps have been sufficient to save them."[18] In any case, while studying Allard's pages more closely, he observed that Allard mentions Julian alone as having been rescued by the Christians: "Devout persons secretly took Julian away." Cavafy's note, "Allard speaks only of Julian," explains why he undertook to revise his poem so as to record the salvation of only one prince instead of two. He was desperately keen to be historically accurate.

Even in the titles of his poems Cavafy strove for exactitude. The folder containing his unique poem on Julian's career as a commander in Gaul bears the Latin title *Hunc deorum templis*. Presumably he was writing from memory what he intended to be a quotation from Ammianus's account of the blind old woman in Vienne, but when he took the trouble to check the text of Ammianus he discovered that he had erred. He then revised the title to give the correct Latin quotation, *Hunc deorum templa reparaturum*.[19]

17. Julian, 131A (p. 101 Budé).

18. Gregory in *MPG* XXXV, col. 549; P. Allard, *Julien l'Apostat* I (Paris: Lecoffre, 1900), 263. It is worth noting that Gibbon, *Decline and Fall*, chap. 19 *ad init.*, gives Julian's age at the time of the massacre as six; Allard also gives it as six, but Migne, in a note, says seven. Socrates (*MPG*, LXVII, 369) and Sozomen (LXVII, 1213) both give the age as eight. Cavafy's poem has Julian at six.

19. Amm. Marc. 15.8.22: *Tunc anus quaedam orba luminibus…exclamavit hunc deorum templa reparaturum.* In the long form of the title Cavafy's handwriting is unclear: *templa* or *templis* could be read, but the presence of *reparaturum* seems decisive to me.

A comparable scrupulosity over a title can be detected in the poem Ὁ Ἰουλιανός ἐν τοῖς Μυστηρίοις, [Julian at the Mysteries], which had previously borne the title Ὁ Ἰουλιανὸς ἐν Ἐλευσίνι [Julian at Eleusis].[20] It has seemed clear to most readers that the initial inspiration for this work of 1896 was Cavafy's study of Gibbon at that very time. The episode of Julian's making the sign of the cross when he encountered demons in an underground cavern occurs in Gregory of Nazianzus, whose original text was in all probability familiar to Cavafy.[21] But it was Gibbon who inferred from Gregory that Julian was at Eleusis: "He [Julian] obtained the privilege of a solemn initiation into the mysteries of Eleusis...."[22] Hence the title "Julian at Eleusis." With the indisputable evidence we now have of Cavafy's study of Allard in regard to the massacre of Julian's family, it becomes almost certain that his study of the same author led to his alteration of the title of his earliest Julian poem. Allard argued at length against the supposition that Julian was initiated into the Eleusinian Mysteries: "Almost all modern historians say that Julian was initiated then into the Mysteries of Eleusis. That does not follow clearly from the text of Eunapius. I find it difficult to accept that Julian was initiated.... Nowhere does he give a hint that he was initiated at Eleusis...."[23] Hence a new title for an old poem.

In what is perhaps the most memorable of the five new poems, the evocation of the boy Julian on the plains of Troy in the company of the Christian Bishop Pegasius, the materials published by Renata Lavagnini again prove the poet's scrupulous concern for scholarship. The primary inspiration in this case must have been Allard, who saw well the implications of Julian's own spare testimony about the episode from his youth: "Without too great an effort of imagination one can picture the two persons chance had brought together. Julian, by the bishop's manner, surmised his secret thoughts: he fixed on him a penetrating look and posed captious questions. Pegasius probably knew by repute Julian's real sentiments...."[24] Although Cavafy undoubtedly knew the actual letter of Julian in which the meeting with Pegasius (who later converted to

20. Cf. G. P. Savidis in Cavafy's *Collected Poems* (n. 5 above), 430.

21. *MPG*, XXXV, cols. 577 ff.

22. E. Gibbon, *Decline and Fall*, ch. 23, Everyman ed., 2: 367.

23. Allard (n. 18 above), I: 330–32. In her note 64 Diana Haas rightly raised the possibility of Allard's discussion as the explanation of Cavafy's change of title.

24. Allard (n. 18), I: 347. Cf. Julian, *Epist.* 19, 79B (pp. 85–87 Budé).

paganism) was described, he found in Allard a congenial speculation about the nature of the encounter. The boy and the man, both nominally Christians, questioning each other amid the pagan shrines of Troy, would have sensed indirectly one another's true disposition. To the religious ambivalence of the scene and the hypocrisy of the players Cavafy added in the work of 1920 a palpable atmosphere of pedophilia by insisting on hidden revelations which the boy and the man surely divined in each other. This was a theme ideally suited to Cavafy's taste and talent; it blended almost perfectly the categories of sensuality and history. And yet Cavafy troubled, ten years after working on the poem, to reexamine the incident at Troy by copying out Bidez's treatment of it in *La vie de l'Empereur Julien*, which appeared in 1930.[25] So once again we can see Cavafy's passion for scholarly acceptability.

In a well-known remark, cited by Malanos, Cavafy is said to have observed that two of his poems remained incomplete for lack of a copy of Gregory of Nazianzus.[26] From what can now be seen of his methods such a remark is by no means as implausible as it might once have seemed. Furthermore, among the seven pieces on Julian that he chose not to publish (nos. 1, 3, 4, 6, 8, 11, and 12 in the present listing), exactly two depend upon Gregory as the principal ancient source. These are no. 1 on Julian at the Mysteries and no. 6 on the salvation of the infant Julian from the murderous soldiers of Constantius. Although it has become clear that Cavafy paid close attention to modern scholarly writing, it has become no less clear that he insisted on verifying his facts by reference to the ancient texts. Just as this means that it would be wrong to speak of a single source for one of his poems (such as Gibbon, Allard, Gregory, or Julian himself), it is wrong to discredit the importance he assigned to the original texts for poems initially inspired by secondary sources. The poem on the mysteries was certainly the result of reading secondary literature (Gibbon), and the poem on the saving of Julian may have been (Gibbon again, or an overly hasty first reading of Allard). In any case, it was Allard's work that drew Cavafy's attention to historical difficulties in his treatment of the two incidents, and he might naturally have wished to check Gregory, the ancient source for both, before proceeding.

25. Lavagnini, 76 (above).

26. T. Malanos, *'Ο Ποιητὴς Κ. Π. Καβάφης* (Athens: Diphros, 1957), 123: Δύο μου ποιήματα ἐναυάγησαν, γιατί δέ βρῆκα Γρηγόριο Ναζιανζηνό στήν 'Αλεξάνδρεια. Cf. Liddell, op. cit. (n. 9 above), 197.

It seems likely from Cavafy's allusion to the *Patrologia* of Migne in the note attached to his draft on Athanasius that at least by November of 1929 he had access to the volumes of Migne, which would have included Gregory's invectives against Julian. If the remark quoted by Malanos is genuine, it must accordingly belong to a time before November 1929 but probably after the work on Ἡδιάσωσις τοῦ Ἰουλιανοῦ [The Salvation of Julian] in December 1923.

The five poems on Julian published in Cavafy's lifetime (nos. 2, 5, 7, 9, and 10) were presumably released to his public because they met his scholarly criteria. No less than three of the five include verbatim quotations from the surviving writings of Julian himself. These are no. 5, which opens with a substantial citation from the emperor's letter to Theodorus on the neglect of pagan gods;[27] no. 9, to which Cavafy affixed a quotation from the *Misopogon* on the Antiochenes' predilection for Christ and Constantius;[28] and no. 10, which is in fact little more than a repetition of a comment by Julian preserved in the ecclesiastical historian Sozomen together with the Christians' witty reply to him (also as given by Sozomen).[29]

The main point of no. 7, mocking Julian's reading of the Scriptures at the very moment of his growing infatuation with Neoplatonist theurgy, depends upon the testimony of Gregory of Nazianzus.[30] Although it is probable, as Diana Haas implies, that Gibbon was the primary inspiration for this poem and that some of the introductory material about Julian's teachers derives ultimately from Eunapius and the ecclesiastical historians, the appearance of the young prince as a lector in Nicomedia is told only by Gregory.[31] To judge from Cavafy's procedure elsewhere, it is highly unlikely that he would have released this poem without satisfying himself that it conformed to Gregory's account. Curiously, the two poems that appear to owe their inspiration to Gibbon, namely this one (no. 7) and the piece on the mysteries (no. 1), both depend upon

27. Julian, *Epist.* 89B (p. 154 Budé): ὁρῶν...ὀλιγωρίαν does not mean "seeing contempt" but rather "seeing neglect (indifference, slighting)" of the cults of pagan deities. Poem no. 5 is also based on Julian's remarks to Arsacius in *Epist.* 84B (pp. 144–47 Budé).

28. Julian, *Misop.* 357A.

29. Sozomen 5.18.

30. Greg. Naz. in *MPG*, XXXV, cols. 551 and 632.

31. See notes 65 and 66 in Diana Haas's article. Compare Gregory's words (*MPG*, XXXV, 551) ὑπαναγνώσκειν and ὑπαναγνώστης with Cavafy's ἀναγνώστης.

Gregory as the principal ancient source. Because Cavafy seems to have had access to Gregory's work in the 1890s when he was reading Gibbon (and when he is known to have written the poem on the mysteries), it is tempting to suppose that the poem on Julian in Nicomedia, although published in 1924, may have been drafted or outlined at that same time. The long delay until publication would closely parallel the fate of the poem on a great procession of priests and laymen (no. 2), published in 1926.

That poem poses more problems than the four other Julian pieces that Cavafy chose to make public. In view of the prominence given to the cross, it is reasonable to identify the work with a version of Ὁ Σταυρός [The Cross] listed as one of the early poems in *The Beginnings of Christianity*. This early poem on the cross was probably written in September 1892 and then revised in March 1917 only a few years before Cavafy's most conspicuous period of preoccupation with Julian began.[32] The subject reflects the poet's immersion in ecclesiastical history during the 1890s. Its description of the Christian celebration at Antioch after Julian's death depends principally upon Theodoret but may also reflect passages in Sozomen and Gregory.[33] The actual ceremony is imaginary, but the spirit of the Antiochene Christians at the time comes through memorably and accurately. Of course Jovian himself was to have trouble with the Antiochenes just as Julian had, but it was hardly to Cavafy's purpose to dwell upon that particular irony. The salutation of Jovian with which the poem concludes is unsettling for anyone acquainted with the history, and Cavafy certainly was acquainted with it. But the historicity of the poem remains intact and provides the occasion Cavafy wanted for exalting what really obsessed him here, the cross, which is equally important as a symbol in another poem from the 1890s, "Julian at the Mysteries." It was not, however, until nine more years had passed after the revision of "The Cross" that Cavafy could bring himself to publish Μεγάλη συνοδεία ἐξ ἱερέων καὶ λαϊκῶν [A Great Procession of Priests and Laity]. But it is worth emphasizing that it appeared in the very same year as another poem on Julian and the Antiochenes (no. 9) and preceded it by just a few months.

32. Cf. Savidis in *Collected Poems* (n. 5 above), 424; also Ἀνέκδοτα Ποιήματα (n. 9 above), 172.

33. Theodoret 3.22. Cf. Sozomen 6.4 and Greg, in *MPG*, XXXV, cols. 708–12, all cited by Diana Haas in her note 69.

The recurrent motifs of the cross and of Antioch lead one to observe that all of Cavafy's Julian poems are restricted to a relatively small number of topics from the life of the emperor. No less than three pieces (nos. 2, 9, and 12) are explicitly concerned with the reaction of the people of Antioch to Julian, and a fourth (no. 5) is based on letters written from Antioch. The fact of Julian's death is the basis of three poems (nos. 2, 3, and 11), of which two (nos. 2 and 3) depict an immediate response to the news, whereas the third (no. 11), in dating the scene to the first year of Theodosius solely by an allusion to the number of years after Julian's death, attempts to suggest how rapidly the emperor's posturing became old-fashioned and absurd. Four of the poems are devoted to Julian's childhood (nos. 1, 4, 5, and 7), and a fifth (no. 8) is based upon a report from the very first year of the young prince's public career (A.D. 355). Indeed, poem no. 8, with its setting in Gallic Vienne, is a reminder that Cavafy nowhere else exploited an episode from the six years that Julian spent in Gaul.

The omission of the crucial years in Gaul, apart from the legend about his arrival there, cannot have been due to the poet's ignorance. He was far too avid a reader of Gibbon and Allard, not to mention Julian himself. It is understandable that Cavafy might not have found inspiration in Julian's battles against obscure tribes and chieftains, but it is not immediately obvious why he took no interest in Julian's dependent relation upon Salutius or in the strange episode of the proclamation of Julian as emperor at Paris.[34] On balance it seems best to assume that the poet had little taste for the western ambience of Gaul and preferred to concentrate on Julian in a Greek context. But even this hypothesis does not explain another notable omission in the work of one who knew the history so well. There is nothing in Cavafy about Julian in Constantinople during the period after Constantius's death and before the journey to Antioch. This was undeniably a Greek environment, and there were rich materials for Cavafy's genius—for example, Julian's ostentatious appearance as a mourner at Constantius's funeral.[35] The travesty of justice at the Chalcedon trials might also have engaged Cavafy's muse: after all, even

34. For Salutius, cf. G. W. Bowersock, *Julian the Apostate* (Cambridge, Mass.: Harvard University Press 1978), 44–45; for the proclamation at Paris, ibid., 46–54.

35. See Libanius, *Orat.* 18.120; Mamertinus, *Panegyric* 27.5; and Greg. Naz. in *MPG*, XXXV, col. 685.

Ammianus Marcellinus, who admired Julian, had to admit that Justice herself shed tears on that occasion.[36]

With most poets it would not be very profitable to ponder historical subjects they choose to omit. But for Cavafy, an avowedly historical poet who was obsessed with Julian, it is worth taking into account that, in spite of turning to Julian twelve times, he concerned himself with a rather small number of topics from the range of those that were possible. They are, as has already emerged, Julian's childhood, Julian at Antioch, and Julian's death. The common denominator for every single one of the poems—what links the principal motifs together—is Christianity. All of the poems, in one way or another, address the issue of Julian's encounter with the Christians. It seems evident that this was all that Cavafy really cared about in Julian's career. Weaknesses of character that the emperor displayed toward other pagans, as in Paris or in Constantinople, held no fascination for him. Similarly, the dramatic effort that Julian made to rebuild the temple at Jerusalem and the equally dramatic termination of that effort amid miraculous balls of flame appear nowhere in Cavafy's oeuvre.[37] Christianity was the real obsession.

The characteristics of Julian that Cavafy chose to underscore are hypocrisy (nos. 1, 4, 6, 7) and puritanical intolerance (nos. 5, 9, 10, 11, 12). The sources provide ample justification for characterizing the emperor in this way, even if many writers have preferred different assessments. Julian was an ascetic who demanded strict adherence to the principles of his new pagan church. He had learned about church organization from his upbringing as a Christian, and it is clear from his writings that he intended to surpass the Christians at their own game.[38] Meanwhile, the Christians of Julian's time were, after all, for the most part yesterday's pagans. They had not changed their way of life all that much.[39] At Antioch they went to the theater and the chariot races, and they celebrated their festivals as they had before. When Julian entered the city he heard

36. Amm. Marc. 22.3.7: *ipsa mihi videtur flesse Iustitia.*

37. On this affair, Bowersock, op. cit. (n. 34 above), 88–90.

38. See W. Koch, "Comment l'empereur Julien tâcha de fonder une église païenne," *Revue belge de philologie et d'histoire,* VI (1927) and VII (1928), published in four installments.

39. See G. W. Bowersock in *Gibbon et Rome à la lumière de l'historiographie moderne.* Publications de la Faculté des Lettres de l'Université de Lausanne, XXII (Geneva: Droz, 1977), 210–12.

the ill-omened wailing of the festival of Adonis.[40] Cavafy understood all this rather better than most historians, in part, of course, because Christian Antioch with its traditional style of life was the kind of city in which he longed to live. He had no problem with the old paganism, robust and free (at least in his view). His poem Ἰωνικόν [Ionic], first composed in the same year as "Julian at the Mysteries," shows a deep feeling for Greek paganism. It was Julian's anti-Christian paganism that Cavafy could not abide. What Cavafy praised in "Ionic" he could find among the Christians of Antioch. The city was a profoundly important symbol for him: its people were immoral (ἀνήθικοι), but their life was delectable (ἐνήδονος). And they were Christian.

They were also Greek. Cavafy's Παλαιόθεν ἑλληνίς, written in the year 1927 and therefore right in the midst of his Julian poems, provides the appropriate commentary. The city of Antioch is proud of its buildings and streets, its kings, its wise men, and its merchants. But it has far more to be proud of: it is Greek from ancient times, παλαιόθεν ἑλληνίς. It has often been observed that the Greekness of Cavafy is that of the diaspora—Alexandria, Constantinople, and (in imagination) Antioch. Greeks of the mainland have tended to admire Julian as their courageous if unsuccessful champion, and on the whole they still do. A young Athenian scholar of today, who has done considerable research on Julian and will shortly publish a book on him, has recently written, "Kavafy...chose to use his poetic gift in order to turn his most private predilections into an art theory, and in Julian's personality he discovered the great negative symbol that would convey to initiates his cult of the Beautiful. Identifying with the Antiochenes of the fourth century, the twentieth-century Alexandrian despises, almost hates, the ascetic emperor for his superior indifference to all that glitters, even gold....Theirs [the Antiochenes'] was certainly not 'a perfectly genuine form of Hellenism,' and Julian was not the first intellectual to denounce their ἀμουσία."[41] This writer goes on to commend the emperor as honest, compassionate, friendly, and fond of family life. Cavafy remains the better historian, but the issues are as alive now as they were in his day or in Julian's.

The Christians of his time could not forgive Julian for arrogating Hellenism—Greekness—to the pagan cause. By forbidding Christians to teach the great Greek classics, he tried to cut them off from their crucial

40. Amm. Marc. 22.9.15.
41. Polymnia Athanassiadi-Fowden, *JTS*, XXX (1979), 331–32.

heritage. Gregory of Nazianzus was quick to protest and as eloquent as always: no one trained in Hellenic traditions could be denied being a Greek.[42] Cavafy from Alexandria must have sensed a kindred spirit in Gregory, the Christian from Cappadocia. But the tide was turning. The very word Ἕλλην would soon be the current word for pagan and would no longer serve for a Greek. Cavafy, like Gregory, belonged to the far-flung community of Greek culture—beyond Greece and embracing Christianity. Cavafy was Ἑλληνικός just as King Antiochus of Commagene in a poem of 1923: Ὑπῆρξεν ἔτι τό ἄριστον ἐκεῖνο, Ἑλληνικός.[43]

Permissive Christianity, then, appears to be the fundamental interest of Cavafy in handling the various Julian episodes. To be a Christian did not preclude being a pagan in the old sense, like the young Syrian in Τὰ ἐπικίνδυνα, nor did it preclude a romance with a pagan like Myris's lover. In Antioch Cavafy found the resolution of the problem he began to solve in 1911 when he started to make his erotic verse public. It was no accident that the historical and sensual categories of his oeuvre tended to merge at times, as the writer of May 1927 observed; for Cavafy was able to interpret his own eroticism in terms of historical examples that preserved for him what he probably found more important than anything else: his Christianity and his consciousness of being Greek. In the Julian poems he struggled for historical accuracy because it was clearly imperative for him to know that there really had been a world that could accommodate a sensualist, both Christian and Greek.

42. Greg. Naz. in *MPG*, XXXV, col. 536A–B. The partisan effort to identify Hellenism with paganism may well go back to the Neoplatonist teachers Porphyry (on whom Cavafy wrote an early poem, now lost [note 10 above]) and Lamblichus.

43. Malanos reported that Cavafy once said to Stratis Tsirkas, Εἶμαι κι ἐγώ Ἑλληνικός. Προσοχή, ὄχι Ἕλλην, οὔτε Ἑλληνίζων, ἀλλὰ Ἑλληνικός: T. Malanos, *Περί Καβάφη* (Athens: Sergiade, 1935), 56. On this remark, see E. Keeley, op. cit. (n. 3 above), 111.

# CHAPTER THIRTEEN

# CAVAFY AND APOLLONIOS

THE TWELVE POEMS THAT CAVAFY WROTE ABOUT THE emperor Julian span his entire creative career, from the 1890s to the year of his death. They illuminate his religious and sexual anxieties, and they also prove the care with which he read the ancient texts that form the core of his poems. Two articles on Cavafy's Julian, by Renata Lavagnini and myself (see chapter 12 in this volume), attempted to open up fresh perspectives on this incomparable poet by tracing the evolution of his reflections on a figure from the ancient past whom he found repugnant. But there is another figure from antiquity who also recurs in Cavafy's work; and if he appears less frequently in the poems than Julian, he is no less powerful a presence. He is someone whom Cavafy admired as the embodiment of his most cherished aesthetic ideals: the sage and miracle worker, Apollonios of Tyana.

The town of Tyana lay within the Roman province of Cappadocia, which was situated in central Anatolia. It is a paradigm of the partly Hellenized and partly barbaric culture of the Greek diaspora which Cavafy, in Alexandria, found so congenial. Apollonios's long life covered most of the first century of the Christian era, and it cannot have been more than a few decades after his death that he became legendary among pagans for his outspoken defiance of Roman authority and his miraculous ability to cure the sick and revive the dead. At least one substantial work, now lost, was devoted in the second century to the exploits of Apollonios; and it is likely that even then he was being cast in the role for which he was obviously suited, that of a pagan rival of Christ. During the early third century, a Greek courtier in the entourage of the emperor

Septimius Severus and his successors composed an elaborate biography of Apollonios of Tyana, replete with the exorcism of demons, the raising of the dead, and an eloquent speech before the tyrant Domitian. This work survives in its entirety. Philostratos, its author, mixed fact and fiction so successfully that the most delicate instruments of scholarship have been unable to separate them.

Four of Cavafy's poems demonstrate that he had studied Philostratos's life of Apollonios with considerable interest. Three of these are included in the published poems that have been admirably turned into English by Edmund Keeley and Philip Sherrard. In order of publication they are "But the Wise Perceive Things About to Happen" (1915), "If Actually Dead" (1920), and "Apollonios of Tyana in Rhodes" (1925). All three are built upon excerpts from Philostratos, who is quoted in each case in the original classical Greek. The first poem is prefaced by a passage from Book Eight, in which it is said that although the gods can tell the future and ordinary mortals can tell the present, the wise perceive what is just about to happen. Apollonios clearly belongs to the category of the wise, and Cavafy is moved to elaborate this extrasensory perception of the privileged few:

> Sometimes during moments of intense study
> their hearing's troubled: the hidden sound
> of things approaching reaches them,
> and they listen reverently, while in the street outside
> the people hear nothing whatsoever.

The second poem has as its title Philostratos's words *eige eteleuta* from the last pages of his work: "There are several versions of [Apollonios's] death, if he actually did die [*eige eteleuta*]." These versions of the sage's death—that he died in Ephesus or in Lindos or in Crete—serve as the inspiration for a characteristically Cavafian monologue:

> "Maybe the time hasn't yet come for him to return
> and show himself to the world again;
> or maybe, transfigured, he moves among us
> unrecognized—. But he will come again
> as he was, teaching the ways of truth; and then of course he'll
> bring back the worship of our gods
> and our elegant Hellenic rites."

The monologue is followed by another characteristic device of Cavafy in which the poet puts a distance between himself and the speaker.

In this case, we are told that the speaker is an impoverished and weak-willed pagan of the sixth century, muttering to himself after a reading of Philostratos's biography.

The third poem is constructed on Apollonios's rebuke to a rich youth in Rhodes who prefers to spend his money on a luxurious house rather than a proper education. Cavafy's verses incorporate the reply of Apollonios in the Greek of Philostratos, which gleams impressively in the midst of the poet's modern idiom:

> "When I enter a temple,"
> said the Tyanian finally, "even if it's a small one,
> I'd much rather see
> a gold and ivory statue there
> than a statue of common clay in a large temple."

The poem concludes with an exclamation of disgust at the idea of common clay.

Cavafy wrote his fourth Apollonios poem in 1920, the very year in which he published "If Actually Dead," but for some reason he never put it into final form; and it remained unpublished until Renata Lavagnini reconstructed it from the drafts some fifteen years ago. In this work Cavafy turned again to the extrasensory powers of the sage. Cavafy's title, "In the Wooded Park," is a direct quotation in classical Greek from Philostratus's biography. While residing in Ephesus, on the coast of Asia Minor, Apollonios had a remarkable vision of the assassination of the emperor Domitian, just as it was taking place in Rome. We can easily see the inspiration for Cavafy's poem by looking at the Philostratean account:

> [Apollonios] was holding a discussion in the woods of the park about noon, the very time when the events in the palace took place. First he dropped his voice, as if afraid; then his exposition lost some of its usual clarity, as happens when a man is distracted by something in the middle of his argument; then he fell silent, as people do when they have lost the thread. He stared hard at the ground, stepped three or four paces forward, and shouted, "Strike the tyrant! Strike him!" It was not as if he was observing some reflection of truth through a mirror, but as if he was seeing the real thing and seeming to take part in the action. The Ephesians were all present at the discussion, and were astounded, until Apollonios, after waiting as people do to see the result of an even struggle,

said, "Don't worry, my friends. The tyrant was slaughtered today."
(Translation by C. P. Jones)

Cavafy's poem of 1920 on Apollonios's vision at Ephesus must have been part of the poet's more general preoccupation at that time with magical perceptions of the death of tyrants. It was precisely in 1920 that Cavafy drafted one of the most striking of the incomplete poems on Julian. It is entitled "Athanasius" and has now been published by Renata Lavagnini. There the great fourth-century saint is depicted in a boat on the Nile during the course of his exile in the year of Julian's death. Two monks are with him, and he is at prayer when he suddenly looks at them and discerns a smile on their faces: they have just learned by intuition that Julian has been killed in Mesopotamia.

It is evident from Cavafy's preparation of the four Apollonios poems in 1915, 1920, and 1925 that throughout this period he turned to Philostratos particularly for themes that would illustrate the privileged knowledge of the sage or, in more general terms, the initiate. But this exploration of the life of Apollonios was not new to Cavafy's spiritual world. The poem on wise men who perceive what is about to happen was published, to be sure, in 1915; but we know that it was first drafted in 1896 and published in the first version in 1899. The poem "If Actually Dead," although published in 1920, was first composed in 1897 and rewritten in 1910. In the original version, the poem consisted only of the monologue in which the speaker anticipates the return of Apollonios. The introduction of a late antique frame for this monologue came later and implies a more detached view on the part of the poet. The early drafts of these works leave no doubt that Cavafy was already well acquainted with the miracles of Apollonios in the 1890s.

It is, in fact, possible to ascertain just when his involvement with Philostratos's biography began. In November of 1892 at Alexandria, Cavafy published an article on Keats, in which he offered a critical assessment of *Lamia*. Keats's poem, which tells the story of a lady vampire who took a beautiful shape and won the love of a certain Menippus, is based on a tale told by Philostratos about Apollonios. The Greek word for the vampire is *lamia*, and this expression, like the whole story, reached Keats through Robert Burton's *Anatomy of Melancholy*, where Philostratos's text is almost literally translated. Apollonios, with his mystic power, was able to recognize the vampire in Menippus's lover and unmask it. "The creature pretended to weep," says Philostratos, "begging him not to interrogate it or force it to confess its true nature. But Apollonios insisted relentlessly until it confessed it was a vampire."

In examining Keats's poem, in which Apollonios naturally plays an important role, Cavafy undertook a thoughtful comparison with the original—and more spare—narrative in Philostratos. He praised Philostratos for swiftly ending the story with the exorcism of the *lamia* and criticized Keats for not knowing when to stop. He judged Keats's addition of Menippus's death altogether unnecessary. It is clear from the essay on Keats that Cavafy's interest in Apollonios was bound up, at least in 1892, with a taste for the supernatural. He believed that Philostratos had provided many precious ingredients for poetry. The life of Apollonios was, he said, "a storehouse of poetic material." In saying this Cavafy was going far beyond an explanation of Keats's choice of subject. He was charting his own course as a poet.

In the preceding year Cavafy had translated Baudelaire's sonnet "*Correspondances*" from *Les Fleurs du Mal*, adding some interpretative verses of his own. As George Savidis and Renata Lavagnini have stressed, the link with Baudelaire is crucial for understanding the esthetic ideals of Cavafy in the 1890s. These included the acknowledgment of a kind of second sight in a poet, a heightened perception that distinguishes such a person from ordinary mankind. For Baudelaire,

> La Nature est un temple où de vivants piliers
> Laissent parfois sortir de confuses paroles;
> L'homme y passe à travers des forêts de symboles
> Qui l'observent avec des regards familiers.

> [Nature is a temple where living columns
> sometimes let inchoate words emerge;
> Man passes that way through forests of symbols
> that look at him with familiar glances.]

For Cavafy,

> The poet's gaze is sharper,
> For them nature is a familiar garden.
> In a dark grove others
> Grope along their difficult way.

The poet sees in the midst of apparent confusion the signs which nature makes intelligible to the knowing.

Apollonios is thus like the poet in his capacity to see through the chaos of the world around him. In reading Philostratos's account of the *lamia*, Cavafy must have been impressed with the gaze that Apollonios cast on Menippus: "Apollonios looked at Menippus like a sculptor [*andriantopoiou dikên*], getting an impression and a view of him. Then, sizing him up, he said, "Ah, you are the beautiful boy that beautiful women chase. You are cuddling a snake and a snake is cuddling you." The penetrating look of the sage is similarly prominent in Keats's poem, but Philostratos's analogy with the scrutiny of a sculptor at work is unique. It may perhaps have inspired one of Cavafy's poems which, although published in 1911, was drafted initially in 1893. Although not concerned with Apollonios at all, it does enlarge upon the rare talent of an imaginary sculptor at Rome to recreate a human image. The poem is titled "Sculptor of Tyana," and Tyana was Apollonios's city.

But it is not only the searching gaze that Cavafy found so important in his reflections on Baudelaire and Philostratos in the early 1890s. It was also the mystery and the magic. Baudelaire's celebrated espousal of the works of Edgar Allan Poe nourished Cavafy's predilection for the genre of the fantastic tale. Lavagnini has pointed out that the marginal notes in Cavafy's copy of *Nouvelles Histoires Extraordinaires* (the French translation of Poe) prove that he had studied carefully Baudelaire's *Notes nouvelles sur Edgar Poe*. In addition, we know that his library included two editions of Poe, which provided between them not only the poems and a good selection of the tales, but also the essay "The Philosophy of Composition." Cavafy's interest in Apollonios's encounter with the *lamia* was accordingly buttressed by his growing appetite for fantastic literature. With the publication of his short story *Eis to phos tis imeras* ("In Broad Daylight"), in an impeccable edition by Lavagnini, we discovered that Cavafy actually went so far as to try his hand at this genre.

"In Broad Daylight" is a tale in the manner of Poe. The setting is, however, peculiar to Cavafy. The story unfolds at Ramleh on the outskirts of late nineteenth-century Alexandria, and the characters are young men of leisure who are preoccupied with money. One of these youths recounts how a mysterious male figure appeared to him in his bedroom in the dead of night: a man "of medium height, fortyish," clad in black and wearing a straw hat. The visitor said that he could show the location of a great treasure, and he instructed the narrator to meet him the next day between noon and four at a certain coffee shop. And when the narrator showed up there, "Horrors [*phriki*]! There indeed was a little coffeehouse, and there indeed he sat." An overpowering vertigo and tension seized the speaker as he beheld "the same black clothes, the same straw hat, the same features, the same glance." As Lavagnini has noted in her commentary on the story, the gaze of the mysterious visitor who appears in broad daylight after his nocturnal epiphany comes straight from Apollonios by way of Cavafy's reading of Keats. In the story the narrator says, "And he, unblinking [*askardamuktei*], was observing me." Just so had Apollonios stared at the beautiful *lamia*, "fix'd his eye, without a twinkle or stir," an expression which Cavafy had earlier paraphrased in Greek as *askardamuktei*. From internal evidence, Lavagnini has ascertained that Cavafy's fantastic tale of Alexandrian youth belongs to 1895–96. It is therefore a natural outgrowth of his reading of Baudelaire, Poe, Keats, and—as an ancient and authentically Greek source for the themes of those nineteenth-century Western writers—Philostratos's life of Apollonios.

Within a year of the composition of "In Broad Daylight," Cavafy wrote the first of his poems devoted explicitly to the figure of Apollonios of Tyana. "But the Wise Perceive Things About to Happen," with its prefatory quotation from Philostratos, can be seen as a natural extension of his work from the paraphrase of Baudelaire's "*Correspondances*" in 1891 to the horror story of 1895–96. The themes of supernatural perception and the privileged position of the elect come together in this poem of 1896. Although the supernatural element dominates in the short story that immediately preceded it, the element of the privileged elect is not absent even there. At the beginning, the narrator classes himself and his friends as superior to others because of their "perfect spiritual development," which allows them to be "simple without ignorance."

The Apollonios theme continued fruitful for Cavafy. In 1897 he wrote the first version of "If Actually Dead." As a monologue without the late antique setting of the subsequent version, this poem constitutes the most fervent of Cavafy's statements of the esthetic ideal which Apollonios represented for him. The poem appears to have brought to an end Cavafy's work on the sage of Tyana during this phase of his career. But the subject was by no means exhausted, as can be seen from his revision of "If Actually Dead" in 1910 and perhaps even from his revision of "Sculptor of Tyana" in 1903. In 1915 came the revision and publication of "But the Wise Perceive Things About to Happen," and five years later came the definitive text of "If Actually Dead," together with the draft of the poem on Apollonios's vision of the murder of Domitian. In all of this work, the themes remain recognizably those of the 1890s, but the poet's increased subtlety in the later years gives new force to those themes. By putting the monologue on Apollonios's death into the mouth of a sixth-century pagan reader of Philostratos, one who was publicly a Christian and privately a pagan, Cavafy hints perhaps at his own experience. Although a Christian, he had become infatuated with Apollonios through Philostratos's biography in a remote time and in an essentially hostile place.

The last, and in many ways most enigmatic, of the Apollonios poems came in 1925, "Apollonios of Tyana in Rhodes." The young man whom the sage rebukes prefers luxury to education and training. In Cavafy's terms it seems that he has forsworn the company of the elect in favor of vulgar ostentation. But what gives the poem its complexity is the fact that Apollonios does not reject ostentation as such: in a small temple he would prefer to see a gold and ivory statue rather than a clay one in a large temple. It is Apollonios's preference for costly adornment (for the right purpose) that provokes the poem's final lines:

> "Of common clay": how disgusting—
> yet some (who haven't been adequately trained)
> are taken in by what's bogus. Of common clay.

The poem concludes, as it began, with attention to proper training or initiation. Cavafy himself had a high regard for opulent objects, as he demonstrated above all in the poem "Of Colored Glass" on a pathetic coronation in late Byzantine times. The empire was so poor that only colored glass could be displayed at the ceremony,

> a sad protest against
> the unjust misfortune of the couple being crowned,
> symbols of what they deserved to have,
> of what surely it was right that they should have
> at their coronation.

This poem was published in the same year as the poem on Apollonios in Rhodes.

Taken as a whole, the writings of Cavafy on Apollonios of Tyana, in prose and verse, extend from 1892 until 1925, in other words from his most youthful literary productions down to the mature work of his last decade. His discovery of Philostratos's biography appealed simultaneously to his taste for the supernatural and to that sense of cultural superiority that he shared with his Alexandrian friends. Miracles and elitism were likewise important to Cavafy as a Christian. The special attraction of Apollonios was rooted in the obvious similarity of the sage of Tyana to the figure of Christ. It was precisely during the 1890s that Cavafy was at work on a series of poems about the beginnings of Christianity, just as he was writing the critique of Keats's *Lamia*, "In Broad Daylight," and the first Apollonios poems. In later life Cavafy confronted the problem of Apollonios and Christ more directly when he added to "If Actually Dead" the Christian speaker who had completed a reading of Philostratos with such admiration. Furthermore, in those later years Cavafy's work shows him increasingly resentful of the frontal assault that the emperor Julian had launched on the Christian church. It was not paganism as such to which he objected, but rather Julian's exclusive paganism, which ruled out Christianity.

Cavafy saw himself as a Christian, but his Christianity had room for pagans just as he wanted pagans to have room for Christianity. Apollonios and Christ: he was drawn to them both. The two unpublished poems of 1920 stand as eloquent testimony to this attraction. Apollonios's miraculous perception of the killing of Domitian and the equally miraculous revelation of Julian's death to the Egyptian companions of Athanasius moved Cavafy in the same way and for the same reasons.

# CHAPTER FOURTEEN

# THE NEW CAVAFY

*Unfinished Poems 1918–1932: Ateli Poiimata,*
edited by R. Lavagnini (Athens: Ikaros, 1994)

IN THE SUMMER OF 1932, WHEN DEATH DREW NEAR TO Constantine Cavafy, who was already recognized as one of the greatest Greek poets of the age, his friends in Alexandria persuaded him to go to Athens for treatment of a throat cancer only recently diagnosed. His arrival in Athens attracted the notice of many of the notable and not-so-notable literary figures in the city. Several of those who met him there wasted no time in revealing what they had learned, even though after a tracheotomy Cavafy was no longer able to speak at all. His last observations had to be transmitted by way of penciled notes. He returned to Alexandria in October of 1932 and died there the following April. It was not long before the world became aware that the poet had left behind a substantial number of unfinished poems.

In the year of his death one interlocutor at Athens published an article reporting that Cavafy had declared to his friends, only six months before he died (and therefore just before his return to Egypt), that he had still to complete no less than twenty-five poems. A decade later another interlocutor, who had been engaged in compiling the poet's bibliography in 1932, wrote that Cavafy had insisted at the time that the bibliography was far from exhaustive. Clearly, time was closing in, and Cavafy did not want to leave the world without a full representation of his achievement. But at the same time he was unwilling, even as he was dying, to sacrifice those lofty standards that had kept him throughout his life from releasing certain works and had in fact repeatedly driven him to revise older pieces.

It was in 1963 that George Savidis announced that the poet's archive, now in his personal possession, contained the sketches of the twenty-five unfinished poems. No poet has ever been more fortunate in the custodian of his memory than Cavafy. Savidis, through an unselfish commitment that exemplified the humanity of this scholar, assured over the years that the Cavafy archive would be made available only to those whose skills and integrity would guarantee an authoritative publication of what survived. He entrusted the unfinished poems to a meticulous philologist from the Institute for Modern Greek studies in Palermo. Renata Lavagnini, daughter of a distinguished Byzantinist and herself a dedicated scholar of Cavafy, has now produced in a single volume the poems to which Cavafy had alluded in Athens. Her research on the Cavafy drafts, including some nearly illegible scraps, has turned up more than thirty poems on which the poet was at work between 1918 and 1932. Her magisterial publication stands as a fitting memorial to George Savidis, who died in 1995.

For everyone who cares about Cavafy's poetry or indeed about lyric poetry generally in the twentieth century, the "new Cavafy" must arouse tremendous excitement. One can only regret that some of the writers—E. M. Forster, W. H. Auden, Marguerite Yourcenar, Philip Sherrard—who so successfully advocated Cavafy's work to Western readers are no longer here to taste the pleasure of this moment. But we can be grateful that Cavafy's finest translator and most acute critic, Edmund Keeley, is very much with us. During the decade of the 1980s, while she was at work on the archive, Lavagnini made known thirteen of the thirty unfinished poems in provisional publications. Seven of these were on Byzantine themes, and four on Julian the Apostate. I was privileged to work with Lavagnini, at the initiative of George Savidis, on a first interpretation of the Julian pieces in 1981. Savidis himself published the text of two of the new poems and established the definitive designation for all of them as *ateli* (unfinished) in contrast with another group, now familiar to all readers of Cavafy—the *anekdota* (unpublished in the poet's lifetime). Now that we can examine all thirty unfinished poems, as well as the few surviving scraps, we can readily agree with their editor when she describes them as a coherent corpus. They are confined to recognizable Cavafian themes and often illuminate one another. They enrich our understanding of the entire published oeuvre of the poet. Nine of the poems are concerned with personal, often overtly erotic, subjects, whereas twenty-one are historical in character (although the personal and erotic elements are present there as well). These poems show, like those already in the public domain, that the triadic distinction that Cavafy once discerned in his work (sensual, historical, and philosophical) collapsed in later years. Eroticism nourished his philosophical view of history (in the Gibbonian sense of history as told by a *philosophe*), and history, in turn, nourished his eroticism.

Cavafy was undoubtedly one of the most historically minded poets of modern times. He read extensively in works of historical scholarship in Greek, English, and French, and he was so attentive to original sources that one of his unfinished poems, on Athanasius's telepathic perception of Julian the Apostate's death, remained unfinished solely because he was unable to locate the precise source of the episode in the Greek *patrologia* of Migne. Cavafy engaged in a lively debate with Gibbon through marginal notes in his personal copy of the *Decline and Fall.* He diligently excerpted the *Cambridge Ancient History*, Bidez's great biography of Julian, and Paparrigopoulos's pioneering history of the Greeks. But even more remarkable than the poet's interest in history were the areas of history that excited his imagination.

As an Alexandrian Greek whose family came from Constantinople, Cavafy embodied the Hellenism of the Near Eastern diaspora. He was enthralled by the ancient history of the Greeks, but not by the Greeks of the Homeric epics, the Greeks of Periclean Athens, or Solon, Plato, and Demosthenes. It was the overseas Hellenism of the centuries after Alexander the Great that attracted Cavafy. He became the poet of the Hellenistic age, of the Roman Empire, and, most remarkably of all, of the Byzantine Empire all the way down to its end in the fifteenth century. For most Greeks of the mainland in the late nineteenth and early twentieth centuries, these were regrettable times when the Greeks were subjugated to alien imperialist powers, times in which the Greeks were no longer themselves imperialist. Their history in this later period was little appreciated and studied. The very word *Byzantine* had a negative ring to it.

There were, of course, exceptions, such as Gibbon's great history, John B. Bury's *History of the Later Roman Empire,* various edifying works on the rise of Christianity, and Paparrigopoulos's history of the later Greeks. These were the books, together with the sources upon which they drew, to which Cavafy turned for inspiration. His interests had been defined early. Already between 1888 and 1891 he had composed a whole cycle of eleven poems on Byzantine themes. The cycle was called *Byzantine Days*, and the poems appear from the titles to have been exercises in a Parnassian style that appealed to the young Cavafy. The first of his twelve poems on Julian, although published posthumously, was actually written in 1896.

These subjects became ever more important as the years went by, and once he had decided to write explicitly about homosexuality (from 1911 onward) he acknowledged an erotic component in his historical tastes. Seferis's famous observation that Cavafy changed in mid-career from a mediocre to a great poet has some basis in the published works, and the simple fact that the folders of unfinished poems show Cavafy at work on nothing drafted before 1918 would confirm that he himself was aware of this change. It was in 1911 with the poem *Dangerous Thoughts* (*Ta Epikindina*) that Cavafy publicly began the poetic exploration of his own sexuality. The poem is a brief monologue of an imagined Syrian student in the reigns of Constans and Constantius in the middle of the fourth century:

Strengthened by meditation and study,
I won't fear my passions like a coward:
I'll give my body to sensual pleasure,
to enjoyments I've dreamed of,
to the most audacious erotic desires,
to the lascivious impulses of my blood...

Let us turn now to the historical pieces among the unfinished poems. They can be divided, for the most part, into four major categories—Hellenistic history, Apollonius of Tyana, Julian, and later Byzantine history. All of these are well represented in the works previously known. But these new poems take us further still into Cavafy's creative world. Each poem provides light on other poems, as a poem ought to do according to a famous methodological comment made by Cavafy in 1927: "light on one poem, partial light on another."

Consider, for example, one of the unfinished Hellenistic poems, entitled *Agelaos*. The notebooks contain Cavafy's own transcription of W. W. Tarn's narration in the *Cambridge Ancient History* on the conference of Naupactus in 217 B.C. The conference is notable, in Tarn's words, as "a last vain appeal made for Hellenic unity against the barbarian." Tarn goes on to observe, "Agelaus' famous speech is substantially genuine, otherwise Polybios would never have put it into the mouth of one of the hated Aetolians." Agelaos had warned the Greeks in vain to join together against a cloud rising in the West. Whether Rome or Carthage emerged victorious in the Punic Wars, that dark cloud was destined to overspread Greece. It is clear from the draft of his poem that Cavafy characteristically took the trouble to go back to the source for the episode, Polybius's *History*. He fashioned lines that speak to his own absorption in the unity of Hellenic culture:

> At the congress of Naupactus Agelaos
> said what had to be said. "Do not fight anymore—
> Greeks against Greeks. The struggle threatening us
> is at hand. Either Carthage or Rome
> will win, and then the winner will turn upon us.
> Philip, O king, you must regard all Greeks
> as your own....be a savior to Greece."
> Clever words, but they didn't do any good.
> In the terrible, accursed days
> Of Cynoscephalae, Magnesia, and Pydna
> many of the Greeks would remember
> the clever words, which didn't do any good.

This poem provides at last a definitive interpretation of a much-discussed poem that Cavafy published in 1931 (although it was probably first drafted in 1916). It is entitled *In the Year 200 b.c.* and begins with a line taken from Alexander the Great's proud message accompanying spoils sent to Athens from his Persian campaign: "Alexander, son of Philip, and the Greeks except the Lacedaimonians...." The Lacedaimonians (Spartans) had not gone with Alexander to serve under a non-Spartan general. The speaker in this poem mocks the independence and isolationism of the Spartans and exults in the great new Hellenic world forged abroad by Alexander, a world in which Greek was heard as far away as India. Superficially this poem seemed to reflect Cavafy's own enthusiasm for the Hellenism of the diaspora, but Edmund Keeley, emphasizing the title's reference to the year 200, had rightly detected a more pessimistic tone in this poem. As he wrote in his book *Cavafy's Alexandria*, "The speaker is delivering his eulogy to the new Hellenism just three years before the last of the Macedonian Philips was thoroughly routed by the Romans at Cynoscephalae, and only ten years before the defeat of Antiochus III the Great at Magnesia, a defeat that established Roman supremacy over the great new world." Keeley's argument for irony and tragedy is magnificently confirmed by the unfinished Agelaos poem. The text by Tarn that had inspired Cavafy was first published in 1930, the year before Cavafy decided to go ahead with making *In the Year 200* public.

Yet another of the new poems is also pertinent to *In the Year 200*. It bears the title *Nothing about the Lacedaimonians*, and it is dated precisely to July of 1930. It is chiefly concerned with the limits of high principle:

> By all means cultivate integrity
> and practice it,
> but in moderation, recognizing that very probably
> you will reach a point at which integrity is unsuitable.
> It's nice and it feels marvelous.
> It's honorable. You'll be a model of integrity
> in many matters and be helpful.
> You'll be deservedly praised: what integrity he has!
> But you should put water in your wine. Don't overdo it,
> because (as you know) "Nothing about the Lacedaimonians."

This speaker manifestly recalls the one in *In the Year 200*, who concludes by asking smugly—"Why should we talk about the Spartans now?" Keeley's already strong argument for understanding this line as ironic applies equally to this new poem. Its title is meant to be a direct allusion to the quotation that begins the other poem: in fact, an earlier draft of the title was precisely *Except the Lacedaimonians*, citing again the actual words of Alexander's boastful message sent on behalf of his army. Lavagnini thought that the final title, *Nothing about the Lacedaimonians*, was some kind of ancient proverbial expression, which she was unable to locate. But it is not. It is simply Cavafy's own reworking of the text of Alexander to fit into the monologue of the speaker in the poem. Like the speaker evoked in 200 B.C., the new speaker finds that the Spartans' principles only served to cut them out of the action. But he was himself blind to the coming subjugation of the Hellenes to an alien power. The new poem reflects a vision of Sparta that is already clear in a famous poem published in 1928, *In Sparta*, where the mother of King Cleomenes III of Sparta agrees magnanimously to go to Egypt as a hostage of the Ptolemies. In the next year, 1929, Cavafy published a second poem on this same subject, *Come, O King of the Lacedaimonians*, celebrating the queen's noble suppression of her personal grief. It is hardly surprising, therefore, to find Cavafy turning yet again to Sparta in his unfinished text of 1930.

The new Julian poems naturally complement the seven that have been known for decades. But they bring forward the tension between the poet's now overt espousal of homosexuality and his equally overt espousal of Christianity. Furthermore, paganism undoubtedly suggested sensuality to Cavafy, and that was why he denounced (as Gibbon had done) Julian's turning the cult of the gods into a desiccated asceticism. Cavafy was well aware of the emperor's Christian childhood. The implications of this emerge dramatically from an unfinished poem, based directly upon a surviving letter of Julian himself, describing a visit he made as a young man to the remains of Troy in the company of a bishop named Pegasius. Both were Christians at the time. When Julian turned later to polytheism, Pegasius too cast off his faith and worshiped the gods. What were the two thinking when they went about the circuit of Troy together, concealing their inmost predilections? I have written earlier about "a palpable atmosphere of pedophilia" in this poem (see chapter 12 in this volume), and Renata Lavagnini has accepted the point:

> They came to the magnificent temple of Athena
> The Christian bishop Pegasius
> And the Christian prince Julian.
> They eyed the statues with longing and emotion,
> But they addressed each other hesitantly
> With allusions, with ambivalent words
> With phrases full of caution
> Because they weren't sure of each other.
> They were constantly afraid of giving something away,
> The false Christian bishop Pegasius
> The false Christian prince Julian.

The unspoken secret that the older man and the adolescent boy shared with each other finds a good parallel, as Lavagnini noticed, in the published poem of 1930 *He Asked about the Quality*. Here the speaker in the poem stops at a shop to make conversation with a handsome attendant:

> He asked about the quality of the handkerchiefs
> and how much they cost, his voice choking
> almost silenced by desire.
> And the answers came back in the same mood,
> distracted, the voice hushed,
> offering hidden consent.

The new Julian poems also include a piece, mentioned earlier, on the telepathy of Athanasius. Remote sensing of this kind is, as we have just seen at Troy and over the handkerchiefs, of the utmost significance for Cavafy. Another of the unfinished poems takes up a similar episode of telepathy at the time of the death of Domitian. In this case the poet returns to the life of the legendary sage Apollonios of Tyana, on whom he had published several pieces in the 1920s. The new work dates from the same period and describes an ecstatic perception of the murder of Domitian in Rome on the part of Apollonios in Ephesus in Asia Minor. The title of the poem is in classical Greek, *Peri ta tôn xustôn alsê,* words taken directly from Philostratus's *Life of Apollonios,* on which Cavafy depended as a source. The poem itself incorporates more of Philostratus's text as the sage cries out in his vision, "strike the tyrant" (*paie ton turannon*). Apollonios, like Julian, was important for Cavafy in his exploration of a polytheism he could admire without compromising his taste for the Church.

The corpus of unfinished poems includes still another piece on supernatural perception among its four treatments of Julian. A blind old lady at Vienne, south of Lyon in France, tells the future emperor about his forthcoming elevation to the throne. The story had been reported by Ammianus Marcellinus, from whom Cavafy drew a Latin title for his poem (*Hunc deorum templis*). This is the only Latin title in his entire poetic oeuvre and must be considered, like the titles in classical Greek from Athenaeus, Philostratus, Plato, Plutarch, and Julian, as an expression of the importance he attached to a historical source. Only one other title in Cavafy is in the Roman alphabet, and that is a citation of Dante attached to an early poem of 1901.

The competing claims of paganism and Christianity dominate many of the published, unpublished, and unfinished poems on Byzantium. The new texts now furnish a commentary on the familiar ones. Attentive readers of Cavafy will remember his extraordinary poem of 1912 entitled *In Church,* appearing in the next year after *Dangerous Thoughts*:

> I love the church: its labara,
> its silver vessels and candleholders,
> the lights, the ikons, the pulpit.
> When I go there, into a church of the Greeks,
> with its aroma of incense,
> its liturgical chanting and harmony,

> the majestic presence of the priests,
> dazzling in their ornate vestments,
> the solemn rhythm of their gestures—
> my thoughts turn to the great glories of our race
> to our glorious Byzantinism (*ston endoxo mas Vizantinismo*).

"Our Byzantinism" was a startling thing to say in 1912 and would have been almost anytime until relatively recently. Yet Cavafy saw the Hellenism of the Byzantine Empire not as a corruption of the Greek polytheist past but as an affirmation of it, to which he willingly linked himself. In one of the so-called unpublished poems, a work of 1914, Cavafy had written about the very last year of the Byzantine Empire, when Theophilos Palaiologos groaned in despair, "I would rather die than live." Cavafy invested this distant and pathetic figure with a new significance for the Greeks:

> Ah, Kyr Theophilos Palaiologos,
> how much of the pathos, the yearning of our race,
> how much weariness—
> such exhaustion from injustice and persecution—
> your six tragic words contained.

"The yearning of our race" and "our Byzantinism" now find their echo in the unfinished poems on Byzantine themes. Perhaps the most resonant of these is another piece with a dramatic date at the very end of the Byzantine Empire. It resumes the lament of the poem on Theophilos Palaiologos but unites with it Cavafy's sexual interests and their complex relation to paganism in a Christian world. The poem, called *After Swimming*, begins with two young men stepping naked from the sea onto the beach. The day is hot, and they are reluctant to put their clothes back on. The various lines drafted by Cavafy show him striving to praise the beauty of their nakedness, their faces, and even their private parts. These lines call to mind a poem titled *Days of 1908*, published by Cavafy just five months before his death. Here a twenty-five-year-old who lives off card games and borrowed money and who wears foul and tattered clothes is said to cool himself at the baths with a morning swim. The speaker remembers him in 1908 as "stark naked, impeccably handsome, a miracle." In the new poem the poet observes that the old Greeks appreciated the loveliness of youth, and up to this point the reader would hardly be aware that *After Swimming* is a historical poem rather than a straightforwardly sensual one.

But suddenly we are told that the boys' teacher was none other than Gemistos Plethon. With this revelation we know that we are in the middle of the fifteenth century. Gemistos was a renowned neo-Platonic philosopher of the period, whose sympathy for paganism aroused the suspicion of the Christian establishment and led ultimately to his exile in Mistra. Gemistos was, of course, himself a Christian, and accordingly his problems meant something to Cavafy. Once Gemistos is introduced into the poem, the charges of paganism from the emperor and the patriarch are mentioned. The poem then concludes with a resounding conjunction of Hellenism and the sensuous young men with which it began:

> On the youth of that time Georgios Gemistos
> had a great influence through his teaching.
> He was very wise and exceedingly eloquent,
> and a spokesman for Hellenic culture.

This is a translation of the poem as reconstructed by Lavagnini. But the drafts show a stunning variant. One version of the final line describes Gemistos as a great lover (*erastis*) of Hellenic culture. In many ways this is a more satisfying text, combining the eroticism with which the poem begins with the Christian master of Greek paganism with which it ends.

The other Byzantine poems also concentrate on the late age of the empire. Although with less overt eroticism, they reflect Cavafy's pride in "our Byzantinism" together with his historical awareness of the forces that worked against what he admired. The two poems concerned with John Cantacuzenus reopen a vein of creativity already known from previously published work and allow Lavagnini now to identify, with good reason, a cycle of Cantacuzenus poems.

In 1341, when the Emperor Andronicus III died, John Cantacuzenus failed to secure the regency for Andronicus's nine-year-old son. For six years there was a struggle for power between Andronicus's widow, Anna of Savoy, who was supported by the Constantinopolitan patriarch, and Cantacuzenus. In two splendid poems already known from Cavafy's published oeuvre, one from 1924 and the other from 1925, the success of Cantacuzenus at the end of the civil war in 1347 is commemorated. The first is a monologue set in that year and delivered by a regretful adherent of Anna's party, who blames his choosing the wrong side on bad advice from the patriarch

with his imposing hieratic presence,
his completely bogus information,
his promises and all his drivel.

The second is an elegiac speech on the occasion of John Cantacuzenus's coronation in the same year, when colored glass was used in place of precious stones. The speaker remarks, "Our afflicted empire was extremely poor," but he finds nothing humiliating or undignified in those little pieces of glass. They seem to him a sad protest against an unjust fate in the collapsing world of Byzantium. Gibbon's words must certainly have inspired the poet here: "Such was the proud poverty of the times, that the absence of gold and jewels was supplied by the paltry artifices of glass and gilt leather."

The two new poems are both dated to 1925 and are therefore of virtually the same date as the two already known. Another important source of Cavafy's interest in Cantacuzenus at that time emerges from the language of the first of these, titled "The Patriarch," which borrows admiring epithets for the emperor directly from the narrative of Paparrigopoulos. The struggle with the patriarch is sharply delineated, by contrasting the characters of the two men, both named John—the "reckless and graceless" John and the "wise, gentle, patriotic, courageous, able" John. Once again we hear the adjective "our" that seems to haunt Cavafy's accounts of Byzantium, as Diana Haas has often observed: "our Byzantinism," "the yearning of our race," "our afflicted empire," and now, of Cantacuzenus, the great man "who ruled our people then."

The second of the new Cantacuzenus poems, entitled *On Epiphany*, is remarkable for its highly Cavafian evocation of the original historical sources for the period. The histories of Nicephorus Gregoras and John Cantacuzenus himself are cited explicitly. The emperor wrote a partisan but well-documented history of his own time, which was complemented by that of Gregoras. Both writers described the death of the emperor's mother, Theodora Cantacuzene, on Epiphany in 1342 during the civil war. Cavafy's poem ends with these sad and scholarly lines in the first person:

The death of Cantacuzene, pitiable as it was,
I have drawn from the History of Nicephorus Gregoras.
In the historical work of the emperor
John Cantacuzenus the story is
somewhat different, but no less sad.

With four poems devoted to John Cantacuzenus in 1924 and 1925, we have to ask what attracted Cavafy so strongly to this rather pathetic figure of late Byzantine history. Something in his reading of Gibbon, Paparrigopoulos, Gregoras, and John had clearly found an echo in himself. I suspect it was the courage of John in successfully resisting the authority of the established patriarchate without sacrificing his faith. After his abdication John went on to become a monk and a historian. He was a man of integrity who held steadfastly to his principles, whose glass ornaments proved him indifferent to ostentation and wealth. He knew that he was part of a decadent and impoverished world, but he maintained the Byzantinism of Cavafy's people, "our people." He was as beautiful in his spiritual nakedness as the disciples of Gemistos were in their physical nakedness. He had the dignity of the Spartans in the face of adversity. His splendor could never die any more than that remembered image of a vagabond youth at the baths in 1908.

Cavafy's poems, particularly the personal ones, have often seemed like snapshots of the past, snapshots in which souls and bodies that have long since deteriorated or turned to dust remain still unspoiled. The photographic parallel had occurred to the poet himself, whose poem of 1913 *Etsi* (Thus), known in English as *The Photograph*, movingly evokes a lost past that, thanks to the camera, is somehow not altogether lost and preserves a beauty that triumphs over a life of degradation:

> Who knows what a degrading, vulgar life you lead;
> how horrible the surroundings must have been
> when you posed to have this picture taken;
> what a cheap soul you must have.
> But in spite of all this, and even more, you remain for me
> the dream-like face, the figure
> shaped for and dedicated to the Hellenic kind of pleasure—
> that's how you remain for me
> and how my poetry speaks about you.

The unfinished drafts now published give us a new poem actually entitled in Greek *The Photograph (I Photographia)*. It is dated 1924 and harks back to the earlier poem of 1913. An unnamed man is looking at the image of a handsome youth on a photograph made in the year 1892. He feels melancholy, but then he is comforted by the fact that there is not the slightest trace of shame (*ntropi*) in the picture:

> Only fools use words like "depraved" and "obscene."

Lavagnini has noticed that in the chronological list of poems that Cavafy left for the years 1891–1925 he recorded a poem, now lost, from January 1904 with the title *The Photograph*. The date of that poem could easily accommodate the setting of the poem we have now retrieved with the same title. What the relation may have been between the two works we can probably never say, but some relation there must have been. The impact of the camera on Cavafy's creative imagination can thus be taken back to a relatively early phase of his career.

The camera of the mind was no less important, as we have seen in the poem *Days of 1908*. Its images were, like photographic ones, reminders of a profligate's freedom from shame. These reminders helped to make him a poet, as he had proclaimed in a poem of 1915: if he had felt shame, he asked, "What kind of a poet, what kind of artist would I be?" We knew already that Cavafy used alcohol to relieve his inhibitions. In *Half an Hour*, a work of 1917, he called it magic. The drafts of the unfinished poems bring us back to this theme in a poem of 1919. Alcohol unlocks an erotic image from the distant past, and the aging poet returns to his preoccupation with shame. Unfortunately, the variant lines make it exceptionally difficult to establish a definitive text, but it is easy to see what Cavafy was after here. He is in a closed house at night. He drinks until his surroundings disappear and he finds himself once again in a street in Marseilles looking at a beautiful ephebe.

> It must have been the alcohol I drank last night,
> It must have been the sleeplessness: I've been tired all day.
> In front of me the dark wooden stand with the archaic head
> vanished, and the door to the dining-room,
> and the red armchair, and the little sofa.
> In their place came a street in Marseilles.
> And my soul, liberated, unconstrained
> was there again and moved about,
> with the image of a sensitive and sensual young man—
> corrupt young man, I must admit.
> My soul felt released. It, poor thing,
> is completely tied down by the weight of age.
> My soul felt released and I saw
> a congenial street in Marseilles,
> with the image of the happy, corrupt youth:
> *he* never felt shame, he really didn't.

It was in 1897, twenty-two years before, that Cavafy had visited Marseilles with his brother John on the way to England, but the memory of that youth had never left the recesses of his imagination. What Cavafy had once called "the magic alcohol" brought it back. The boy had felt no shame. Early drafts of this poem show Cavafy commanding himself to feel none too.

The city of Alexandria, in which Cavafy spent the better part of his life and where so many of his memories were formed, was the subject of Keeley's illuminating monograph. Among the new texts there is one that speaks directly of the city, and with this it will be appropriate to conclude. The poem is dated to December of 1927. It proudly proclaims the poet's commitment to the later ages of Hellenism:

> My imagination goes now
> not to Alexandria of the Ptolemies,
> but of the fifth and sixth centuries.
> Alexandria is a very important and vivacious place
> in the sixth century and the start of the seventh,
> until the arrival of the Arab power (*o krataios Aravismos*).
> They still speak Greek well…
> It would not be unnatural for us
> to look at that age with such feeling:
> we have now brought back
> Greek speech to its own soil.

In a variant drafted for the final lines, Cavafy had expressed himself even more directly:

> I am a Greek poet, and a Greek of the city
> who did my Hellenic work on its soil.

Cavafy saw himself as the heir of a great tradition. Aristomenes, a prince from western Libya, was the imaginary subject of a poem written less than a year after these lines. The man was a pretentious poseur who fancied Greek dress, culture, and language, but he lived in constant terror of making solecisms in Greek. When he did, as Cavafy puts it,

> the Alexandrians, in their usual way,
> would start to make fun of him…

So the poor man went about constipated from unspoken talk. Aristomenes was an outsider whose embarrassment was a tribute to the enviable culture of the Alexandrians. The arrival of Islam made a difference, as this newly revealed poem makes clear in its explicit reference to Arab power. Even so, Cavafy's poem *Exiles*, from 1914, shows him reflecting on the survival of Greek among the Hellenic few as late as the ninth century. The city was not what it had been, but nonetheless

> In the evenings we meet on the sea front,
> the five of us (all, naturally, under fictitious names)
> and some of the few other Greeks
> still left in the city.
> Sometimes we discuss church affairs
> (the people here seem to lean toward Rome)
> and sometimes literature.
> The other day we read some lines by Nonnos:
> what imagery, what rhythm, what diction and harmony!

Nonnos, that great epic poet of Dionysiac mythology in Christian Egypt of the fifth century, appears here as the writer to whom a handful of Alexandrian Greeks turn in the ninth century for inspiration. It was similarly to the Hellenic world that flourished in Nonnos's day and that continued to flourish all over the Byzantine Empire in the days of the caliphs that Cavafy turned for his inspiration as he sat in twentieth-century Alexandria. Through Cavafy the city would recapture the ancient glory of the Hellenes.

# CHAPTER FIFTEEN

# THE LATER MOMIGLIANO

WHEN ARNALDO MOMIGLIANO DIED ON SEPTEMBER 1, 1987, the intellectual life of many countries suffered a severe blow. To scholars and thinkers in Italy, France, Germany, England, Israel, and the United States, Momigliano was not only an historian of renown but a personal friend. His cheerful smile, rumpled suit, and omnipresent shoulder bag (overflowing with pencils, papers, and books) were a familiar sight—charming and a little frightening at the same time. Behind the amiable and chaotic exterior was one of the most vigorous and discerning minds of the twentieth century. The shuffling manner and hearty laugh of this expatriate professor concealed an erudition unmatched in our time, an intellect that was relentless and uncompromising, and emotional needs that were fed equally by love and rage.

Momigliano was a man of many worlds, and that is probably why his impact was so enormous. Born in Caraglio (near Cuneo), south of Turin, he came from a distinguished Jewish family of intellectuals from Piedmont, and he considered himself throughout his life an Italian who was different from most Italians. Although he became a well-known figure in the intellectual life of Italy in the 1920s and '30s and wrote his first book at the tender age of twenty-two, his exile from Italy in 1939, after he had lost his university position the previous year, left him with an unceasing hatred of the Fascists and of those whom he suspected of actively collaborating with them. The loss of members of his family at the hands of the Nazis nourished a hostility to the Germans that he overcame only by an admirable triumph of mind over emotion in the last years of his life. From 1939 onward, Momigliano built a new life in England, ultimately becoming professor of ancient history at the University of London and a fellow of All Souls in Oxford. As a sensitive outsider, he understood the English in many ways better than they understood themselves; and this understanding helped him to accept the fact that, no matter how long he stayed in England, he would always be an outsider. After the war he renewed his contacts with Italy and developed close relations with the Hebrew University in Jerusalem, and then, gradually, he extended his activities to the New World.

So turbulent and diverse a background made Momigliano the ideal interpreter of other great scholars who had suffered from exile, alienation, or racial prejudice. His sympathetic assessment of the German exile Beloch, who lived in Italy (married to an American wife), or his assessment of the achievement of the Russian exile Rostovtzeff in terms of his experience of the Russian Revolution, or his interest in the Jewish family of another Russian exile, Elias Bickerman, were all grounded in his own personal experience. As Momigliano grew older, his work was less and less confined to the mainstream of Greek and Roman history, in which he had begun his career. It turned more to the history of historiography, the politics of scholarship, and the art of biography from antiquity to the present. In his ancient studies, instead of looking at the conquests of Alexander the Great or the majestic parade of Roman consuls, Momigliano turned increasingly to those who lived at the edge of the Greco-Roman world—to the Celts, to the Iranians, and above all to the Jews. When a group of his colleagues presented him with a volume of essays in his honor in 1983, the work was aptly titled *Tria corda* ("Three Hearts"). Momigliano had at least three, even if there was no nation in which he felt truly at home.

The title *Tria corda* is echoed, no doubt deliberately, in the title of the last volume of essays to appear from the pen of Momigliano. (He actually did write with a pen: not for him the typewriter or the word processor.) The book is called *On Pagans, Jews, and Christians* (Wesleyan University Press, 1987). It appeared posthumously, just after the eighth installment of the monumental series of his collected articles published in Italy under the formidable title *Contributi alla storia degli studi classici et del mondo antico.* The appearance of Momigliano's final book, with its reference to three religious worlds, provides a good occasion for considering the last phase of his career. All the essays in the volume were written within seven years of his death, during a period distinguished by an ever closer attachment to North America and, in particular, the

University of Chicago. In this decade, when Momigliano was well beyond the normal retirement age, he came annually for extended visits as an honored professor at Chicago; and there, amid congenial company, he took up new studies on the history of religion, a subject to which he devoted much of his last years. From Chicago Momigliano traveled to other major intellectual centers in North America. He cherished his membership on the editorial board of the *American Scholar* and rarely missed its semiannual meetings. Because the trans-Atlantic period of Momigliano's life so closely coincides with the period in which he wrote the papers in *On Pagans, Jews, and Christians*, the link between the two might be worth exploring.

Momigliano's serious involvement with America began in 1962, when he delivered the Sather Lectures at the University of California at Berkeley. His topic was, for him, a traditional one: "The Classical Foundations of Modern Historiography." The titles of his lectures show that, after a cursory glance at Persian and Jewish historiography in the opening lecture, he trod the well-worn ground of Herodotus, Thucydides, the Roman annalists, and Tacitus. These lectures were never published in his lifetime, and friends of Momigliano knew better than to inquire when they might be. A reference to these unpublished lectures in a newspaper article several decades later was sufficient to bring down an avalanche of abuse upon its author. For one who committed so much of his work promptly to publication, the failure to publish the Sather Lectures can only mean that Momigliano was not satisfied with them. Although some parts appeared as articles, the lectures presumably lacked, in his eyes, the fresh and stimulating perspectives that were characteristic of virtually everything he saw fit to publish, and their posthumous publication reinforced that supposition.

When Momigliano came to Harvard for a term in 1965, under the auspices of the departments of classics and history, he offered two seminars that, like the Berkeley lectures, were clearly rooted in his earlier work. But even as he taught those seminars, the Harvard experience perceptibly changed Momigliano's intellectual orientation. Probably for the first time in his life he discovered an academic community that did not share (at least did not at that time) his own sense of the importance of Italian culture and thought after the Renaissance. There was virtually no student interest in his seminar on Vico, the eighteenth-century Italian philosopher. Momigliano complained bitterly on one occasion that professors of Italian in America were almost all ex-barbers. It was undoubtedly true that for Americans, even very educated ones, in the 1960s an allusion to Italians suggested principally the Pope, the Mafia, or immigrant labor. It was a rude shock for Momigliano to realize that a nation such as the United States, which had been built in part on the foundations laid down by ancient Rome, should have so little interest in the civilization of modern Italy. In subsequent decades the situation has changed dramatically, and Italian culture of the modern era is not only widely appreciated in America but now very fashionable. There can be no doubt that Momigliano himself played some part in effecting this change as he taught and lectured with increasing frequency in the United States throughout the '70s and '80s. The problem of the relation between classical and modern Italy never deserted Momigliano, as can be seen from the lecture he delivered in Chicago just two years before his death: "Classical Scholarship for a Classical Country."

The other seminar which Momigliano gave in that term at Harvard in 1965 was on the odd collection of biographies of Roman emperors that is known as the *Augustan History*. These biographies, generally short, unreliable, and salacious, have posed problems for students of ancient history for centuries. Momigliano himself wrote one of the most influential modern articles on the subject, which he labeled "an unsolved problem of historical forgery." His choice of this topic for his other Harvard seminar reflected his deep reluctance to accept the new consensus that was forming around the opinion of Sir Ronald Syme that the *Augustan History* was the work of an impish scholar who deliberately and good-humoredly perpetrated a hoax on the literate world.

Momigliano was as deadly serious in his scholarship as he was ebullient in personal relations. He found it difficult to understand why anyone of erudition would waste his time writing bad biographies as a joke. Although he resisted Syme's view in print almost to the last, in that seminar of 1965 he proved markedly tolerant of views that diverged from his own. He formed a close rapport with the excellent group of students that gathered around him. That seminar could be described as his first major impact on American scholarship. At the same time, his students had their own impact on him by encouraging him to look away from the old preoccupations of the date and purpose of the *Augustan History* and to think more broadly in terms of ancient biography, the great models of Suetonius and Plutarch, and larger problems of characterization and personal description in the ancient world.

Three years later Harvard invited Momigliano back for one of the first sets of the newly established lectures in honor of Carl Newell Jackson. For this occasion Momigliano chose as his subject "The Development of Ancient Biography." His choice of subject was clearly dictated by his experience in the seminar of three years earlier, and this turning to biography represented a new direction in his research on the ancient world. Biography was an ideal subject for him because of his long-standing interest in the history of classical scholarship. He had himself contributed a series of important biographies of major scholars to the *Enciclopedia Italiana*, and these, as well as other memoirs of great figures of the past, profited from the warm humanity that Momigliano brought to his vast learning. This means that he came to the scholarly study of biography as a biographer himself.

Momigliano's audacity in fastening on the subject of biography in the late 1960s and early 1970s must be appreciated in the context of the academic historiography of that period. Biography and personality were very much out of fashion. Even intellectual history had died a slow death, and professors were generally beating the drums for social and economic history. But Momigliano went his own way. Such was the force of his scholarship, to say nothing of his personality, that others followed. Having retired from his chair at the University of London, Momigliano found ready audiences for his reflections in both the United States and in Italy. The topics that he chose for his seminars and lectures in these two countries, although separate, were interrelated. This undoubtedly tells us something about the mutually supportive stimulation provided by the two environments and their educational systems. In Pisa over many years he pursued a series of investigations of major scholars of the late nineteenth and early twentieth centuries—their work, their preoccupations, their intellectual legacy. This was a natural extension of his own earlier work as a biographer (with the *Enciclopedia Italiana* and elsewhere). In the United States Momigliano continued his work on biography as a genre, work he had really started there.

Stunned by the implications of a book called *Metahistory* by the American historian Hayden White, Momigliano also took up in America an attack across a broad front against the historicism that White espoused. For one who had for so much of his life been concerned with ideas, Momigliano appeared in his trans-Atlantic years as a great champion of facts and *Realien* against the view of history as rhetoric that was put forward in the writings of White. Once again Momigliano went his own way, and others followed.

Finally, in the American phase, Momigliano turned more and more, perhaps as a result of the increased attention he gave to the personality of scholars and the nature of biography, to the spiritual springs of human action. Now in his seventies, he took up the systematic study of religion as if he were a young scholar embarking on a career. The causes of this turn to religion as a subject of historical inquiry in Momigliano's final decade are inevitably complex, but the fact that he was spending so much of his time in the New World, which had spawned more than its share of religions (especially Mormonism and Christian Science, as well as a variety of exotic sects) certainly played a role. Another impetus came from Momigliano's distinguished colleague at the University of Chicago, Mircea Eliade, who invited him to contribute chapters on the historiography of religion as well as on ancient religion to his *Encyclopaedia of Religion*. This was a great challenge to Momigliano, one that caused him considerable difficulty, as he readily admitted to those who were close to him. He had already written some material for the *Cambridge Ancient History* on early Roman religion, but what Eliade required was something more wide-ranging and more accessible.

Religion and Momigliano, as displayed in the pages of *On Pagans, Jews, and Christians*, his last book, were in many ways an odd conjunction. He was not himself a noticeably religious person, although he knew his Bible well. He was obsessed by his own Jewishness, no doubt as a result of the terrible upheavals of the war; but it was an obsession that had little of the religious in it. In the first paper in *On Pagans, Jews, and Christians*, he declared emphatically and proudly that he saw nothing special in holy writ: "Let me admit from the start that I am rather impervious to any claim that sacred history poses problems which are not those of profane history. As a man trained from early days to read the Bible in Hebrew, Livy in Latin, and Herodotus in Greek, I have never found the task of interpreting the Bible any more or any less complex than that of interpreting Livy or Herodotus."

On one occasion when Momigliano attempted to explain the achievement of a great classical philologist in terms of religion, he made probably the most disastrous misinterpretation of his entire career. In his obituary of the classical scholar Eduard Fraenkel, Momigliano argued that this expatriate German Jew had spent his life in fulfilling the holy obligations of Judaism through his dedication to scholarship. Nothing could have been further from the truth. Fraenkel was indeed a Jew but preferred not to think about it, and in the end he took his own life rather than survive alone after the death of his wife. If there was any Jew for whom Judaism meant little, it was Fraenkel.

Momigliano's error in the Fraenkel matter and his own professed view of sacred texts help to explain some of the more surprising judgments that appear in *On Pagans, Jews, and Christians*. One thing he understood well from his own background was the hard work that observant Jews put into studying their religion. He knew that the education of a Jew took time and much reading, and similarly he knew that Christians had to be trained in the faith. For both, sacred texts had to be studied, pondered, and interrogated. He knew, too, that the pious, once educated, could engage in debate or even polemic, just as scholars do. And so religious education seemed to Momigliano an important part of understanding religion. It was not surprising, therefore, that he ran into serious problems when he turned his attention to paganism.

In one of his essays written for Eliade's *Encyclopaedia*, Momigliano tried to take account of competing cults and rituals, both official and private, in the world of paganism. After briefly enumerating exotic gods from Anatolia and Egypt, healing deities such as Asclepius, temple miracles, magic, astrology, and even Zoroastrianism, Momigliano wrote, "The real difficulties in understanding the atmosphere of paganism in the Roman Empire perhaps lie elsewhere. It remains a puzzle how, and how much, ordinary people were supposed to know about Roman religion. The same problem exists concerning the Greeks in relation to the religions of individual Greek cities.... People who tell us something about their own education, for example, Cicero, Horace, and Ovid, do not imply that it included a religious side." In his paper on ancient biography and the study of religion, Momigliano was driven again to the problem of the education of pagans in their own religion and concluded that the only way we could ever find out was through biography (or autobiography). "We need personal stories," he wrote, "whether biographical or autobiographical, personal education, personal religious commitments. Punctual relations between social life and personal experience (dreams included) are what we want to know." I suppose that the strange locution "punctual relations" means something like "points of contact."

The problem is simply that religious education, as it is known to Jews or, to a lesser extent, to Christians, did not exist in the upbringing of ancient pagans. Momigliano was trying to apply a category familiar to him from his own historical studies of Judaism to the Greeks and the Romans. Ultimately he recognized that this simply would not work.

He grappled with the problem once again in one of his more eccentric papers of the 1980s, a paper that begins in a characteristically insouciant way: "I woke up one winter morning to ask myself: 'What do I know about what people believed in Athens, Rome, and Jerusalem in the first century B.C.?'" This seemingly innocent question presupposed that there had to be a belief or beliefs shared by people in each of those three cities in the first century B.C. That was a highly questionable presupposition, and Momigliano found himself in even greater difficulty when he rephrased his question to take the form: "What was the place of Hope and Faith in Athens, Rome, and Jerusalem in the first century B.C.?" These concepts, which became so integral to Christian thought by way of Judaism in later centuries, scarcely provide the key to understanding the views of Greek and Roman pagans.

Momigliano found himself increasingly frustrated in trying to locate something that could be described as religious thought among the pagans. Practices, initiations, cultic rituals, sacrifices could all be described and assigned a role in their daily life, but religious education and any religious thought that might lie behind it were hard to find. Momigliano was far too perceptive a historian to confuse the ruminations of philosophers (Plato, Aristotle, or Cicero in his *De divinatione*) with the kind of reflection he had in mind, but philosophical writing about the gods was just about all there was. This did not form the basis of a religious education. So ultimately Momigliano was forced to the conclusion that somehow the Jews, and by extension the Christians, were different: "The mere fact that one had to study in order to be pious is a strange notion which made Judaism increasingly intellectual—not what cults were known for in the Graeco-Roman world. It favored separation of the learned from the ignorant, and it caused (and allowed) basic doctrinal disagreements; in the end it introduced schism and excommunication. But, to confine ourselves to the first century B.C., we should recognize that, while in Athens and Rome thinking about religion usually made people less religious, among Jews the more you thought about religion, the more religious you became."

Cultic practices, rituals, processions, and sacrifices were religion as action rather than religion as theology or belief. Piety in these terms was always difficult for Momigliano to comprehend, and no amount of personal biography would ever help to make it more comprehensible. The cults of the emperors in the Roman world have long been an intractable subject for historians of antiquity, but the anthropological approach, as represented by Simon Price's important book on the imperial cult in Asia Minor (*Rituals and Power*, 1984), has provided a more persuasive interpretation of the acts that comprised the cult. Price's work appeared after Momigliano was already well advanced on his own. Although he was quick to grasp its importance, ritual and ceremony, like the archaeological remains that allow us to document it, were not congenial subjects for Momigliano, who was above all a scholar of texts and ideas. Momigliano was more at home in a bookshop than in a museum, in a library than at an excavation site.

Momigliano once told me that it was obvious that the Christians must have fully understood the imperial cult because, after all, they too believed that a man was a god. I have often been troubled by this arresting observation, which seems to me so patently wrong even though on the surface it is so entirely reasonable. At the least it shows the dangers of comparing the rituals of polytheism with the theology of monotheism. A similar kind of disconcerting rationalism lay behind Momigliano's attempt to understand why monotheism was not conducive to a coherent universal state (with everyone believing in one god), whereas polytheism seemed to accommodate easily a multinational state such as the Roman Empire. Most historians of the past had scarcely thought to pose such issues.

As a result of his extensive reading, Momigliano was also too ready to believe that there was a lively hostility to the Christians on the part of pagans from the second century A.D. onward. He could see anti-Christian polemic in a passing jest of the satirist Lucian and, more seriously, infer anti-Christian polemic when pagan writers said nothing at all about the Christians. He was thus able to argue most implausibly that Diogenes Laertius wrote his *Lives of the Greek Philosophers* as a defense of Greek paganism against the increasingly sophisticated Platonic theologians of early Christianity. But the shrill polemics of the early Christian apologists reflected their status as a minority wanting to be recognized. The pagans had no need for such diatribes and chose most of the time not to notice the Christians unless they got in the way—something the martyrs learned to do with ever-increasing skill.

Momigliano's problems in wrestling with the history of religion arose from his essentially intellectual view of it. A moving survey of the Jews of Italy takes up in detail the intellectual leadership of Jews in his homeland in the nineteenth and twentieth centuries. There are affecting examples from his own family—Felice Momigliano, who was a professor of philosophy at the University of Rome, and Attilio Momigliano, who was an interpreter of Dante, Ariosto, and Manzoni. This is a history of Jews as intellectuals with Judaism as no more than a background. The point becomes very clear in the penultimate paragraph of this survey when Momigliano admits, "Talmudism had practically ceased to interest Italian Jews at the end of the eighteenth century.... In fact, Jewish culture was seldom transmitted in the sense we Jews intend it to be transmitted. If the Jews themselves know so little about their own Judaism, they can hardly complain that their neighbors understand it even less."

Momigliano's esteem for great Jewish intellectuals and scholars was best exemplified in my experience on the day when I took him to meet Shelomo Goitein, the distinguished commentator on the Arabic documents of the Cairo Geniza and the Jewish society it revealed. In a remarkably perceptive paper on Gershom Scholem, reprinted in Momigliano's last book, he had speculated on similarities and differences in the German background of Scholem and Goitein—even though he had at that time never met Goitein. In November of 1981, when the Goiteins received both of us for afternoon tea, Momigliano had the satisfaction of knowing that his speculations about Goitein were all completely accurate. The respect that Momigliano showed to this formidable Jewish Arabist was as moving to witness as it was instructive. Goitein, the older scholar, treated Momigliano with the solicitude of a professor toward a favorite student, and Momigliano responded with respectful admiration. Shortly afterward I received a letter from Momigliano: "You organized a perfect day, if perfect days can be organized, and I am most grateful. The visit to Goitein will be something to treasure for both of us." I have never seen anyone before whom Momigliano was so humble. The meeting with Goitein obviously touched something deep. What that was, I suspect, was a total and uncompromising dedication to scholarship.

Until his final decade Momigliano had never confronted the inadequacy of explaining religion as an intellectual activity. *On Pagans, Jews, and Christians* is a memorial of that confrontation. His attempt to understand polytheism exposed many sensitive nerves in himself. He had come to these new and disquieting problems in the American years by way of the study of biography that he launched in the Harvard lectures of 1968 and through the invitation of Eliade to contribute to the *Encyclopaedia of Religion*. He was nourished in his studies by the companionship and stimulation of the Committee on Social Thought at the University of Chicago and by the many friends and colleagues whom he had come to know

over more than twenty years of visits to America. Apart from the extraordinary arsenal of erudition that Momigliano brought to every subject he
touched, his work was always distinguished by the clarity and candor of
the questions he posed. Looking for the views of an ancient Athenian on
faith and hope in the first century B.C. may seem bizarre or even pointless, but it was a stage along a road of historical inquiry that many other
historians would have hurried past.

Momigliano's last years were devoted to arguably the most difficult
studies he had ever undertaken. It is possible that he might never have
undertaken them at all without the support of the environment in Chicago. Certainly his last book is as much an intellectual autobiography as
it is a work of scholarship. And, as Momigliano himself has taught us,
the personal revelations are exactly what we need to understand such an
extraordinary man and the world in which he wrote.

# CHAPTER SIXTEEN

# A Modern Aesop

*Travels with Herodotus,* by Ryszard Kapuściński

RYSZARD KAPUŚCIŃSKI DIED IN 2007 AT THE HEIGHT of his powers. Beginning as a local reporter for the Polish newspaper *Sztandar Młodych,* or the *Banner of Youth,* he rose to international eminence with his reports from many of the most turbulent places on the planet, and at the age of seventy-four, when he died, he was universally acknowledged to be as great a writer as reporter. He was a journalist like no other, an incomparable observer whose literary brilliance transformed his reporting into something like the magical realism of fiction—into magical realist nonfiction, which in some ways has an even greater sting.

Emerging from the stifling repression of communist Poland in the 1950s, Kapuściński took up assignments in India, China, East Asia, sub-Saharan Africa, and Latin America. After his tour in China he switched employers and joined the Polish Press Agency, which gathered news and intelligence from all parts of the world. Amid so many alien cultures Kapuściński saw not only what was happening abroad, but also what the West needed to know. With the instincts of a novelist and an allusive style forged under the eyes of Polish censors, he wrote with equal facility about Soviet penal colonies, the fall of the Shah of Iran, the court of Haile Selassie (in an amazing book called *The Emperor*), and a bloody conflict between Honduras and El Salvador over soccer.

In 2004 Kapuściński published the last and perhaps the most unusual of all his books, *Travels with Herodotus*. This is a work that is full of autobiographical reflections—therefore highly personal, and yet no less full of historiographical reflections about the Greek "father of history"—that constantly keep the reader at a distance from Kapuściński himself. This double engine of autobiography and Herodotean reading generates an almost Brechtian effect of alienation. In the end we learn relatively little about either Kapuściński or Herodotus. Yet the oscillation from one to the other generates the kind of enchantment that only magic kingdoms can create. Kapuściński's premise, however, is that there is no Shangri-la. Although everything is exotic, it is frequently barbaric. Kapuściński's foreigners are as inscrutable and merciless as those in Herodotus. The question that keeps arising is why we should be reading now about all these strange peoples, separated by two and a half millennia.

The author himself is the common denominator, of course. It is he who experienced the bewildering cultures of India, China, and Africa, as they are described in this book, and it is he who is assiduously reading Herodotus in all those disparate places. The ostensible reason for this conjunction is that when Kapuściński received his first assignment as a journalist outside Poland, his supervisor presented him with a copy of Herodotus for reading along the way. The gift proved to be portentous. He would have us believe that he kept company with Herodotus throughout his journeys for more than two decades after his first trip abroad in 1956. Just as he begins with the assignment that first took him beyond the borders of Poland, he begins at the same time with the opening of Herodotus's investigations. In a dazzling manipulation of narrative structure, he traverses the ancient historian's world in tandem with his own travels. The Massagetae and the Scythians stand side by side with the Indonesians, Congolese, and Iranians, and we move seamlessly from a concert by Louis Armstrong in Khartoum to the storming of Babylon by Darius the Great. With unerring instinct Kapuściński brings his own story to an end just as he takes us through the grand finale of Herodotus, with its account of the Greek defeat of the Persian invaders under Xerxes. In the last pages we are artfully taken to Bodrum in modern Turkey, which just happens to be the site of ancient Halicarnassus, the home of Herodotus.

Kapuściński romanticizes Herodotus in a traditionally European way. Since the historian is imagined to have come from "a land of sun, warmth, and light, of olive trees and vineyards," Kapuściński cannot resist the idea that "someone born here must naturally have a good heart, an open mind, a healthy body, a consistently cheerful disposition." He thinks that Herodotus, as a child of his culture and his climate, sat at hospitable tables "in large groups of a warm evening to eat cheese and olives, drink cool wine, converse." This is Goethe's *Kennst du das Land, wo die Zitronen blühn?*—"Do you know the country where the lemon trees bloom?"—but with a Greek referent and a Polish accent.

Kapuściński asks us to believe that the events described by Herodotus so absorbed him when he was in the Congo "that at times I experienced the dread of the approaching war between the Greeks and the Persians more vividly than I did the events of the current Congolese conflict, which I was assigned to cover." Yet this is a conflict that Kapuściński himself characterizes by "frequent eruption of gunfights, the constant danger of arrest, beatings, and death, and the pervasive climate of uncertainty, ambiguity, and unpredictability." He says that "the absolute worst could happen here at any moment and in any place." Did all that really pale before the Persian Wars?

One may question whether Kapuściński was really reading Herodotus all the time he was covering the trouble spots of the globe for the more than twenty years chronicled in this book. Yet he is clearly concerned to impress upon his reader the impact that Herodotus had upon him and to draw, by the constant collocation with himself, a parallel. We have to wonder what the point of this exercise is. Kapuściński drops important clues as he goes along. The first is his emphasis on the international scope of Herodotus's inquiries. (It is worth remembering that the Greek word *historiê* for this particular historian means "inquiry" or "investigation," rather than what we would call history.) For Kapuściński, Herodotus "enters the stage as a visionary on a world scale, an imagination capable of encompassing planetary dimensions—in short, as the first globalist." A little later, multiculturalism is added to globalism as part of Herodotus's baggage. This multiculturalism "was a living, pulsating tissue in which nothing was permanently set or defined, but which continually transformed itself, mutated, gave rise to new relationships and contexts." And from Herodotus the globalist and Herodotus the multiculturalist we move next to Herodotus the journalist: "How did he work, i.e., what interested him, how did he approach his sources, what did he ask them, what did they say in reply? I was quite consciously trying to learn the art of reportage, and Herodotus struck me as a valuable teacher."

Finally, toward the end of his book, Kapuściński opens up something quite different in Herodotus. When asked what struck him most about the Greek history, he replies, "I answer that it is its tragic dimension." This leads him to a comparison with Herodotus's contemporaries— Aeschylus, Sophocles, and Euripides. And comparisons with drama and myth lead straight to the fundamental problem of sorting out history from fiction. Herodotus discovered long ago, says Kapuściński, that "people remember what they want to remember, not what actually happened." Accordingly, "getting through to the past itself, the past as it really was, is impossible....The past does not exist. There are only infinite renderings of it." This explicit repudiation of the old ideal of objectivity about history, of Ranke's *wie es eigentlich gewesen* ("as it really was"), encapsulates the lessons that Kapuściński draws from Herodotus as he understands him.

Not everyone has read Herodotus this way, as an early hero of subjectivity and relativism. Some have seen him as the first anthropologist, who gave the results of his fieldwork among alien peoples such as the Egyptians or the Scythians. But at the same time he brought his work to a triumphalist conclusion with the Greeks' resounding defeat of the Persians. There was nothing relativist about that. For Herodotus it really did happen, and it was important. The very directness of his reportage is an impediment to Kapuściński's view of him. Herodotus often says he cannot vouch for the accuracy of what he reports, though he reports it all the same—but when he can be sure, he tells us what happened. Such transparent reportage poses a problem for Kapuściński, and may, in the end, explain why his Herodotus is made to look increasingly like Kapuściński himself.

In the opening pages of his book, before we hear of the fateful gift from his supervisor at *Sztandar Młodych*, Kapuściński recalls that he attended the lectures on ancient Greece by Professor Izabela Bieżuńska-Małowist at Warsaw University in 1951. He found no trace of Herodotus in what he describes as his "careful notes" on these lectures, but he assumes that he must have made a momentary appearance. It happens that I knew Bieżuńska-Małowist, and she was a superb and widely admired scholar. Perhaps Kapuściński missed a lecture or two in those dark days at the university, but we can have no doubt that Herodotus appeared significantly in that course at Warsaw. Even if the city lay in ruins, as Kapuściński says, and libraries had gone up in flames, Bieżuńska-Małowist knew her Herodotus well and would have given him the prominence he deserved, even with due regard for the ever-vigilant secret police.

In beginning as he does, Kapuściński wants to draw attention to the suppression of the translation of Herodotus that Seweryn Hammer had made in the mid-1940s and deposited with the Czytelnik publishing house. He knows that the text had been sent to the typesetter in the autumn of 1951, but the book did not actually appear until the end of 1954, after Stalin's death. He assumes that a Polish censor had blocked its publication, and hence, when the translation came into his hands just before he left the country in 1956, he at last had access to this forbidden fruit. Kapuściński suggests that Herodotus had been suppressed "because all our thinking, our looking and reading, was governed during those years by an obsession with allusion." Every word had "a double meaning, a false bottom, a hidden significance."

I must say that reading the text of Herodotus as a text "utterly different from what was clearly written" takes a colossal effort on the part of someone reared outside a totalitarian regime. Herodotus was the most direct and candid, if sometimes credulous, of all ancient historians. If there was one thing he was not, it was allusive for the purpose of conveying hidden meanings. Still, his tales of bloodthirsty tyrants and insatiable imperialist rulers could indeed be read as cautionary for a modern regime, and conceivably the Polish censors might have been fearful of the inspiration readers might draw from reading about Periander, Croesus, or Xerxes.

In an interview in 1997, Kapuściński acknowledged that he practiced Aesopian writing, by which he meant that one text served, rather like a fable by Aesop, as a means of conveying to knowledgeable readers a message about something else. His book on Haile Selassie, by his own admission, was "not about Ethiopia or Haile Selassie—rather, it's about the Central Committee of the Communist Party." In taking Herodotus as his mentor and guide during his many travels as a journalist, he is both claiming for himself the Greek historian's multiculturalism and reporting style and, at the same time, imputing his own Aesopian methods to his ancient predecessor. *Travels with Herodotus* is a beguiling work in which Kapuściński undertakes to cleanse the ambivalence of his own journalism by examining it through the lens of his Greek predecessor. He wants his voice to be Herodotus's voice, and this is probably why he can say, "I actually became attached not so much to the book, as to its voice, the persona of its author." The identification of the two becomes even more pronounced when Kapuściński writes that Herodotus "decides, probably toward the end of his life, to write a book because he realizes that he has amassed such an enormous trove of stories and facts that unless he preserves them, they will simply vanish." This is exactly what Kapuściński chose to do near the end of his own life, and to validate his enterprise by the linkage with Herodotus.

But the Aesopian drive, which Herodotus utterly lacked, never left Kapuściński. Through the interleaved tales from Herodotean antiquity and his own travels there are clearly subtexts that any alert reader is bound to detect. Kapuściński obviously could not stop himself from including the kind of double meanings that were natural to a man who had grown up in a universe of repression and persecution. Consider his retelling of Darius's campaign against the Scythians, who, as Kapuściński says, loved the steppe and boundless space. Their king told Darius that because they have neither cities nor farmland, they have nothing to defend, and therefore they saw no need to go into battle. Kapuściński accurately describes the resulting confusion of Darius as "the collision of two military styles, two structures." One is the monolithic organization of the Persians' regular army, whereas the other is "the loose, mobile, ever-shifting configurations of small tactical cells." The latter is "an amorphous army of shadows, of phantoms, of thin air." Kapuściński was writing after the invasion of Iraq by the so-called coalition of the willing, to which Poland provided a conspicuous contingent.

Again in retelling the story of Cyrus's invasion of the Massagetai, north of Iran along the Amu Darya, Kapuściński says that in sending first the most unfit and ill-equipped of his army against the Massagetai, "he is in effect condemning these people to death." Darius similarly used weak and ill-prepared troops as part of a prearranged conspiracy to break down the resistance of Babylon. After an initial wave in which a thousand men were easily annihilated, Darius sent another two thousand, who were decimated according to Darius's plan. The merciless exploitation of young soldiers was evidently another theme that appealed to Kapuściński Aesopian instincts. As he remarks, "It is an interesting subject: superfluous people in the service of a brute power."

This interesting subject provokes reflections on spying as well as on warfare. Someone who is searching for significance in life can, according to Kapuściński, find life more meaningful if he works covertly for the authorities and thereby acquires "the comforting sense of immunity." In this way, "the dictatorial powers, meantime, have in him an inexpensive—free, actually—yet zealous and omnipresent agent-tentacle." Here is the psychology of all those who worked for the Stasi in East Germany or for Polish intelligence under the communists. Kapuściński is at his most Aesopian in this passage, since we now know that he himself worked as an intelligence agent for the Polish communists during the travels that he describes in this book. That is probably why he supposed that a man in Cairo who offered to show him a mosque had to have been an undercover agent. Because he thought that a visit to a mosque was preferable to a visit to the police station, he accepted the man's offer, only to be robbed after climbing a winding staircase to the top of the minaret. This episode, oddly reminiscent of Hitchcock's *Vertigo*, suggests that Kapuściński was more likely to imagine that a solicitous man in the street was a spy than a thief. That is highly revealing. It is also very unlike Herodotus.

What Kapuściński shares with Herodotus is his insatiable curiosity about other peoples and other cultures. If some readers of Herodotus have found him naïve in his uncritical registering of strange customs and tales, Kapuściński is naïve in the same way. He dares to pose questions that a more sophisticated writer would avoid. "What sort of a child is Herodotus?" he asks. "Does he smile at everyone and willingly extend his hand, or does he sulk and hide in the folds of his mother's garments? ... What did a little Greek living two and a half thousand years ago play with? A scooter carved out of wood? Did he build sand castles at the edge of the sea?" This last question, which Kapuściński raises early in his book, proves to be portentous at the end, when he tries to explain Herodotus's (and doubtless his own) passion for travel and foreign peoples. "Where did this passion of Herodotus come from? Perhaps from the question that arose in a child's mind, the one about where ships come from. Children playing in the sand at the edge of a bay can see a ship suddenly appear far away on the horizon line and grow larger and larger as it sails toward them. Where did it originate? Most children do not ask themselves this question. But one, making castles out of sand, suddenly might."

The childlike wonder of Herodotus clearly appealed to Kapuściński, who cultivated it in himself as an antidote to all the Aesopian deviousness with which he grew up. Sometimes it rings hollow, as in the vacuous passages on olive trees and conversation under the Mediterranean sun. Sometimes it is worse than hollow, as when Kapuściński writes sympathetically about the recent theory of the Afro-Egyptian origins of Greek civilization. But at other times it has a startling clarity and power. Amid the collapse of colonial government in the Congo, when Belgian administrators were being replaced by "a dark, deranged power, which most frequently assumed the guise of drunken Congolese military police," Kapuściński dares to say "how dangerous freedom is in the absence of hierarchy and order." As a Pole who grew up under communism, he must have thought often about the relation of hierarchy to freedom. When he comments on the dangers of freedom in the Congo, his words inevitably, and probably consciously, carry an Aesopian burden. But he says nothing about how the hierarchy and order that he wants should be imposed in order to allow freedom to flourish.

So ultimately this enchanting autobiography, in which a courageous and innovative journalist positions himself as a twentieth-century Herodotus, seems sadly superficial. It has the evanescence of a child's fantasy or a conjuring trick. Underneath its shimmering prose, in which Kapuściński interweaves tales from ancient Greece with the horrors of the modern world, beats the unquiet heart of a fundamentally decent man and an uncommonly gifted observer. In the end the reader fails to learn very much about him, and that was doubtless his intention. But he is an unforgettable companion, even if he shows himself to be no Herodotus. The old Greek had, after all, a tremendous story to tell: the first global conflict between East and West, and the Greeks' ultimate triumph over the Persian invader. History did not furnish Kapuściński with so satisfying a conclusion, or indeed with any conclusion at all.

# CHAPTER SEVENTEEN

# AUDEN ON THE FALL
# OF ROME

WHEN THE EDITORS OF *LIFE* MAGAZINE PROPOSED that W. H. Auden write an essay on the fall of Rome,[1] they caught the poet at a moment when this subject was much on his mind. Someone perhaps knew this, and knew as well that it was a subject that had occupied him on and off over several decades. Auden wrote the essay in March 1966, but, regrettably, *Life* rejected the piece, and it was published for the first time, together with this introduction, in 1995.[2]

1. A series of essays under the collective title, "The Romans," ran in *Life* from Mar. 3–June 17, 1966.

2. Auden typed the text himself double-spaced on 17 folios of 8-1/2 × 11 inch paper, and, either then or later, made some corrections, deletions, and additions in pen. Although his essay was rejected (and presumably sent back to him), *Life* retained a Xerox copy for their records. The magazine had a policy of burning all defunct files once they were ten years old. The text of this essay comes from the *Life* Xerox of the original typescript, retrieved from the magazine's archives by a senior editor around the end of 1976, shortly before the files for 1966 were due to be destroyed. (The original typescript probably does not survive.) The title is not written in Auden's hand, though the words may be Auden's. The Xerox from which this text is taken is now in the collection of Robert A. Wilson. After *Life* had rejected the essay, Auden's New York agents, Curtis Brown, tried to get it into print elsewhere: they submitted the piece to *The Atlantic Monthly* on Aug. 25, 1966. But on Sept. 13, 1966, that magazine also declined it.

Writing in *The New Republic* in September of 1944, Auden had offered his observations on the long road that led from Augustan Rome to the Augustinian city of God. He was reviewing a reprint of a book by Charles Norris Cochrane titled *Christianity and Classical Culture*, first published in 1940. Auden acknowledged having read this book many times, and he added, "[M]y conviction of its importance to the understanding not only of the epoch with which it is concerned, but also of our own, has increased with each rereading."[3] With its high-flying ideas, abstract thought, and murky argumentation, Cochrane's book was heavy going even at the time, but it was widely admired in a world that showed great respect for Toynbee's *A Study of History*.

In the last years of the Second World War and the years that followed, any synthesis that appeared to offer a comforting, yet profound, explanation of the violent upheavals of history provided welcome reading. There can be few today who read Cochrane's book, despite the obvious importance of its theme. The grand progression that he postulated from "reconstruction" to "renovation" and on to "regeneration" is hardly likely to persuade a historian of the 1990s. But it clearly spoke to Auden and, in particular, to Auden the Christian. Whenever he returned to the theme of the Roman Empire and its apparent collapse, the shadow of Cochrane was all too visible.

In 1944 Auden believed that the present time was "not so unlike the age of Augustine."[4] He drew attention to the planned society, rampant criminality, bureaucracy, religious persecution, and even "a new Constantinism," which would impose religious instruction in the schools in order to cure juvenile delinquency. Self-satisfied Christians of the fifth century A.D. were presiding over the dissolution of the world they thought they had saved, and the parallel that Auden saw with his own time soon found poetic expression in his poem "The Fall of Rome" (1947). There, for example, he represented self-righteousness, selfishness, and bureaucracy in tough and sardonic verses:

Cerebrotonic Cato may
Extol the Ancient Disciplines,
But the muscle-bound Marines
Mutiny for food and pay.

3. "Augustus to Augustine," *Forewords and Afterwords* (New York: Vintage, 1989), 33. Henceforth *FA*.
4. "Augustus to Augustine," *FA* 39.

Caesar's double-bed is warm
As an unimportant clerk
Writes *I DO NOT LIKE MY WORK*
On a pink official form.[5]

Auden shared with the twentieth-century Greek poet C. P. Cavafy a poetic interest in the declining Roman Empire and an awareness of its relevance to contemporary events. It is not surprising to find Auden writing a preface for a new translation of Cavafy's work in 1961. He was clearly impressed by Cavafy's perception, highly unusual when he wrote, that the Christians enjoyed a traditional pagan way of life with considerably more brio than most of the pagans who struggled against them in late antiquity. "After Constantine," wrote Auden, "it was the Christian who had a better chance than the Pagan of getting on in the world, and the Pagan, even if not persecuted, who became the object of social ridicule."[6] Like Auden himself, Cavafy was both Christian and homosexual, and explicit about both. It is clear that Auden detected a kindred spirit, even if he was unable to read the Greek poet in his original language. The encounter with Cavafy evidently moved Auden to adopt a noticeably more positive view of the early Christian Empire than he had formed from his repeated readings of Cochrane's work.

In late 1965 the editors of the newly established *New York Review of Books* had the inspired idea of inviting Auden to review a recent set of lectures delivered in Belfast by the Regius Professor of Greek at Oxford, E. R. Dodds, under the title *Pagan and Christian in an Age of Anxiety.*[7] This book paid obvious tribute to Auden's *Age of Anxiety,* and it took up Cochrane's themes in a far more lucid and original way than Cochrane's own work. Dodds allowed Auden to find a middle ground between his original rejection of the Christian Empire and the more sympathetic treatment evoked by Cavafy. Dodds had proclaimed, in fairness to his readers, that he was an agnostic who could not share "the standpoint of those who see the triumph of Christianity as the divine event to which the whole creation moved."[8] In his review, published early in 1966, Auden responded to Dodds's challenge by declaring at the outset that

---

5. *Collected Poems* (London: Faber and Faber, 1991), 333. Henceforth, *CP91.*
6. "C. P. Cavafy," *FA* 342.
7. Cambridge: Cambridge University Press, 1965.
8. Quoted by Auden, "Heresies," *FA* 41.

he was an Episcopalian but did not believe that Christianity triumphed either.[9]

A clear echo of Auden's reading of Cochrane can be heard in his judgment, "I consider the adoption of Christianity as the official state religion, backed by the coercive powers of the state, however desirable it may have seemed at the time, to have been a 'bad,' that is to say, an un-Christian thing."[10] But he then went on to put in a good word for Irenaeus, who came to the defense of the heretical Montanists "not, surely, because he agreed with them but because, gentle soul that he was, he disliked persecution, even of cranks."[11]

Toward the end of the Dodds review, Auden returned to the positive side of the Christianization of the Roman world. He emphasized that the Church was open to all men, "without regard to social class, education, or their past lives."[12] In a truly Cavafian spirit, he declared that the Christian faith was really a more "this-worldly" religion than any of its competitors. It was obvious that, in reflecting on Dodds's lectures, Auden had enlarged his positive assessment of Christianity in the final epoch of the Roman Empire.

Clearly Auden was a brilliant choice for the *Life* essay, and it is sad that the editors found the piece he provided unsuitable for their audience. The essay is a thoughtful and exciting extension of Auden's previous reflections. Some parts of it, especially the pages on classical idealism, are warmed-over Cochrane without much change from what Auden had written in his review of 1944. But there is much that is fresh and original. Auden himself saw fit to link this essay with his earlier work by ending it with a complete quotation of the poem "The Fall of Rome" from 1947.

In 1966 people could still talk about the fall of Rome without embarrassment. The expression came straight from Gibbon, and for two centuries historians took it for granted that Rome had declined and fallen. Most would probably have agreed with Gibbon in blaming the Christians and the barbarians for what happened. But with the publication of Peter Brown's *The World of Late Antiquity* in 1971[13] and a rising tide of relativism in historical interpretations of the Roman Empire, the Gibbonian view

---

9. Ibid.
10. Ibid.
11. Ibid.
12. Ibid., 47.
13. London: Thames and Hudson, 1971.

of decline and fall soon yielded to a vision of restructuring, regrouping, shifting of boundaries, and the emergence of new perspectives that transformed the end of Rome into the rise of late antiquity. Transformation replaced decline and fall.

Auden's essay stands interestingly on the brink of this great change in the historical interpretation of Gibbon's problem. He knew his *Decline and Fall* well and borrowed, although with evident discomfort, from Gibbon's rosy account of the Antonine age. He cites Gibbon on occasion and even rephrases the famous lines at the end of chapter 2 of the *Decline and Fall* on the poverty of social and intellectual life in the second and third centuries A.D.[14] Two hundred years earlier Gibbon himself would have had no difficulty in subscribing to Auden's observation, "the price paid for this tranquillity was a general decline in intellectual curiosity and invention."

But, significantly, amid the echoes of Gibbon and Cochrane, there are unmistakable adumbrations of the new view of late antiquity that was to emerge in the 1970s. Auden was making his way toward this interpretation by way of Cavafy and the lectures of Dodds. Both are quoted in his essay for *Life*—with reference to Neoplatonism (Dodds was, in fact, among the most distinguished scholars of Neoplatonism in his day), and with reference to the puritanical views of Julian the Apostate as ridiculed in a poem by Cavafy. Auden had already quoted this poem in his introduction of 1961:

> Was it possible that they [the Christians of Antioch] would ever renounce
> Their lovely way of living; the variety of their
> Daily amusement; their magnificent
> Theatre where they found the union of art
> With the erotic propensities of the flesh![15]

Auden now gives the translation of John Mavrogordato, rather than the Rae Dalven version for which he had provided an introduction. Although the poem has been still better translated by Edmund Keeley,

14. Edward Gibbon, *The History of the Decline and Fall of the Roman Empire*, ed. D. Womersley (Penguin, 1994) I: 83–84: "If we except the inimitable Lucian, this age of indolence passed away without having produced a single writer of original genius.... The decline of genius was soon followed by the corruption of taste."

15. "C. P. Cavafy," *FA* 343.

the Mavrogordato translation well conveys Cavafy's admiration for the sensuality of Christian life when it was threatened by the pagan austerities of Julian. This positive view of the early Christian Empire clearly found a resonance in Auden.

Still more arresting is Auden's own assessment of the role of Christianity in reviving the cultural life of the Empire from the torpor into which both Gibbon and he believed that it had fallen. In his essay for *Life*, Auden, the avowed Episcopalian, declared with pride, "One may like or dislike Christianity, but no one can deny that it was Christianity and the Bible which raised western literature from the dead." In a fervent reformulation of the argument at the end of his review of Dodds, he developed the social implications of Christian doctrine:

> A faith which held that the Son of God was born in a manger, associated himself with persons of humble station in an unimportant Province, and died a slave's death, yet did this to redeem all men, rich and poor, free men and slaves, citizens and barbarians, required a completely new way of looking at human beings; if all are children of God and equally capable of salvation, then all, irrespective of status or talent, vice or virtue, merit the serious attention of the poet, the novelist, and the historian.

These lines, like virtually all Auden's critical prose, reflect his personal tastes. It is where these tastes are kept from view, as in the routine paragraphs on ancient technology or the comments on classical idealism borrowed straight from Cochrane, that Auden's piece becomes disappointingly pedestrian. But the passion and originality that suffuse most of it show him grappling with issues that had concerned him deeply for at least twenty-five years (after he first read Cochrane). Several important themes that show up here were to reappear again in the poetic work of Auden's final years.

Some of these themes are so prominent that the *Life* essay can serve as a kind of commentary on them. For example, in the second paragraph of the essay on the fall of Rome, Auden admits, "By heredity and temperament, I think of the Romans with distaste." But he then goes on to say, "The only classical latin poet I *really* like is Horace." He denounces Roman architecture and expresses a preference for the "rolling English road." It is perhaps not surprising that the greatest master of twentieth-century lyric in English should have admired the undisputed master of Latin lyric in antiquity. But this casual remark serves as a kind of prelude to a poem that Auden wrote two years later, "The Horatians." Here he competes with Horace on his own turf by writing verses based on a complex Horatian meter (Asclepiadean stanzas). His taste for the "rolling English road" is reaffirmed in this tribute to Horace as a poet with a knowledge of local topography, whose tastes "run to / small dinner-parties, small rooms, / and the tone of voice that suits them." He even manages to link his favorite poet with his Anglican faith:

> how many have
> found in the Anglican Church
> your Maecenas who enabled
>
> a life without cumber.[16]

This luminous tribute to Horace of 1968 was echoed again in one of Auden's last poems, titled "A Thanksgiving." These are lines in which Auden contemplates the poetic models that had inspired him over the years and those whom he now requires:

> Who are the tutors I need?
> Well, *Horace*, adroitest of makers,
> beeking in Tivoli.[17]

Apart from Horace, Auden confesses that in his opinion there were not many interesting writers in the Roman Empire or late antiquity. He does manage to single out the *Pervigilium Veneris* as a little masterpiece (a judgment in which most critics would concur). But the great surprise in his review of Latin literature is his praise for the poet Maximian: "finally, in the sixth century after the West has fallen, one really remarkable poet, Maximian." Auden strengthens his observation by quoting from one of Maximian's elegies just before the concluding section of his article. A girl in Constantinople bursts into tears upon discovering the ageing poet impotent. When the writer tells her that his personal inadequacy need hardly cause her such grief, she admits that her tears are really not for her own deprivation but for "the general chaos." She represents Maximian's failure as a symbol of the creative failure of the world at large.

It is nothing less than astonishing that Auden should see in Maximian one of the few great poets of the late age of Rome. Many learned classical

16. *CP91* 772.
17. *CP91* 892.

scholars have gone to their graves without ever having read a line of Maximian's verses or even having heard his name. Possibly the brief account in F. J. E. Raby's *History of Secular Latin Poetry in the Middle Ages* (1934) led Auden to this highly obscure poet. It is not easy to come by a text of his verse in Latin, let alone in translation. Classical scholars who have actually studied the elegies of Maximian have generally not thought much of them. The standard classical encyclopedia pronounces this poet *ein mittelmässiger Kopf* ("a mediocre fellow").[18] But it is easy to see why he appealed to Auden. This is a poet of declining powers, who sees himself and the world around him disintegrating, who tries to live with the passion he once felt and can no longer express. There is something unmistakably Horatian about the elegies of Maximian (who looks superficially more of an Ovidian). His complaint that he is no longer what he once was echoes the famous words of Horace in the first poem of the fourth book of *Odes* to the same effect, "*Non sum qualis eram*" (cf. Maximian, less stylishly, "*non sum qui fueram*"). These words must have spoken eloquently to Auden, who, at the end of his life, left those heartbreaking lines, first published by Edward Mendelson in the preface to *Thank You, Fog*:

> He still loves life
> But O O O O how he wishes
> The good Lord would take him.[19]

The quotation from E. R. Dodds in Auden's essay on the fall of Rome arose from a long-standing interest in Neoplatonism and Gnosticism. In 1966 he was convinced that the social unrest of the day—especially the drug culture of the hippies—bore some resemblance to the peculiarities of the philosophical movements of late antiquity that became, for most purposes, substitutes for religion. In 1972 Auden composed a poem for Dodds under the title "Nocturne." This poem, invoking young radicals plotting to blow up a building and airplanes imagined as metal mosquitoes, cries out for a lost innocence. There is a sense of doom, the advent of night, that echoes the pessimistic conclusion of the *Life* essay. There Auden wrote, "I have no idea what is actually going to happen before I die, except that I am not going to like it." The beginning of the poem for Dodds asks:

---

18. Pauly-Wissowa, *Realencyclopädie der classischen Altertumswissenschaft* 14.2 (Stuttgart: Druckenmüller, 1930), 2533.

19. W. H. Auden, *Thank You, Fog* (London: Random House, 1974), viii.

Do squamous and squiggling fish,
down in their fireless houses,
notice nightfall? Perhaps not.[20]

In the following year, the year of his death, Auden took up the subject again in "No, Plato, No," a kind of poetic reprise of all that Cochrane had taught about matter and mind. In fact, the pessimism with which Auden ends his *Life* essay includes a condemnation of public taste for prehistoric archaeology. This judgment is, in its way, as deeply felt as Auden's condemnation of heroin addicts and beats. For him it was Greco-Roman archaeology that held human interest. The taste for the prehistoric (Neolithic or Bronze Age) represented yet another departure from the humanity he prized above all.

This passing reference to archaeology foretells another of Auden's latest poems. In *Thank You, Fog* there are verses from 1973 entitled simply "Archaeology." It becomes clear here that what directed Auden to the whole subject of excavation was the problem of ascertaining from the remains left behind what people long ago were really like:

From murals and statues
we get a glimpse of what
the Old Ones bowed down to,
but cannot conceit
in what situations they blushed
or shrugged their shoulders.

What can one infer about rituals—some abominable, but some perhaps not?

There's nothing the Crucified
would like less
than butchery to appease Him.[21]

How, in short, do we know the past? History may not be the answer. In his last years, Auden seems to have suspected that history was apt to get everything wrong. He did not want succeeding generations to believe everything they read in history books. He must have remembered that Gibbon had defined history as "little more than the register of the

20. *CP91* 879.
21. *CP91* 895–96.

crimes, follies, and misfortunes of mankind."[22] Archaeology of the right kind could therefore be a kind of consolation:

From Archaeology
one moral, at least, may be drawn,
to wit, that all
our school text-books lie.
What they call History
is nothing to vaunt of,
being made, as it is,
by the criminal in us:
goodness is timeless.[23]

## The Fall of Rome

*W. H. Auden*

The Roman Empire is an historical phenomenon towards which no Westerner can feel either indifferent or impartial. My distant ancestors were barbarians from Scandinavia, which was never under Roman rule. I was born in Britain where the Roman culture was not strong enough to survive the Anglo-saxon invasions, and which broke away from the Roman Church in the sixteenth century. It must be significant, I think, that the countries which went Protestant at the Reformation were precisely those which had been least influenced by the culture of *pagan* Rome.

By heredity and temperament, I think of the Romans with distaste. The only classical latin poet I *really* like is Horace. I find their architecture, even in ruins, as oppressive and inhuman as the steel-and-glass buildings of to-day. I prefer "the rolling English road" made by "the rolling English drunkard" to the brutal straight line of the Roman road or the thru-way. One reason why I like Italy and the Italians so much is that, aside from their unfortunate addiction to rhetoric, I cannot imagine a people *less* like the Romans of antiquity.

We open a classical atlas and note that the Roman Empire stretched from the Scotch Border to the Euphrates. We tour Europe and look at the ruins of gigantic buildings, acqueducts, roads, fortifications. We read

---

22. *Decline and Fall* (Womersely), 1: 102.
23. *CP91* 896–97.

descriptions of Roman banquets. On the basis of such evidence, it is natural to imagine the Empire as a society like our own: highly affluent, humming with industry, and bustling with commerce. Such a picture, however, is false.

By modern standards, the population figures were small. In the early fourth century the population of Rome itself was between one half- and three-quarter million, that of Antioch, the third city in the Empire, about two hundred thousand. Though the Empire contained one or two industrial and trading cities, its economy was based on agriculture, and its agricultural techniques were primitive. The only technical advance made by the Romans was the application of dryfarming methods in North Africa. They possessed no plough capable of cultivating heavy clay soils, and no wheel-barrow. Rotation of crops had not been discovered, so that the fields had to lie fallow every other year. It would seem that some kind of reaping machine was invented, but it was hardly used; the standard harvesting tool was the sickle. Before the time of Augustus an efficient water-mill had been invented, but in most of the lands round the Mediterranean the water-supply was neither copious nor constant enough to permit of its use. In the Second century Rome ground its wheat by donkey-mills and it was not until the Fourth that these were replaced by watermills supplied from the acqueducts. In the country wheat continued to be ground in hand querns. Techniques of manufacture were equally primitive; spinning was done on distaff and spindle, cloth woven on hand-looms, pottery moulded on the wheel, metal hammered out on the anvil.

The Empire possessed an excellent road net-work but, since the horse-collar had not been invented, goods could only be transported by ox-waggons moving at the speed of two miles an hour. Perishable goods, like fruit and vegetables, therefore, could not be transported at all, meat could only be transported salted or on the hoof, and transport costs were high; a journey of three hundred miles doubled the price of wheat. Nor was transport by sea much easier. The techniques of ship-building and navigation were such that the Mediterranean was closed to shipping from mid-November till mid-March, and for only two months in the year was sailing considered fairly safe. Under such conditions only the State could afford to transport necessities for any great distance; private trade was either in luxury goods or for a local market.

Under the Empire, wealth was probably more evenly distributed than it had been in the late days of the Republic when, according to Gibbon, "only two thousand citizens were in possession of any independent substance." There must have been a number of small landowners like Horace, whose Sabine farm was run by a foreman and eight slaves, and had five tenant farms attached to it. The disparity of wealth between the classes, however, remained very great. Rome in the fourth century contained eighteen hundred family houses and forty-five thousand tenement buildings. There were a small number of immensely wealthy men, most of them senators, and a vast number of slaves, peasants, small tenant farmers, living near the subsistence level. The precarious situation of the small man was aggravated by the tax system. The financial needs of the Government were mostly met by a tax on land, levied at a fixed rate. A big landowner with estates scattered over the Empire could suffer a loss here through civil disturbance, a loss there through a bad harvest, and still be able to pay his taxes and show a profit; a tenant farmer with a single piece of land, visited by similar misfortunes, could easily be ruined and forced to sell.

All of this meant that the Empire operated on a narrow margin of financial safety. The wars of the Republic had been wars of shameless aggression in which, as Gibbon says, "the perpetual violation of justice was maintained by the political virtues of prudence and courage," but they had paid: money, slaves, plunder of all kinds, had poured into Italy. The stabilisation of the frontiers under the Emperors put an end to such adventures; henceforth the Roman army was maintained for the purposes of defence, and a defensive war, though normally more commendable than an offensive, is a dead financial loss.

So long as the barbarians outside the frontiers remained too weak or too afraid to attack, so long as no ambitious army commander started a civil war in a bid for power, so long as it suffered no natural catastrophe like an epidemic of plague, the Empire could just manage. But any prolonged war or serious catastrophe strained its resources to breaking-point.

Political stability depended upon the Emperor being approved of both by the senate and by the army. So long as he commanded the loyalty of the army, an emperor could, of course, ignore the wishes of the senate or cow it into submission, and some emperors did, but such a procedure was always risky. By tradition, senators of pretorian rank were put in command of all the legions except the one in Egypt, and senators of consular rank were appointed as governors of all the major frontier provinces, so that they were in a good position, if they found an emperor really intolerable, to start a military revolt; if that failed, senators were rich enough and influential enough to hire an assassin.

It was also highly desirable that an emperor should reign for a long time, on account of the custom of the donative. Upon his accession an emperor was expected to present every soldier in his army with a substantial sum in cash; consequently, a succession of short reigns meant a ruinous drain on the Treasury.

In every respect the age of the Antonines was lucky. The senate, who distrusted the hereditary principle, and the army, who tended to be loyal to the last emperor's legitimate heir, were able to agree because the Antonine emperors were childless. Each was able to please the senate by nominating as his successor someone from among their members of proven ability and, by adopting him into his family, to secure the support of the army. Furthermore, most of them lived to a ripe old age. In the hundred-and-twenty-one years between the accession of Vespasian and the death of Marcus Aurelius, there were only eight emperors, the average length of a reign was fifteen years, and only one, Domitian, died a violent death.

Even during this period of peace and tranquility, however, there were signs that all was not well economically. Since the reign of Augustus, the State had kept down the expenses of administration by entrusting local government to city councils who served without pay, on the assumption that in every city there were enough persons of substance with the civic pride and patriotism to undertake the task willingly. The pride and patriotism were there alright, but there was less money than either the State or the cities imagined. The sums spent by the city councils, in jealous competition with each other, upon public buildings, water-works, free public entertainment, exceeded their resources and, by Trajan's time, the State found it necessary to appoint auditors to keep a check on extravagance. The two campaigns, lasting less than a year each, in which Trajan conquered Dacia, were small-scale affairs, but to pay for them, he had to debase the coinage, a practice continued by his successors with the inevitable results.

Culturally, too, something was lacking. The Augustan settlement had put an end to an intolerable state of anarchy and, for two centuries at least, made it possible for a citizen to live what the Greeks would have called an "idiotic" life, that is to say, a private life free from political cares, but the price paid for this tranquility was a general decline in intellectual curiosity and invention. In the field of technology, for example, the characteristic Roman contributions, the use in architecture of the arch, the vault and concrete, the use of pumps and archimedian screws for draining mines, the arts of surveying and road-making, the military techniques of the legion, the techniques of organising large disciplined bodies of men for labor or war, all of these ante-date the Empire. During the five centuries that it lasted, the only new inventions we hear of are an improved siege-engine and the use of heavily-armed cavalry. In 370 an anonymous inventor of a portable pontoon bridge and a paddle-wheel war-ship driven by oxen offered his services to the State but was, apparently, ignored.

Then, in the arts, where there can be no progress, only blossoming or sterility, the Imperial flowers, it must be admitted, are few. The poets, for example, who are still widely read with both admiration and pleasure are Lucretius, Catullus, Virgil, Horace, Propertius, Ovid. All of them grew up under the Republic, and the youngest of them, Ovid, is dead by A.D. 17. After them, who is there? Seneca (d. 65), Martial (c. 104), Juvenal (c. 140); readable, but hectic, strained, and basically unpleasant. Then nobody for two hundred years. In the fourth and fifth centuries, a mysterious little masterpiece, the *Pervigilium Veneris,* and some poets, Pagan and Christian, like Prudentius, Ausonius, Paulinus of Nola, Claudian, who wrote one or two nice pieces, but are very minor figures. Finally, in the sixth century after the West has fallen, one really remarkable poet, Maximian. The list is not long.

Serious trouble began during the reign of Marcus Aurelius with a long campaign along the Danube and an outbreak of plague. After his death, disaster followed disaster. Invasion by Frank and Goth and Berber, peasant revolts in Gaul, frequent civil war, anarchy and galloping inflation.

The picture drawn by St. Cyprian (200–258) is probably not much exaggerated.

> The world to-day speaks for itself; by the evidence of its decay it announces its dissolution. The farmers are vanishing from the countryside, commerce from the sea, soldiers from the camps; all honesty in business, all justice in the courts, all solidarity in friendship, all skill in the arts, all standards in morals—all are disappearing.

For the next hundred years few of the emperors were even competent and none were nice. In the seventy-three years between the death of Severus and the accession of Diocletian there were twenty legitimate emperors, not counting their nominal co-regents, and a host of usurpers. The average length of a reign was two-and-a-half years. Claudius died of the plague, Valerian was taken prisoner by the Persians, Decius fell in battle against the Goths; all the rest, and almost every usurper, were assassinated or lynched or killed in civil war. Great areas of land went out of cultivation—they may have been of poor quality, but hitherto they had been found worth cultivating—, and the denarius sank to 0.5% of its value in the second century.

Diocletian, Constantine and his successors managed for a time to stop the anarchy, but at the cost of a wholesale regimentation and immobilisation of society under which any personal freedom ceased to exist, a rate of taxation which destroyed all private initiative and sense of civic responsibility, and forcible conscription of peasants, who were branded like cattle so as to make it easier to recognise deserters. The main victims of the inflation were the city governments whose income was derived from long-term mortgages and fixed rents, and government employees on salary. Diocletian increased the size of the army, but attempted to cut down expenses by paying it in kind. During the first two centuries, equipment and rations were issued to a soldier against stoppage of pay, yet he could still hope to save half of his pay, and requisitions of food or material from the cities were paid for. Under Diocletian promotion in the army was rewarded by an increase not in pay but in rations, and requisitions were not paid for. Both the soldier and the civil servant were much worse off than they had been earlier, and the temptation to plunder and peculation became correspondingly greater.

The time was long past when candidates eagerly stood for election to municipal office. Men had now to be compelled by law to serve, and edict after edict, threatening with fines and confiscations officials who evaded their responsibilities by hiding out in the country, show that this was in fact what was happening.

By 380 the Government had to forbid the construction of new city buildings until the old ones had been repaired; in 385 it had to undertake to pay a third of the cost of such repairs. Some idea of what it must have been like to be a citizen in the time of Theodosius can be gained from the following edicts.

> Landowners found harboring persons who have left their legal
> domicile, or evaders of military service, shall be burned alive. (379)

Anyone who cuts down a vine or limits the productivity of fruit-trees
with the intent of cheating the tax-assessors shall be subject to capital
punishment, and his property shall be confiscated. (381)
Anyone who thrusts himself into a position to which he is not
entitled shall be tried for sacrilege. (384)

By 404 the State had become impotent to maintain even elementary
law and order, for an edict of that year authorises all persons to exercise
with impunity the right of public vengeance against the common enemy
"by exterminating malefactors, brigands, deserters, wherever they may
be found."

The partition of the Empire into an Eastern half and a Western half
did not take place officially until after the death of Theodosius in 395,
but from the time of Diocletian they had begun to go different ways, and,
once they did so, the collapse of the West could only be a matter of time.
The West was much poorer than the East, and its frontiers much longer and more difficult to defend. Invasion followed invasion. In 410 the
Goths under Alaric entered and sacked Rome. In 476 a boy who bore the
names of the founder of the Republic and the founder of the Empire,
the emperor Romulus Augustulus, was deposed by the barbarian king
Odoacer and retired to a villa in Ravenna. Turnus was avenged at last.

The decline of the Roman Empire has been attributed to many causes:
defects in the economy, a falling birth-rate, the dessication of the grass-
lands in Asia which set the barbarians in motion, Christianity, etc, and
there is something to be said for them all. The question remains, however, whether there was not some radical defect in the fundamental principles upon which the Empire was originally based which in the long run
were bound to bring it to disaster.

The Imperial civilisation derived its categories of thought, its concepts
of Nature, Man and Society from Greek idealist philosophy. (Epicurean
materialism of the Lucretian kind died an early death.)

Classical idealism postulates two co-eternal principles, Mind and primordial Matter. Matter-in-itself is an amorphous meaningless flux upon
which Mind imposes forms or patterns, aside from which, Matter is nothing or all-but-nothing. The imposed forms which impart to Matter the
nature of body do not in the process lose their formal character but
remain timeless and immutable. Matter-in-motion, moreover, resists the
imposition of forms, and can never furnish perfect copies. The material

cosmos is a world of becoming which never quite becomes; it remains an inadequate reflection of the truly real and intelligible world. The latter, the divine and truly real, whether as Plato's Ideas or as Aristotle's Unmoved Mover, is self-sufficient, without either knowledge of or concern for anything but itself. To account for the existence of form and order in the cosmos, Platonism postulates an intermediary demiurge, the World Soul, which looks upward to contemplate the archetypes and downward to impose them on Matter; Aristotelianism postulates an inherent wish for order in Matter. While "God has no need of friends, neither indeed can he have any," all things are "in love" with God and become as orderly as it is possible for things in motion to become, inanimate beings like the stars by making their movements regular, living beings by trying to live an existence in conformity to the species or type to which they belong. For man alone, by virtue of his reason, the divinely real can become an object of experience and through that experience the master of his destiny. To live according to reason is, however, immensely difficult and calls for a heroic effort by the "super-ego." The "Id," the energies of the body are hostile, and no help can be expected from the Divine. Knowledge of the true and the good, which are not apparent to the senses, presupposes a longing for it, and this longing is to be found only in a few individuals. Plato's Philosopher and Aristotle's Great-Souled-Man are both social freaks.

To classical idealism, motion, processes, change as such are misfortunes: the perfect does not move. The consequences of such a view for science, politics, art and history are serious. It permits the study of mathematics and logic, and the classification of biological and social types, but experimental investigation of nature must be a waste of time, since the real truth cannot be found in the imperfect copy. Corresponding to the antithetical pair Mind–Matter, in its cosmology, classical idealism sees history and politics as an interaction between timeless Virtue and mutable Fortune. To call the historical circumstances in which man finds himself Fortune, implies that, like primordial matter, they are unintelligible; to attempt to discover what has caused them to be what they are or to predict what may follow from them must be a waste of time. Then, since few men possess Virtue, the majority must be persuaded to lead a life they do not and cannot understand by habituating them to laws and telling them "noble lies." The peace and happiness of mankind depend upon a tiny élite. On them falls the task of discovering and maintaining the perfect form of State, of which there can be only one, under which human beings will lead the life proper to their species. All that is essential about an individual is the "type" to which he belongs, and this type cannot change, only repeat itself. An individual can progress from ignorance to knowledge, but communal or social development is ruled out. The goal of "creative" politics is to conquer Fortune and so put an end to history, a task so formidable that only a superman can accomplish it.

Supermen the Roman Emperors tried to be. Cicero and others might make fine speeches about Natural Law before which all men were equal, but their words had very little to do with Roman reality. Roman Law may be a fascinating subject of study for lawyers, and, since I know nothing about them, I am willing to believe that in certain sectors of Civil Law, like laws of contract and testament, the Romans made great advances. What I do know is that debtors were treated as criminals. In the two legal domains of most concern to the average man, Criminal Procedure and Administrative Law, that is to say, decrees concerning taxation, military service, the rights and limits of freedom of speech and movement, I cannot see that the Roman record is anything to boast about. Its criminal procedure was brutal and inefficient, relying largely upon informers and torture, and did not make the faintest pretence at equal treatment for all. If, in its later days, the Empire became legally more democratic, this was a democracy of slavery; the use of the lash was no longer confined to the lower orders.

As for Administrative Law, the citizen had no say whatsoever in its decrees, and no right of protest. Since the emperor was both the executive and the legislative head of the State, there was nothing, theoretically, to stop him issuing any decree he liked; "what is pleasing to the Prince," says Ulpian, "has the force of law." Moreover, since he was regarded as a sacred being, any violation of his decrees could be interpreted as an act of treason or sacrilege, the one offence for which a member of the *honestiores*, or upper classes, could be tortured and executed; a number of emperors made use of this legal possibility.

Classical idealism cannot tolerate the arts as gratuitous activities; either they must be reduced to didactic instruments of some ethical or political purpose, or they must be suppressed. Plato had the intelligence to see this clearly; Aristotle in his *Poetics* merely betrays his utter misunderstanding of his subject.

Roman literature, both in verse and prose, was an aristocratic art addressed to a small highly sophisticated audience. This in itself was not a fault. Once the age of the bard reciting tribal lays in the hall of his chief is over, and until printing has been invented and literacy has become common, literature cannot be anything else. Indeed, a "courtly" period is probably necessary if a language is to realise its full possibilities. In writing for a small critical circle, the classical Latin authors discovered what could be done with Latin, the wealth of its conjunctions and subordinate phrases, the flexibility of its tenses and word-order, which make it such a superb instrument for organising facts into a logical and coherent whole. The defect of Latin literature was not its way of treating facts, but the extraordinar[il]y small number of facts it considered worth treating. It averts its face from all experience save that of the highly educated and the politically powerful. The literature of the middle-ages had an equally small audience, but readily drew its material from popular sources. *The Canterbury Tales* were written for a courtly audience, but its characters are neither courtiers nor figures of farce. As W. P. Ker has written:

> Classical literature perished from a number of contributory ailments, but none of these was more desperate than the want of romance in the Roman Empire, and especially in the Latin Language.... "The Gothic mythology of fairies," as Dr Johnson calls it, was no less the property of Italy than of the North. In any mountain village the poets might have found the great-great grandmothers of those story-tellers for whom Boccaccio in his *Genealogy of the Gods* offers a courteous defence. The elves and fays of Italy, *Lamiae*, as Boccaccio calls them, might have refreshed the poets. But the old wives and their fairy tales are left unnoticed, except by Apuleius.

And Apuleius, one must add, was only interested in their gruesome or grotesque elements.

What was a limitation in the poets was quite fatal to the historians. It is significant that history was regarded by the Romans, not as the matrix from which all literature is derived, but as a handmaid to literature. One may admire the Roman historians for their style, or enjoy their scandalous gossip, but for historical understanding one looks to them in vain. As Gibbon remarked: "They said what it would have been meritorious to omit, and omitted what it was essential to say." Conceiving of the human individual as a specimen embodying a type, in abstraction from all those concrete features and relations which give him an historical existence, they assumed that men are free to choose between arbitrary and abstract alternatives of "vice" and "virtue," that there is nothing to stop them, if they wish, from living the life of their great-grandfathers. Of their historical approach, Erich Auerbach says:

It does not see forces, it sees vices and virtues, successes and mistakes. Its formulation of problems is not concerned with historical developments, either intellectual or material, but with ethical judgements. It shows an aristocratic reluctance to become involved with growth processes in the depths, for these processes are felt to be both vulgar and orgiastically lawless....The ethical and even the political concepts of antiquity (aristocracy, democracy, etc) are fixed aprioristic model concepts.

One symptom of this approach is the complete lack of interest shown by the classical historians in what people actually say, all the idiosyncracies of phrasing and vocabulary which reveal the personality of the speaker. Face-to-face dialogue goes unreported by them. When they do employ Direct Speech, it is a set piece of oratory written in the style of the historian himself.

One may like or dislike Christianity, but no one can deny that it was Christianity and the Bible which raised Western literature from the dead. A faith which held that the Son of God was born in a manger, associated himself with persons of humble station in an unimportant Province, and died a slave's death, yet did this to redeem all men, rich and poor, freemen and slaves, citizens and barbarians, required a completely new way of looking at human beings; if all are children of God and equally capable of salvation, then all, irrespective of status or talent, vice or virtue, merit the serious attention of the poet, the novelist and the historian. St Jerome, trained in the classical rhetorical tradition, might find the Bible "uncouth," but in his translation he made no attempt to "classicalise" it. (Only the sixteenth century humanists were crazy enough to try that.) Old Testament stories, like Abraham and Isaac, or David and Absalom, New Testament stories like Peter's denial, did not fit into any of the classical stylistic categories; to translate them called for a quite different vocabulary, even a different syntax.

Most of the writings which have survived from the third and fourth centuries are polemic theological journalism, Neo-platonists versus Christians, Christians with one interpretation of their faith against Christians with another. From being an obscure sect, disliked by the mob, as oddities always are, and suspected of horrid secret rites, but people no man of education would give a thought to, by the reign of Marcus Aurelius Christians had become numerous enough and influential enough to be taken seriously both by the authorities and by intellectuals. Persecution, hitherto sporadic and incoherent, became a deliberate planned policy under the more serious-minded emperors. Intellectuals like Celsus and Porphyry felt that Christianity was a cultural threat serious enough to deserve attack, and, on the Christian side, there were now converts like Tertullian and Origen educated enough to explain and defend their beliefs. Reading their polemics today, one is more struck by the points upon which they agreed than by their differences.

> Wilt thou yet take all, Galilean? but these thou shalt not take,
> The laurel, the palms and the paean, the breasts of the nymphs in
> the brake:
> Breasts more soft than a dove's, that tremble with tenderer breath;
> And all the wings of the Loves, and all the joy before death.

So Swinburne. But his contrast between jolly, good-looking, sexy, extrovert Pagans on the one hand, and gloomy, emaciated, guiltridden, introvert Christians on the other is a romantic myth without any basis in historical fact. The writings of Christian and Pagan alike during this period seem to indicate that, as Joseph Bidez says;

> Men were ceasing to observe the external world and to try to under-
> stand it, utilise it, or improve it. They were driven in on themselves.
> The idea of the beauty of the heavens and of the world went out of
> fashion and was replaced by that of the Infinite.

Such an attitude is consonant neither with orthodox Platonism nor with orthodox Christianity. Despite its latent dualism, orthodox Platonism held that the material universe was in some manner a manifestation of the Divine. The cosmos, says Plato in the *Timaeus*, "is the image of the intelligible, a perceptible god, supreme in greatness and excellence and perfection." For the orthodox Christian, God created the world "and saw that it was good," and "The heavens declare the glory of God and the firmament showeth His handiwork." But in the third century, both among Pagans and among those who imagined themselves to be Christians, radical dualistic theories began to take hold. "Some held that the cosmos had been created by an evil spirit, or by an ignorant one, or by bodiless intelligences who had become bored with contemplating God and turned to the inferior; others concluded that it had somehow fallen into the power of star-demons." (*E. R. Dodds*) The incarnation of the human soul in a fleshly mortal body was felt by many to be a curse and accounted for as being either a punishment for an earlier sin committed in heaven, or the result of a false choice made by the soul itself. Consequently, to an increasing number, the body became an object of disgust and resentment. Among some Christians there was a tendency to make a heretical substitution of Lust for Pride as the archetypal sin, and to see in violent mortification of the flesh, not a discipline, but the only road to salvation. A fascination with the occult, with astrology, spiritualism, magic, was wide-spread. Both Pagans and Christians took oracles and "belly-talkers" seriously. Reading the Christian polemics of the third century, one gets the impression that the Church was in grave danger of going crackpot. Only one writer, Irenaeus, can be called orthodox, as orthodoxy was to be defined in the next two centuries. The fact that the Councils of Nicea and Chalcedon were able to arrive at the credal definitions they did, suggests, however, that the most vociferous and articulate Christians were not typical of their third century brethren. Not all, not even the majority, can have been Gnostics who believed that Christ's body was an optical illusion, or crypto-materialists like Tertullian, or crypto-idealists like Clement, or indulged in glossolalia like Montanus, or castrated themselves like Origen, or behaved like the Marcionite, who always washed his face in his spittle to avoid using water, the creation of the demiurge.

The fiasco of Julian's attempt to establish his solar monotheism, and the ease with which his successors suppressed pagan worship—there were very few Pagan martyrs—suggests that, by the time of Constantine's so-called conversion, Christianity as a faith had already won out over its competitors, Neo-platonism, Manicheeism and Mithraism. For this victory many explanations can be given;—the impression made by the courage of the martyrs, the refusal of the Church to limit its membership to a spiritual or intellectual élite, or to make mystical experience necessary to salvation, the opportunities it offered to any man of talent and character to rise to high office in its hierarchy, its superior ability to give its converts a sense of belonging to and being needed by a community, and its philosophical superiority. *Credo ut intelligam* is a maxim which applies to all experiences except that of physical pain, and the Christian creed made better sense of human experience than the others. Far from Constantine and his successors contributing to this victory, they very nearly ruined it. The greatest disasters which have befallen the Church, disasters for which we have not yet finished paying the price, were the adoption by Theodosius of Christianity as the official State religion, backed by the coercive powers of the State, and the mass, often forcible, conversions of the barbarians in the centuries that followed.

Constantine and Theodosius took up Christianity for a purely pagan reason; they hoped that the "Christian" God would ensure them political and military success; a view neatly diagrammed by Blake in his re-translation of Dr Thornton's translation of the Lord's Prayer.

> Our Father Augustus Caesar, who art in these thy Substantial Astronomical Telescopic Heavens, Holiness to thy Name or Title, a reverence to thy Shadow. Thy Kingship come upon Earth first & then in Heaven. Give us day by day our Real Taxed Substantial Money bought Bread; deliver from the Holy Ghost whatever cannot be Taxed; for all is debts & Taxes between Caesar & us & one another; lead us not to read the Bible, but let our Bible be Virgil & Shakespeare; & deliver us from Poverty in Jesus, that Evil One. For thine is the Kingship, or Allegoric Godship, & the Power, or War, & the Glory, or Law, Ages after Ages in thy descendants; for God is only an Allegory of Kings & nothing else. AMEN.

As Charles Cochrane has written:

> To envisage the faith as a political principle was not so much to christianise civilisation as to "civilise" Christianity; it was not to consecrate human institutions to the service of God but rather to identify God with the maintenance of human institutions, represented in this case by a tawdry and meritricious empire, a system which, originating in the pursuit of human and terrestrial aims, had so far degenerated as to deny to men the very values which had given it birth, and was now held together only by sheer and unmitigated force. So far from rejuvenating *Romanitas*, the attempted substitution of religion for culture as a principle of cohesion served merely to add a final and decisive element to the forces making for the dissolution of the Roman order.

The eremitic movement, and the monastic movement which succeeded, it, were essentially movements of protest not against Paganism but against worldly Christianity. Before we condemn the desert hermits, as the humanists of the eighteenth and nineteenth century did, for refusing to accept their civic responsibilities, we must remember what, especially for the better educated and better off, who might have become magistrates or civil servants, taking such posts involved. A magistrate had to inflict torture; a bureaucrat could not live without taking bribes. Even what seems to us their most peculiar and repellant trait, their horror of washing, might be more understandable if we knew more about how men and women behaved in the public city baths. To anyone who took his faith seriously, the urban life of the "Christian" Empire must have seemed an appalling spectacle. It was now worldly advantage to be labelled a Christian, and there must have been a great multitude who, counting upon a death-bed repentance to cancel their sins, continued to enjoy gladiatorial shows, wild-beast fights, obscene mimes, etc. Cavafy's description of the reaction of the citizens of Antioch to a visit from the emperor Julian is probably not far from the truth.

> Was it possible that they would ever deny
> Their comely way of living; the variety
> Of their daily recreations; their splendid
> Theatre where they found the union of Art
> With the erotic propensities of the flesh!
>
> Immoral to a certain, probably to a considerable extent,
> They were. But they had the satisfaction that their life
> Was the much talked-of life of Antioch,
> The delightful life, in absolutely good taste.
>
> Were they to deny all this, to give their minds after all to what?
>
> To his airy chatter about the false gods,
> To his annoying chatter about himself;
> To his childish fear of the theatre;
> His graceless prudery; his ridiculous beard.
>
> Most certainly they preferred the letter CHI,
> Most certainly they preferred the KAPPA—a hundred times.
>
> (translated by John Mavrogordato)

Most people's idea of the Desert Fathers is derived from what they have heard about Simeon Stylites, and this is unjust to them. To begin with, few of them were mendicants; most earned their modest keep by weaving palm-leaf baskets and mats. Lunatics and spiritual prima donnas were, it is true, to be found among them, but many anecdotes reveal that they were recognised for what they were by their saner and humbler brethren. At its best the movement produced characters of impressive integrity and wisdom, with great psychological understanding, charity and good-humor. Nor was excessive mortification ever encouraged by the Church authorities. An early canon condemns those who abstain from wine and meat on fast-days for "blasphemously inveighing against the creation." We owe the Desert Fathers more than we generally realise. The classical world knew many pleasures, but of one which means a great deal to us, it was totally ignorant until the hermits discovered it, the pleasure of being by oneself. Nothing could better illustrate the relentlessly public character of classical civilisation than an anecdote of Augustine's, in which he tells of his utter astonishment when he saw a hermit reading to himself without pronouncing the words aloud: this was a new world. Again, they seem to have been the first people in history to appreciate the beauties of wild nature, and the first to make friends with wild animals instead of hunting them.

Though it did not reach its full development until after the collapse of the West, the monastic movement had already started. It began to be realised that, while solitary withdrawal could be valuable for certain exceptional persons and for certain periods in their lives, man was a social animal who normally needed to live with others. The problem was one of devising a kind of social organisation which would be neither totalitarian, based on collective egoism, nor competitive, based on the egoism and ambition of the individual. At its best, the monastic movement solved this problem better than any other social form before or since. Its drawback is of course that it has been limited so far, to the celibate. Perhaps it has to be: perhaps family life and communal life are incompatible, except under catastrophic conditions. But the matter deserves more attention than we give it.

"Histories of the downfall of Kingdoms," said Dr Johnson, "and revolutions of empires are read with great tranquility." I am not sure that to-day it would not be more accurate to say "with great excitement." On the evidence of contemporary historical novels (a surprising number are concerned with the fall of Rome) and science fiction, it would seem that what really fascinates us to read about is a post-catastrophic society and landscape—abandoned ruins of once great cities, bad lands, roads overgrown with grass, individuals and small groups, which have been brought up in a civilised society, learning how to cope with life under barbaric conditions. It is noticeable, too, that there is a far greater public interest in neolithic or bronze-age archaeology than in Graeco-roman archaeology.

I can guess at various reasons for this change of taste, some good, some alarming. Compared with our great-grandfathers, we are far more suspicious of worldly success, far less willing to believe that economic, social and racial inequalities are in conformity with the laws either of nature or of God. When we read the *Aeneid*, we can recognise as they did the magnificence of the verse, but we are repelled, as, apparently, they were not, by Virgil's identification of Right with Might. We agree with Burckhardt.

> "This or that hall-way would have to be the most beautiful if only because it leads to our room." What coldness and heartlessness there is in this attitude: the ignoring of the silenced moans of the vanquished who, as a rule, had wanted nothing else but to preserve what had come into being. How *much* must perish so that *something* new may arise.

How much more moving to us than Virgil's description of the military triumphs depicted on Aeneas' shield is the following incident in one of Maximian's elegies. Sent by Theodoric as an envoy to Constantinople, he picks up a girl. He is getting on in years and proves impotent. The girl starts to cry. He tries to comfort her by assuring her that she can easily find a more adequate lover. "It's not that," she says, "it's the general chaos of the world."

I think a great many of us are haunted by the feeling that our society, and by ours I don't mean just the United States or Europe, but our whole world-wide technological civilisation, whether officially labelled capitalist, socialist or communist, is going to go smash, and probably deserves to.

Like the third century the twentieth is an age of stress and anxiety. In our case, it is not that our techniques are too primitive to cope with new problems, but the very fantastic success of our technology is creating a hideous, noisy, over-crowded world in which it is becoming increasingly difficult to lead a human life. In our reactions to this, one can see many parallels to the third century. Instead of gnostics, we have existentialists and God-is-dead theologians, instead of neo-platonists, devotees of Zen, instead of desert hermits, heroin addicts and beats, (who also, oddly enough, seem averse to washing), instead of mortification of the flesh, sado-masochistic pornography; as for our public entertainments, the fare offered by television is still a shade less brutal and vulgar than that provided by the amphitheatre, but only a shade, and may not be for long.

I have no idea what is actually going to happen before I die except that I am not going to like it. Some ten years ago I tried to express my forebodings in a short lyric entitled *The Fall of Rome:*

The piers are pummelled by the waves;
In a lonely field the rain
Lashes an abandoned train;
Outlaws fill the mountain caves.

Fantastic grow the evening gowns;
Agents of the Fisc pursue
Absconding tax-defaulters through
The sewers of provincial towns.

Private rites of magic send
The temple prostitutes to sleep;
All the *literati* keep
An imaginary friend.

Cerebrotonic Catos may
Extol the Ancient Disciplines,
But the muscle-bound Marines
Mutiny for food and pay.

Caesar's double-bed is warm
As an unimportant clerk
Writes I DO NOT LIKE MY WORK
On a pink official form.

Unendowed with wealth or pity,
Little birds with scarlet legs,
Sitting on their speckled eggs,
Eye each flu-infected city.

Although elsewhere, vast
Herds of reindeer move across
Miles and miles of golden moss,
Silently and very fast.

## PRINCIPAL SOURCES

Auerbach, Eric, *Mimesis*
Cochrane, Charles N., *Christianity and Classical Culture*
Dodds, E. R., *Pagans and Christians in an Age of Anxiety*
Gibbon, E., *Decline and Fall of the Roman Empire*
Jones, A. H. M., *The Later Roman Empire*
Ker, W. P., *The Dark Ages*
Rostovtzeff, *The Social and Economic History of the Roman Empire*
Singer, Charles (editor), *The History of Technology, Vol II.*

# SELECT BIBLIOGRAPHY

## GIBBON AND THE EIGHTEENTH CENTURY

Bowersock, G. W., John Clive, and S. R. Graubard, eds. *Edward Gibbon and the Decline and Fall of the Roman Empire.* Cambridge Mass: Harvard University Press, 1977.

Craddock, Patricia. *Young Edward Gibbon, Gentleman of Letters.* Baltimore: Johns Hopkins University Press, 1982.

——. *Edward Gibbon: A Reference Guide.* Boston: G. K. Hall, 1987.

——. *Edward Gibbon, Luminous Historian 1772–1794.* Baltimore: Johns Hopkins University Press, 1989.

Ducrey, Pierre, ed. *Gibbon et Rome à la lumière de l'historiographie moderne.* Geneva: Droz, 1977.

Folkenflik, Robert. *Samuel Johnson, Biographer.* Ithaca: Cornell University Press, 1978.

Pocock, John G. A. *Barbarism and Religion.* Vol. 1, *The Enlightenments of Edward Gibbon.* Cambridge: Cambridge University Press, 1999.

——. *Barbarism and Religion.* Vol. 2, *Narratives of Civil Government.* Cambridge: Cambridge University Press, 1999.

——. *Barbarism and Religion.* Vol. 3, *The First Decline and Fall.* Cambridge: Cambridge University Press, 2003.

——. *Barbarism and Religion.* Vol. 4, *Barbarians, Savages and Empires.* Cambridge: Cambridge University Press, 2005.

Womersley, David, *Gibbon and the "Watchmen of the Holy City": The Historian and His Reputation 1776–1815.* Oxford: Clarendon Press, 2002.


## SIGN LANGUAGE IN ITALY AND ANTIQUITY

de Jorio, Andrea. *Gesture in Naples and Gesture in Classical Antiquity.* Translated, with introduction and notes, by Adam Kendon. Bloomington: Indiana University Press, 2000.

## BERLIOZ

Barzun, Jacques. *Berlioz and the Romantic Century.* Boston: Little Brown, 1950.
Cairns, David. *Berlioz, 1803–1832: The Making of an Artist.* London: Deutsch, 1989.
——. *Berlioz, 1832–1869: Servitude and Greatness.* London: Allen Lane, 1999.


## LEAR

Noakes, Vivien. *Edward Lear: The Life of a Wanderer.* London: Collins, 1968; revised and enlarged edition. Stroud: Sutton, 2004.


## BURCKHARDT

Cesana, Andreas, and Lionel Gossman, eds. *Begegnungen mit Jacob Burckhardt / Encounters with Jacob Burckhardt.* Basel/Munich: Schwabe/Beck, 2004.
Momigliano, Arnaldo. "Introduction to the *Griechische Kulturgeschichte* by Jacob Burckhardt." In *A. D. Momigliano: Studies on Modern Scholarship*, edited by G. W. Bowersock and T. J. Cornell, 44–53. Berkeley: University of California Press, 1994 [Cornell's English version of the Italian original].


## CLASSICS BETWEEN EUROPE AND AMERICA

Briggs, Ward W., ed. *Soldier and Scholar: Basil Lanneau Gildersleeve and the Civil War.* Charlottesville: University Press of Virginia, 1998.
Dyson, Stephen L. *A History of Classical Archaeology in the Nineteenth and Twentieth Centuries.* New Haven: Yale University Press, 2006.
Marchand, Suzanne. *Down from Olympus: Archaeology and Philhellenism in Germany 1750–1970.* Princeton: Princeton University Press, 1996.
Winterer, Caroline. *The Culture of Classicism: Ancient Greece and Rome in American Intellectual Life 1780–1910.* Baltimore: Johns Hopkins University Press, 2002.


## CAVAFY

Haas, Diana. "Cavafy's Reading Notes on Gibbon's *Decline and Fall.*" *Folia Neohellenica* 4 (1982): 25–96.
——. *Le problème religieux dans l'oeuvre de Cavafy. Les années de formation 1882–1905.* Paris: Presses de l'Université de Paris—Sorbonne, 1996.
——. *Grand Street* (Spring 1983). Entire issue devoted to Cavafy.
Keely, Edmund. *Cavafy's Alexandria.* Cambridge, Mass.: Harvard University Press 1976; rev. ed. Princeton: Princeton University Press,1996.
Savidis, George (ΓΠ. Σαββίίδης). Μικρὰ Καβαφικά Athens: Hermes 1985 (vol. 1), 1987 (vol. 2).
Savidis, Manolis. *The Official Website of the Cavafy Archive,* containing Greek texts and various translations of both poems and prose, as well as selected published essays about these works: http://www.cavafy.com/.

## MOMIGLIANO

Brown, Peter. "Arnaldo Dante Momigliano, 1908–1987." *Proceedings of the British Academy* 74 (1988): 405–42.

Dionisotti, Carlo. *Ricordo di Arnaldo Momigliano*. Bologna: Il Mulino, 1989.

Miller, Peter N. *Momigliano and Antiquarianism: Foundations of the Modern Cultural Sciences*. Toronto: University of Toronto Press, 2007.

Steinberg, M., ed. *The Presence of the Historian: Essays in Memory of Arnaldo Momigliano*. History and Theory *Beiheft* 30. Wesleyan University, 1991.


## KAPUŚCIŃSKI AND HERODOTUS

Bowersock, G. W. "Herodotus, Alexander, and Rome," *The American Scholar* (Summer, 1989): 407–14.

Dewald, Carolyn, and J. Marincola, eds. *The Cambridge Companion to Herodotus*. Cambridge: Cambridge University Press, 2006.

Kapuściński, Ryszard. *Travels with Herodotus*. New York: Knopf, 2007.

Strassler, Robert B., ed. *The Landmark Herodotus*. New York: Pantheon, 2007.


## AUDEN AND THE FALL OF ROME

Auden, W. H. *Forewords and Afterwords*. New York: Vintage, 1989.

Brown, Peter. *The World of Late Antiquity*. London: Thames and Hudson, 1971.

———. "The World of Late Antiquity Revisited," *Symbolae Osloenses* 72 (1997): 5–30.

Cochrane, C. N. *Christianity and Classical Culture: A Study of Thought and Action from Augustus to Augustine*. Oxford: Clarendon Press, 1940.

Dodds, E. R. *Pagan and Christian in an Age of Anxiety*. Cambridge: Cambridge University Press, 1965.

# INDEX

*Compiled by Jacob L. Mackey*